1

Later EVERYDAY CREATIVITY™ *Books*
From RUTH RICHARDS

———

Eminent Creativity, Everyday Creativity, and Health
(Co-Edited, with Mark Runco)

Everyday Creativity and New Views of Human Nature
(Edited)

Everyday Creativity and the Healthy Mind (forthcoming)
(Authored)

EVERYDAY CREATIVITY

COPING AND THRIVING IN THE 21ST CENTURY

everyday creativity
coping and thriving in the 21st century

DR. RUTH RICHARDS

"If we had a keen vision of all that
is ordinary in human life, it would
be like hearing the grass grow or
the squirrel's heart beat, and we
should die of that roar which is the
other side of silence."

--GEORGE ELIOT (MARIAN EVANS CROSS)

ISBN 978-1-365-68095-3

First edition: 1994/2017

PRINTED IN THE UNITED STATES OF AMERICA

www.lulu.com

To Lauren Jo Richards-Ruby Coffing, Jacob Coffing,
the memory of Sandow S. Ruby,
other inspirational family and friends
and for Chippy, Petey, Rosie
and the benefit of all beings

CONTENTS

———————————

PREFACE

"LOST BOOK" FOUND
(2016)

If we write a lot over the years, something may get lost. Here is a whole book that got lost! It was my first major work for a broader audience—to complement quite a few academic papers, chapters, and a very complex monograph. The title, here, is *Everyday Creativity*, a construct for which I have since become known.

The subtitle is: *Coping and Thriving in the 21st Century*. Now we are well into that 21st century!

Meanwhile I have also edited or co-edited two books (one right after the "lost book," with Mark Runco, *Eminent Creativity, Everyday Creativity, and Health*). There is now, today, another co-edited volume on the way. Plus I am also finishing another book. The title again begins with *Everyday Creativity*. To my delight, over the years my creativity work, on my own and with colleagues including Dennis Kinney, Ph.D., at McLean Hospital and Harvard Medical School, has received attention, and even, early on, a feature by Daniel Goleman in the Tuesday Science Times section of *the New York Times*. I was honored in 2009 to be awarded the Rudolf Arnheim Award from Division 10 of the American Psychological Association, for Outstanding Lifetime Accomplishment in Psychology and the Arts.

A lifetime award sounds final—but I am not all that ancient, nor am I done! I am also Fellow of three APA divisions, an active presenter, researcher, and author and, still, years after the lost book, am working to help the construct of *everyday creativity* become better understood. Not a fad or a frill, not a rare talent for only artists or scientists, or a handful of famous people, *everyday creativity* is a fundamental capability we all have, in fact our human birthright. Our "originality of everyday life" includes even our everyday off-the-cuff ability, to adapt, shift, modify, improvise, and try a bit of this, and of that. It is a survival capacity, although it is a great deal more as well. Yet if it weren't for our creativity, many of us would, in fact, be dead.

Beyond that, looking at you and me, at the creator, and our creative *process,* here is our ability to be fresh and present, to see life anew, to be consciously aware, and richly aware of our options, to go beyond biases and preconceptions, to imagine new worlds, and to–most truly—come alive. Not surprisingly this is also very good for us. Plus—as I was already showing back in 1994—very good for our world.

Now, enter this 1994 lost book.

Everyday Creativity: *Coping and Thriving in the 21st Century*, was actually commissioned by a Big Name Publisher, and under a different name. Upon completion though, my original editor had left. The follow-up editor (who told me she had earlier done only fiction) had a very different idea. I was not going to dismantle this first book, which has its own integrity. (Plus I didn't especially like the new idea.) I was all the more resistant, remembering late nights, early mornings, a young child, and a cross-country move, all during the writing.

The new editor, the Big Name Publisher, and I ended up parting ways. I must have tried with another publisher, because of an outline I found from early 1995, based on the completed book, perhaps to go with a query, and carrying the present title.

This 1994 book somehow went missing (maybe a box in the basement). In the last several years, I found it again, and said "This isn't bad!" I made a couple of bound copies (afraid it would go missing again—this time, I'd have to lose three of them) and decided sometime to publish it. Now at last, and with the new publishing options, here we are.

Actually, I have gotten other benefit from this lost book as well by telling its story in a writing seminar at Saybrook University. Along with giving some pointed advice.

This present book is word for word as written. The only part I had not finished (or begun, alas) was a bibliography. Thus I am including one drawn from my final integrating chapter for the Runco & Richards (1997) edited *Eminent Creativity*, *Everyday Creativity, and Health.*

I very much hope you will enjoy this 1994 book on *everyday creativity*. And if you do, there are now others…

Ruth Richards
Brooklyn, NY
October 31, 2016

PREFACE

EVERYDAY CREATIVITY
(1994)

There are many books about how to be creative. This is one too. But it is also about much more, about why to be creative, and the central question of what creativity is in the first place -- this vastly unrecognized and unappreciated resource, broad and powerful, and present in everyone of us in at least embryonic form. Nor is this some hyperbole designed for the over-promotion of creativity. As we shall see, creativity, as much as any other characteristic, is what makes us human. And, very truly, creativity may also help keep us alive.

We shall talk a lot about everyday creativity. Everyday what? Just blink and it is there. At least when one has learned to see it. This is the invisible creativity of modern life, unrecognized by those who think that Van Gogh, Einstein, Beethoven, and only a few others "had it." This is the creativity that often surrounds the very person who insists, "I'm just not very creative." It is not a special skill or talent to try a little of in art time, or music time, and then put away in a box on the shelf. It is the way you get through a day, find your way out of the woods, cope with a difficult boss, feed everyone when there's nothing to eat, help your child learn, and keep yourself sane. And when everyday creativity is known and acknowledged, it can become even more powerful yet.

Everyday creativity is truly a survival capability of the 21st century. But we shall go even further and argue that such creativity is a driving force of evolution -- one that goes hand in hand with, but is different from, the evolution of flesh and blood creatures like us. We are speaking of creativity in its disembodied and ethereal form, be this in books, magazines, movies, on the airwaves, or in a note scrawled to a friend -- of creativity as the evolution of information.

The book has two themes that weave through the particular topics. The first involves the continuous flow of originality that surrounds us and the second theme the forces of awareness or unawareness which can connect us to, or disconnect us from, this flow. As we pursue these themes, we shall step back and forth through what have been called the "Four P's" of creativity: the creative product, person, process, and the press of the surrounding world or environment.

These are essentially four different lenses on the issue. What is it that we are doing (creative product)? Are particular people doing more of it? (creative person)? Just how is it happening anyway (creative process)? And are there circumstances that make this easier or harder to do (environmental press)?

Indeed we find that the essence of everyday creativity is not all that remote or bizarre, and that creative products -- whether these be things, ideas, or behaviors -- lie in profusion all about us. As a first step, we can learn to see these better. We look at two core qualities and three optional qualities which such creative products might have.

For more perspective, we compare our own everyday creative efforts to those of so-called persons of "genius." Can such exceptional efforts, even be compared? Yes, indeed -- there is a common core. We consider what is similar and different, and what we may mean by "genius" in the first place. Does this imply we can sometimes create things showing at least a wisp of creative genius? Here, we suggest the answer is yes. It can be very important to know this, as well as reasons why one might view such the so-called genius as impossibly remote, different, unapproachable, and able to do things that we might not even be able even to understand, never mind imagine.

Indeed, it makes sense that if creativity affects our very survival, its forces will be found at many levels and in many activities. We cannot place our species survival in the hands of a few specialists in remote offices or laboratories. We are talking a grass roots phenomenon, one that defines -- and preserves -- our very humanness. Creativity allows us, each one of us, to adapt to changing environments and conditions. This occurs through the incredible power of our minds. We generate new information, new ideas and possibilities for living, which fuel both our growth individually and in groups. This can be compared to the generation of new living organisms, in our biological evolution. Yet these "births" of new information are much more powerful and plentiful in our individual lives and lifetimes than are the biological kind. Here is an evolution we can readily shape. How then shall we proceed?

In the big picture, our human diversity is the substrate upon which this evolving creative process acts. It is the fertile soil we end up either enriching or degrading, depending upon whether we embrace a creative style of living, and value in each other the combined possibilities we all represent.

In fact, depending on our own values and orientation, we might view a certain "unusualness" in some people -- including our own selves -- as threatening and abnormal, on the one hand, or rich with possibility, on the other. Similarly, we might see certain behaviors in a negative way, as primitive, childlike, and immature, again on the one hand, or productively unusual on the other. Parts of the "creative process" can be interpreted in these various ways. We shall see why and when this can happen.

With few exceptions, most of us can develop a greater appreciation of the diversity of human nature, and of the "normality" of this diversity. This includes an appreciation of the rich possibilities within each of us -- both suspected and unsuspected. What is needed is not only a tolerance for, but an eager courting of, some of the wild creative processes that we can (if we want) tap into. We may end up balancing on the edge of some complex mental reorganizations, far from the safe forces of mental equilibrium -- far from the certainty of what we thought we knew. The mind, after all, is a complex adaptive system, and a little chaos, properly placed, may be a healthy part of the mix.

Indeed, in the interests of creativity, we may even at times figuratively work toward mental "avalanches" of ideas in certain areas of our thinking. We may stir things up intentionally, and watch them collapse into a new order. Here, we consider ways to raise the chance of such a "shake up." Possibly, this is what creative insight is all about.

Now making an about-face, we look at some of the forces of conformity we encounter regularly, including a great many we take for granted. Here is where our environment may try to put the brakes on our creativity. And our creativity can be suppressed in insidious ways. Often, we do it to ourselves, without a clue, and help others do it to us as well. How important it is to bring these patterns to light. In a very real sense, we are giving up our creative birthright. This, fortunately, we can work to correct.

A natural focus then becomes education. How can we use this formal opportunity in order to blossom? To create an environment that nurtures our creativity -- which helps us fill ourselves out in our own unique ways, rather than be channeled into little socially acceptable set of skills and ways of thinking. Learning is about a lot more than doing well on the Scholastic Aptitude Test (SAT's). But at times you would never know this. Here is a limited view indeed of human possibility.

The other general theme of the book involves specific forces of awareness vs. unawareness which can connect us to a flow of originality around us, or at times even screen it from us completely. Our lack of awareness can also divide us from parts of ourselves. Indeed, it can make us feel dead, instead of alive.

Our awareness can certainly be recruited through the intensity of emotions such as fear, anxiety, or anger. But a happier road back in involves gentle realizations of qualities such as discrepancy, novelty, or pleasing balance. An important part of this is an aesthetic of everyday life, an instinctive appreciation of what is fit, fight, appropriate, elegant or beautiful. We all have the aesthetic sensors for this -- and a potential for joy in finding these aesthetic places and moments. Indeed, the proposal is made that beauty, broadly defined, may stand in the relation to the birth of new information as sexual attraction to the birth of new organisms. Beauty interests us, says come a little closer, bids us to commit ourselves and be changed, and in the process, to give of ourselves creatively to this greater world of information. We can learn, much better, how to respond to this call.

As we raise our sensitivity to these sometimes subliminal cues, we may look at other ways in which we become frankly blind, deaf, and otherwise senseless of what is transpiring around us. These include automatisms we may cheerfully practice -- unknowingly, of course and conceptual prepackagings of the ways in which we see the world. It is as if we were constantly wearing blinders or, at times, even a complete blindfold.

Then too, there are evolutionary limitations in our ability to sense certain qualities and dimensions of time, space, stability, and change. We are all victims of these limitations -- they are all part of what was once our basic survival equipment. Presumably, they served their purpose well back in our prehistory. But they are sometimes acting to our detriment now, in the modern world. How amazing that we often don't even know it.

Modifying such patterns is one task of our conscious evolution. If we are not genetically adapted to the modern world -- well, that is too bad -- we are not going to solve this through our genes. We will only solve this through changing how we see ourselves, how we process information, and how we act. This evolution -- and possibly revolution - - involves an evolution of information. This may be the most important task we have. Luckily, we can change our thinking a lot faster than our genes. Our creative development is key to this.

As another part of the problem, we look at ways our psychological defenses may screen us from parts of our reality, and from parts of ourselves -- from the most upsetting parts, of course. Our defenses may also separate our thoughts from our feelings. As one part of this, they may divide our feelings from important events we need to see in our age of increasing mechanization, specialization, dehumanization, and disorder. These mental tricks may help things look better in the short run, but they ultimately shackle our creative potential. They sidetrack processes of self-discovery and change that are not only psychologically healthy, but physically healthy as well. Our very immune systems can be affected. Could you live longer by being more open, less defensive, and creative? You'd better believe it.

And there is a different sort of "defense," if you will, which we can also get around. This is a way we all defend ourselves, one could say, from our human condition, rather than from our individual issues. It basically involves thinking what we like, and meanwhile "chasing the blues away." It can even reach the level of consensual delusion. The problem is, the blues may come back in force. This is particularly critical at this point in our history, where so many rapid global changes, including an unprecedented assault on our environment, is proceeding relatively unchecked. Meanwhile we cheerfully focus on activities and pleasures that keep us preoccupied, and which may even make matters considerably worse. How much better to wake up to all of this. It is not that we cannot care - - we don't necessarily even see it to begin with. Enter again our conscious evolution, and a wide range of new possibilities.

Is this all grim and horrible -- a confrontation with disasters, belt-tightening, self-denial, and new levels of stoic unpleasantness? On the contrary. Out of a perspective of relationship, caring, and the ultimate promise of love, we look at how our creative selves can find entirely new realms of pleasure and joy, of identity, self-awareness and meaning, and of loving connections in our lives, while also helping each other and the world we live in.

CHAPTER 1

MORE CREATIVE THAN WE THINK

The mind has more cards than it has been playing.

--RICHARD TARNAS, *PASSION OF THE WESTERN MIND*

I was driving through the California Redwoods along Highway 101, the Redwood Highway. Up a mountain, into a redwood grove, and around a turn, is a place called Confusion Hill. You pay your money, climb a steep slope, and enter a crooked little house.

The next moment, you feel dizzy, disoriented, very very heavy, and you wonder why this ball at the end of a string is hanging sideways. Not exactly sideways, but way off at an angle, straining on its leash. You know you're in this place, but the feeling is bizarre. It still doesn't make sense. For your senses tell you that down is that way, and up is this. And now a marble is rolling uphill. You even start it rolling uphill yourself! And you see water flowing along a series of chutes that each seem pointed up, one after another, the water falling a tiny bit from one upgoing chute to the next, stairstepping its way up into a wishing well.

Confusion Hill. But the confusion is in our heads. How quickly we may take things for granted. The ceiling is up, the floor is down, and gravity works. Even when the evidence starts piling up that things aren't quite what they seem, we still can't believe it. As far as we're concerned, the floor will stay right down where it is supposed to be. But we yield with one little concession: a ball is hanging "sideways." As much as we can manage, we keep seeing what we expect to see.

How do we get from here to creativity? Easily. As with the crooked little house, we often see everyday life the way we expect it to be. Yet everyday creativity means seeing the familiar in new, and in meaningful, ways.

All around us are things we see one way, and not another. We get up to fix breakfast—ho hum, another day—we figure out the day's chores, fix a leaky faucet, rush off to work, solve a tricky problem at the office, talk to a friend who is having a problem, make some calls, pick up the place, grab a snack, and end up exhausted. Finally we get a break and go off to see a movie. At last we'll get some creativity.

But it's a bad movie.

Yet the creativity wasn't at the movies at all. It was back there between the breakfast and the chores, in the office, on the road, and on the telephone. This is the creativity of our everyday lives which we may easily overlook. Creativity happens all the time, and in the most mundane places. But we must learn to see it.

Then there are the creative chances lost. Experiences unexperienced, actions untaken. We are too numbed and unaware; we miss their importance, or even their existence. If we indeed want more creativity in our lives, we need to mark our creative moments consciously. We need to include them in our sense of self, reward them at work and at home, and build them even further, in ourselves and in others. For up is up, and down is down (and they often are). But for creativity, we must learn to see—and to think—in some totally new ways.

In this book, we go forth to tease out two interacting dynamics we sometimes sense only dimly: First, the complex flow of originality around us, viewed as a force in evolution. And, secondly, the forces of awareness vs. unawareness which can connect us to or disconnect us from this flow, and indeed, can divide us from parts of ourselves.

Originality

———

How often do you hear people say, "I'm just not very creative." Then they elaborate, with something like "I just can't paint a picture." Or they confess, with some self-deprecating laughter as if it really didn't matter—"I never could carry a tune." First of all, they can probably do a lot more than they think. still...

This is not it! Everyday creativity is about originality, and this is actually as familiar as our reflection in a mirror. It is about doing things in new and different ways—and this can happen anywhere, and about anything. It is how we get through the day, deal with a difficult boss, and how we enjoy ourselves a little, even at the worst of times. It is there even a bit in speaking a sentence. Indeed, originality is a primary factor in our everyday lives. Yet we are so used to originality, that we may not give it a thought, or give ourselves much credit.

We seem to be giving up part of our birthright. Think about it. Why should "creativity" be reserved for "art time," "music time, " "science time," or heaven forbid, only an "elective" period at a school, then placed in a box on the shelf, framed in a museum, spoken of only in terms of movie stars, famous authors, playwrights, a scientist or two on the front pages of the papers. Why should it be boxed and kept away from us?

Should a few notable people be doing all our seeing and thinking for us? Telling us how to live? Does this somehow keep our lives more stable and predictable, and also perhaps the life of society? Here is creativity viewed largely from the outside. At the movies, on TV, in a song, in a book. While within we pursue our sometimes routine grey-colored and worry ridden lives.

Our Creative Adaptations

We are, in fact, creatures evolved and adapted through creativity. No one is telling us the details of our day. We are not creatures preprogrammed to know automatically how to build a nest or a make a dam across a stream although we may "automatically" know a lot more than we think we do. Rather, we have smarts, flexible changing creative smarts, to cope in new ways with changing environmental conditions and challenges in the world around us.

This is what the biologist T. Dobzhansky, in *Mankind Evolving,* has called our "phenotypic plasticity," our range of many real-life choices. In essence, this is the vast multitude of possible ways we can each of us turn out—the uses we can make of our biologic and genetic potential. To find food when the land is empty, to see the lion before it pounces, to keep warm in the icy winter. And thus we are able to live all over the world, in a wide range of climates and terrains, and display a dazzling diversity of cultures.

Survival and Information

It only took one of us human beings, in effect, to start the first fire. Meanwhile, certain others tried and failed, and a few others people eventually found some alternative ways to create fire. Meanwhile, most people weren't working on fire at all, but were busy with something entirely different.

Yet how quickly each home had a fire burning.

This is a happy division of labor, for how quickly we can buzz with the results of our efforts, and share them back and forth with each other, literally throughout space and time. Perhaps you recently lit a fire in a fireplace; you didn't have to invent the match. How readily a notion like "fire" or "match" or "spark" and "friction" can become intertwined with a culture, surviving long after its discoverer is forgotten. The information has developed a life of its own.

Indeed, with culture, a bottom line can be life or death. Our physical survival is certainly linked to our genes, our genetic material or our DNA. But it is also linked to our memes or the "units" of information we continually generate and share with each other. The presence or absence of critical information can make all the difference in whether the genes themselves survive—in whether in fact we live. Just think of the people above who learned to start fires, and the people who did not.

We suggest, by parallel with biodiversity, that the living diversity we reflect in our ability to create—through the kaleidoscope of our many interests and talents and life choices—may be our surest safeguard against an unpredictable future.

Generally speaking, the more memes we can create, the better.

We Are Meme-Makers

A bit more about these memes. Richard Dawkins, in his book, *The Selfish Gene*, compared these bits or "units" of information to our genes, or DNA, speaking at least metaphorically. It can be useful to think in terms of these little packets of information or ideas, if not necessarily accurate.

Memes make up the likes of an idea, a tune, an equation, an image. The English language is a particularly powerful group of these, or a "meme-complex." This set of interconnected words and rules, of English, French, or Japanese, for instance, tends to get passed on as a whole. This passing on is done formally too, in schoolrooms and study programs, in the hopes that no one will miss out. Think of the first two of the "three R's" (Reading, 'Riting, and 'Rithmetic).

The passing on (or "replication") of memes can be rather interesting. As with genes, or DNA, information can literally be copied, say from brain to brain (you tell someone), book to brain (they read it), or book to Xeroxed pages (copies made for later reference).
But now come up with "a cure for cancer," and watch it move! A "population explosion" of memes is unlike anything else. Unlike our genes, which change only when new human beings

are created, we can produce memes constantly. Then they can move at extraordinary rates, via TV, radio, satellite transmissions, the Internet, and so on, and can show up virtually anywhere, multiplying numerically around the world wherever the equipment is installed to receive them. They can proliferate in books and magazines and newspapers, and via word of mouth, and over the telephone. They can be issued and reissued, recorded and replayed. Sometimes the effects are widespread, dramatic, and almost instantaneous, as with the announcement of "President Kennedy's assassination."

Whatever the dominant culture will record, we are constantly passing all sorts of information around between ourselves, for our own reasons -whether over the dinner table, at work, on the phone, in a letter, or in a formal report. We may use sounds, symbols on paper, electrical pulses. Just think of the conversations crisscrossing a room, those travelling in the daily mail, or, indeed, speeding on the Internet. We are engaged in a constant buzzing and spinning of webs of information, off by ourselves and with others.

Even information we consider "private" is often shared with someone (even through a glance of agreement!), and is thus potentially hooked into the greater network of ideas which mutually influence each other. It is may be hooked in directly, or through its effect on someone else's thinking. It may seem "like nothing," but before one even knows it, it may sometimes undergo explosive multiplication and influence a great many strangers many thousands of miles away.

Creativity and Memes

Pursuing the meme and gene analogy, aspects of creative thinking may be compared to sexual reproduction! That is to say, the "combining" of memes (the putting together of information in new ways), can be compared to the "recombination" of genes (the reshuffling and selection of morn and pop's DNA to make a new offspring). The possibilities with memes seem at least as dazzling.

It helps to think of creativity in Arthur Koestler's terms, as a "bisociation." This is a sudden insightful bringing together of two totally different frames of reference. We'll use "stick" and "tool" as examples. Here is a chimp is behind a barred door, and a banana lies on the other side, well out of reach. The chimp has a stick, but right now, the stick is only a stick. The chimp is getting hungrier and hungrier, but there's no way to reach the fruit.

Suddenly the frame of reference shifts. The stick is a tool! With this insight, it can be done. The chimp reaches, hooks, and retracts the fruit. Information has been combined in a novel way. Stick and tool (in the chimp's symbolic vocabulary) have been joined. And the chimp is eating a tasty snack.

One may compare genetic "recombination." In the genetic union and reshuffling of DNA from father's sperm and mother's egg, predetermined pairs of genes, from each parent, meet and get shuffled and sorted to determine the offspring.

By contrast, memes, or pieces of information, can be linked together in creative thought in what truly is an infinite number of combinations of two, three, or more pieces. One can combine anything at all, without limit, drawing all at once, on a fantastic assortment of memes spanning, at the least, millions of miles and millions of years. One can work with pure fantasy, somebody else's fantasy, worlds of mathematical formalisms, scientific models of the universe, new organisms, societies and cultures, parallel universes, histories of worlds known and unknown. Whatever.

Yet with this achievement of human imagination and symbolism also comes considerable dangers and responsibilities.

Watching Out

Clearly, the possibilities abound for us as human beings. As the sociobiologist E.O. Wilson says, we humans have so dominated our environments for the last ten-thousand years that all manner of variety is possible in what people can do. Not so for the ant or the termite. There is no margin for error, or experimentation. The slightest inefficiency in nest building, odor trails, or other functions, and they are gone—finished off as a species by a competing predator. We've got the room to explore.

But the downside to this dominant position is that we could make some big mistakes and not necessarily know it.

Colluding with disaster, even as we make some serious missteps, may be our own feelings of powerlessness as individuals. We have become so habituated to the flexible creative options we do have that we may take them for granted. We are not the creative ones, one might think; we don't have any power. And the little triumphs of our own day may seem just like everyone else's, and just like yesterday's triumphs, and therefore of no real significance—except, perhaps, that they are helping to keep us alive.

Fortunately, we, as human beings, can not only think, but we can think about thinking. We can reflect on our creativity, and make the most of it. We can decide what is working, what isn't, and what we want to do next. We can also decide what it is time to wake up and see. As the saying goes, "This day is the beginning of the rest of your life."

Even at the moment when we are saying "I'm not very creative," we are probably performing one of our primary functions on this earth: to keep generating that originality—everywhere from our kitchen to the workplace, and in our own unique patterns—playing with it, weeding it out, and deciding what parts to keep. The laws of electromagnetism? The sonnets of Shakespeare? Pistachio ice cream? Love and marriage? Home schooling? Multilingual theatre? Hi-top sneakers? The latest slang words? Perhaps. Children carrying guns? No way, forget it.

Indeed, we have not only been adapting to our environments. We have been adapting those environments to us. One thing that we, all of us, do very well is to create new worlds, in our homes, in our schools, down the block, in the next state, in outer space, in our libraries and in our heads.

Our children are born not only into a house and a block and a neighborhood, but into the vastness of cultures, subcultures, and personal cultures to which we most definitely contribute. And which we can also change. It's that constant metabolism of growth and change to which we each add our essential part—and not just the art class on Saturday afternoons—which is the measure of our originality.

Awareness

Here is the second shining strand in our topic. Or perhaps the first. Because before we may act, we must see.

I was struck recently by my instant attention to an orangeish grey cloud masking some hills across the San Francisco Bay, in Marin County, California. "Fire!" I reacted. But it was not. It was just fog in slanting sunlight. "Yet it could have been fire," I reflected, "and my mind—in fact, all our minds must have a built-in trigger, a warning for fire, because this is something we can't afford to miss."

Certainly, awareness and survival are linked. How acutely we can become aware of potential dangers, ominous changes, a raising of voices, a flashing of weapons.

Yet our awareness may be useful for a great deal more. Consider beauty, consider love, or the sudden shock of a discrepancy. Do we sense fear?—or is it curiosity, and excitement? Any of these can wake us up. We shall argue that awareness can serve a great many diverse and exhilarating functions, often going hand in hand with creativity. Survival may be the ultimate goal—individual, species, or cultural but this may be achieved at times in some subtle and indirect ways.

How Aware?

Nonetheless, our personal awareness can often be quite limited. You think not? Take a closer look around you right now. The view out the window, the cup on the table. I am looking myself, and saying, oh yeah, I had hardly noticed.

Our culture and biology have equipped us with an amazing range of selective filters. These are useful in their place, for without them we would drown in a morass of information. Yet, according to Aldous Huxley, that which makes it through "is a measly trickle of the kind of consciousness which will help us to say alive on the surface of this particular planet."

Our periods of awareness are especially important considering how readily we can habituate to the things that are unchanging in the world around us. You see the same panorama of distant mountains every day on vacation, let us say. You've gone on vacation precisely to see something new, and the first day the mountains are there, and the second and the third and the fourth. But by the fifth day they are only sort of there, and by the end of the week, they are starting to fade away into invisibility. At least they are fading, until you actively remind yourself to look.

This is how it goes. We have seen something, we've coded it, it's not particularly changeable from day to day, and our minds have just too many other things to do to be bothered with having to notice this again, yet one more time.

Worse yet, we can even forget things in chunks, once we have boxed them up together in categories. Things such as "cars," or "rocks," or "horses," or "crowds." The particular instances can "become" the class name—to be attended to or forgotten as a whole. We can meanwhile lose all consciousness of the individual items themselves, the shiny red automobile, the jagged boulder, the animal leap, the helter-skelter run of a family of four jumping into a pounding surf. Now here is the family of four, to be sure, running and laughing and jumping right in front of us, but there are too many other people there too, going all ways at once as they yell and call back and forth to each other over the sand; it's a "crowd." And it's gone. Poof. Once again, we've got too much on our minds to notice.

We Only See the Changes

In fact, we're a little like the pigeons who may be strolling that same beach, jerking their heads regularly as they move. If it weren't for the jerking, and thus for the movement of the static environment in the pigeons' visual fields, the birds would actually not see anything. A pigeon can become frightened if an animal, say a cat, just stops and waits motionless, poised to pounce. The lethal potential has peaked, yet the cat has suddenly become invisible.

And here we are, the carefree human beings who think we're seeing everything around us -- and may even, heaven forbid, at times think we can control it. How little we're often seeing. Our visual systems are designed to respond to changes and to edges, to dark-light boundaries. Even our emotions have this design (with certain important exceptions, to be discussed in the chapter on "mood swings and creativity"). The newness and the vividness of an experience are all- important qualities. Within limits, even the goodness or the badness of our life circumstances may fade off into the background. We adapt, for that's our job. Yet what then is left?

I find one study particularly compelling, in which a person looks at an image, of a face, let's say. It is not in the external world this time, but projected by a tiny device onto a contact lens the person is wearing. Held immobile against the eye, this image disappears. People who meditate may tell you that this is just what they are trying to do at times, by focusing their attention. To calm the world of perceptions and look behind the curtain. How little we may know of what is behind the curtain!

At other times, some people may be trying to look more intensely at the world around them, and to see it more truly, with gr eater freshness and immediacy. The intent is to encounter directly one's experience, and one's self as experiencer, without all of our habitual assumptions, shortcuts, deceptions and blindnesses, and mental detours to the past and future from the present. How very much more there is to see. Seeking this can be most surely creative.

As mentioned, danger can awaken us to the moment. But there may be much happier and gentler ways -- and these may rouse us, despite ourselves, even when we're most numbed out with routine, and are automatically going through our days.

Aesthetic Awakening

Our resonance with beauty—how quickly beauty may awaken us.

We're not talking here about only a pretty picture or ornament. We're including any appealing set of perceptions, sensations, or mental transformations of our reality or our imaginations, viewed in the broadest possible terms. An old run down factory can be beautiful. So can the crumbs from a muffin. A friend's answer to a question. A pile of freshly dried clothes. A weather report. There is something right, fitting, harmonious, good, that makes us want to turn our head back and have another "look." It appeals to us, for some reason out of an infinity of possibilities.

Beauty, thus defined, may touch all realms of human experience the harmony of numbers, the balance of nature, the flights of our fancies -- and with our sense of curiosity, excitement, adventure, or discovery. And perhaps also with connection, tenderness, and caring, as we'll discuss. Aesthetics, involving "the appreciation of beauty," (Oxford American Dictionary) may be a central "way in" for us, to see more, and to see ever more deeply of our everyday world. It may help us decide what to attend to, and what to remember.

Aesthetics—viewed here as an everyday survival mechanism—should certainly not require a graduate degree. One should be born with some talent for it. (An advanced degree could even hurt if it led to more conceptual "prepackaging.")

A rather "cute" dictionary definition of aesthete from the *Random House Dictionary* goes: "A person who has or affects high sensitivity toward the beautiful in art, poetry, etcetera." First we'll dispense with "affects" (with affectation or pretension), since we're interested in the real thing.

Now put your lens on the "etcetera." John Dewey, educator and philosopher, saw aesthetics everywhere—the ultimate result of being alive. These are the accents of one's days—the experience of vital new balances in the flow of life itself. And also in oneself, as one reaches a new equilibrium with one's world. To Dewey, in *Art as Experience,* works of art were "refined and intensified forms of experience."

Indeed, if it moves you, then you, in some way, have been changed.

Dewey spoke of the aesthetic in the raw—the many everyday events that can hold our enjoyment, for instance, "... the men perched high in air on girders, throwing and catching red-hot bolts.... how the tense grace of the ball-player infects the on looking crowd... the zest of the spectator in poking the wood burning on the hearth and in watching the darting flames and crumbling coals."

The above is intensely visual. Yet one needn't paint it for it to "count." Indeed, as Ralph Waldo Emerson said, "The eye is the best of artists." Dewey went further to propose that the physical works of art may actually get in the way of aesthetics. The process or context that gave life to the moment can be lost.

Consider a postcard you might have purchased of a dramatic vista where you were vacationing. Did you notice later how pale and flat the view had become? Certainly, the postcard is pale and flat. But beyond this, one is no longer standing in the wind, surrounded by the mountains or open sky, smelling the mixed smells of nature, sharing the moments with one's companion, or by oneself. The moment is more than a view. It is a multidimensional experience echoed by a multidimensional transformation within oneself.

The Many Uses of Beauty

We turn briefly from visual delights to a mathematical delight. The mathematician Henri Poincare, explained the great and harmonious pleasure he could find in his creative search for new mathematical forms; this aesthetic sense was also an indispensable guide:

"Among the great numbers of combinations blindly formed by the subliminal self.... only certain ones are harmonious, and, consequently, at once useful and beautiful. They will be capable of touching this special sensibility of the geometer... (giving) them occasion to become conscious."

This adaptive value and usefulness of beauty or rightness or order (be it in mathematics, how well the corn is growing, the smile of a child making a discovery, or the elegant graphing of a series of numbers), is central to the present view of everyday creativity. The aesthetic of everyday life. We shall view beauty, fitness, a sense of elegance, there are various descriptions and experiences of this, as a particularly joyous part of our everyday survival equipment. It helps us to attend, value, record and remember.

And to act. As Emerson said, "Go out of the house to see the moon, and 't is mere tinsel; it will not please as when its light shines upon your necessary journey."

Or, Emerson again, "ever does natural beauty steal in like air, and envelop great actions." How we love to remember the challenge we successfully met it's the ultimate happy ending. Pragmatically speaking, as the event fades into the past, its illumination with aesthetic glory may help mark it as special, to be remembered and, when necessary, repeated.

Aesthetic appeal, broadly defined, may even serve as a deliberate draw -- inviting us to come closer, perhaps to act. It urges us to notice and remember, to think, to process and transform, and thereby somehow to be creative ourselves, producing yet further aesthetic possibilities.

We shall consider this as an hypothesis: That the pull of beauty may be to the birth of new memes what the drive of sexual attraction is to genes.

Consciousness Raising

For creativity—just as with the tilted house at Confusion Hill one needs a shift in perspective. And a new set of new rules. This may involve reclaiming parts of our creative birthright.

We need, first, to remove any blinders we have on. We are many of us blinded through lack of practice; our culture has not valued our creative seeing. We are also blinded to a considerable degree by our natures, by perceptual filters bestowed by evolution. The lapses can be so extreme that we even lose touch with some growing global dangers, as we'll see. Fortunately there is much we can do to overcome these l imitations, a process which has been called our "conscious evolution."

The next step is to amplify that underdeveloped and intuitive sense of those messages we are receiving -- those subtle hints that something is new, startling, moving, and important, and which make us look, wonder, and care.

We are good at getting the sudden messages that arrive by trumpet. Fear, shock, surprise, and excitement, let's say. But there's so much more—think of the total body calm and peace one may find half-hearing the raindrops outside, during a cozy nap on a Sunday afternoon. How often does one let this scene fade into the background, unconscious and unnoted. We may, all of us, in our culture, need more "practice" in valuing such aesthetic moments, and bringing them to conscious awareness.

There is much more to be said. But it is suggested here that an appreciation of beauty, in the broadest sense, can be an aid in survival, for every one of us. It can direct as well as reflect, our search for viable forms and changes in the world around us, and enrich our own creative choices. Beauty can resonate with the ultimate purposes of our existence. It is information alive in the universe.

Where We Are Going

We have said this book is about two interacting processes: the flow of originality that surrounds us, and our awareness of this fundamental dynamic and our part in it.

The exploration will take us through the rich generation of diversity in our world, and its role in a proposed process of evolution that involves information, and not genetics. We are all a part of this process, whether participating consciously or not. By making our participation more conscious, we may find important increases in personal meaning, efficacy, and our psychological and physical wellbeing.

We will also confront huge areas of personal distortion, "blindness," or non-perception. These are "shortcuts" or "detours" that may be useful to us at times, but often work to numb, deaden, or screen us from the world around us, and divide off parts of our experience.

Still, we can automatically preserve certain "ways in," through what is connected and important to us. We can multiply these and open our eyes and minds further through an aesthetic we'll call connected awareness. The more open one becomes, the more natural it can feel to perceive and produce creatively, to enjoy this, and to feel -- and actually to become -- more healthy and more alive.

It may also feel increasingly crucial to think creatively about creativity and what we're doing with our considerable creative power s and ultimately to work toward our "conscious evolution" in a world of confusion, crisis, and accelerating change.

CHAPTER 2

WHEN IS IT CREATIVE?

If I had to define life in a word, it would be: Life is creation.
--CLAUDE BERNARD

The incident below seemed "wrong" at the time, and highlighted the difference between what may be publicly acclaimed as "creative" and quietly passed by.

A few years ago, I was visiting my friend Deborah, her husband Lee, and their two daughters—an unusually creative group of people—at their rural home in New Hampshire. I was at the house alone when the phone rang. It was a local reporter wanting to interview Deborah about "creativity."

"Deborah lives next door to a well-known landscape painter," the reporter explained." I thought she could comment on what it's like to live next to such a creative person."

"What!" I thought. "Live next to a creative person? Deborah is one of the most creative people I know." I was astonished. How could the reporter overlook Deborah's own creativity, even as a sideline to the interview. Deborah's talent, I reasoned, was known in town as well to some extent, because Deborah gave art classes for kids at the house. Yet at the time all that I did was take the reporter's message. I regret to this day—all the more as I write this now—that I didn't say anything more.

After I hung up, I thought about Deborah and Lee's lifestyle, so overflowing, good-natured, and fun. As it occurs, Deborah has also worked as a professional artist and quilt-maker, and Lee has sculpted and marketed stone vases and candlesticks. Yet this needn't have been true, nor was it so at the time of this incident.

I looked around the house, not a regular house at all, but an old country factory Deborah and Lee had redone. On several walls were Deborah's colorful story-telling quilts -- animal tales, fanciful scenes, a portrait of the family as rabbits. (This joke-turned-quilt marked the younger child's birth.) One quilt was a version of a small pond, complete with snap-on lily pads. If all I had seen were the quilts, this would have been enough.

But the whole living space was an inspired work by these two people, and not, I might add, by some professional remodelers. I thought of Deborah and Lee with hammers and paintbrushes, turning their inner pictures of this home into a reality. They transformed a grimy workroom into a huge white sunny space with picture windows and, in one corner, an open kitchen area. At the other end was a large step-down solarium, with wicker love-seat and matching chairs, bright sunshine streaming through a jungle of tropical plants. Two highlights were a giant fern and a large rubber tree. There was a sense of peace and escape, and of magic.

The furniture was as much a process as an arrangement. Chairs and rockers, and some giant floor cushions sort of floated around the room in clusters, to wherever they were needed, loosely circling around the room's centerpiece: a shiny blue wood-burning stove on a raised brick platform, with logs piled nearby. It almost visibly radiating warmth. One could exist in this friendly environment at a scattering of heights and locations, moving through a circulating sea of perches. The two children had also contributed. A wall that might have been wallpapered was, instead, a mosaic arrangement of their paintings and drawings. Suspended from the ceiling nearby was a little ocean scene, a hanging gallery of child-fashioned cardboard fish, painted and glistening in bright patterns of color, and splashed with glitter—a school of magic fish turning slowly on threads from the ceiling.

And on it went. Here were the toys. I especially liked the building blocks the girls had made themselves—made with obvious adult assistance--a pile of homemade crazy shapes sawed with childish delight from planks and beams, along with a few more regular shapes. These they had sanded and then painted in wild colors: phosphorescent lime and hot pink, one with stars, one with stripes, and a bunch that glowed in the dark. Certain blocks had a child's name added here or there. Most were overflowing from a low box, but others were stacked nearby in a gravity defying tower, just begging for someone to help them fall.

Then there was a reading area, another kiddie corner, with books everywhere, some open on the floor or on top of large throw pillows, others shelved carefully with kiddie logic, so the same sizes were lined up together. lying open among the others was a blank-paged book the older girl had been writing in. Why not, after all? Do only "authors" write? Only big people with printing presses? Not in this little world.

I thought about the artist next door, the landscapist. No doubt the paintings were attractive, perhaps even remarkable. But they were also very much what people tend to imagine when they hear the word "creativity." What about this living environment of creativity and change at Deborah and Lee's house, radiating with human energy—even when the family was out. The joy of creation sprang from each little detail, as well as the caring of these people for each other.

It's not that one would have expected the reporter to know the details of this creative home environment. But if she had, how much would she have valued the creativity displayed here? Would the reporter have asked another neighbor to comment on Deborah's home, and on "what it's like to live next to such a creative person"? Would the feature have seemed as newsworthy? I suspect not.

The Mystique of "Traditional" Creativity

Let's face it. Some people who are looking for "artistic creativity" won't give much thought to the sort of artistic process seen at Deborah and Lee's house. At the same time, they may be impressed by a "landscape painting," however unoriginal it is. Such is the mystique of oil on canvas (or an impressionistic watercolor sketch) that even a landscape done essentially by formula could elicit sighs of admiration from certain visitors.

"I didn't know you were so creative," you can hear someone say. I have seen it happen. Think of the ultimate mechanical exercise: "painting by numbers." The "artist" takes paint from little capsules or containers, each with a number, like "11"or "16,"for a certain blue-green or yellow, and applies the paint to outlined cartoon-like areas on a canvas that are printed with the same numbers. The autumn woods magically appear, with a log cabin in the distance." I didn't know you were so creative," the artist is told. I have seen this happen too.

These are in no way comments against the more "traditional" visual arts. They are actually a particular passion of mine. But there is painting and there is painting, just as there is writing and writing, or different levels of creative home design, or of teaching students. It's not the activity per se, but how it is done. This will be a recurring refrain.

At best, our visual artists (or for that matter our poets or our musicians, or our social critics, home designers, or innovative teachers) can function like our extra sense organs. They can be our, extra eyes, and extra ears. These artists and seers can mark the progress of culture, celebrate its achievements, warn us of our oversights, and foretell its many possible future developments. They may, with exquisite talent, bring out feelings we might only vaguely sense, and take us mentally to where we would never otherwise go.

But this does not mean every artist will take us on such a voyage.

At the same time, even a bustling and innovative at-home achievement, such as the creative home and learning environment of Deborah and Lee's, may de facto be taken by some people as "ordinary." Ordinary, and therefore, not special. It's done at home, it's leisure time, unpaid, untrained, unofficial, among a great many other biases and stereotypes, which may be playing a role. But what a terrible thing we may be perpetrating here on some of our finest achievements.

It makes an interesting thought experiment to wonder how the local newspaper reporter might have viewed Deborah and Lee's work the very same work -- if it had been commissioned at the kilobuck level as a design for an innovative new "flex space for multiage living and learning." Let's add, for good measure, that a special TV news feature was being filmed for a regional television "newsmagazine" show on "home environments for the future," with a tentative title for this segment of "an extension of you that also extends you." A weighty recommendation?

Are we letting other people decide things for us? Here are two "core" criteria for everyday creativity which one may apply—to followed by a lot of qualifications.

"Core" Criteria for Creativity

We will talk first about the end-result, about the final outcome of what a person does creatively, or the so-called creative product. This is the first of "four P's," representing four common lenses or viewpoints through which people have often looked at creativity. We will turn in a bit to the creative process and person, as well as the environmental press or conditions which can work for—or against—creative activity. Creative products can come in a great many forms: physical objects (for instance, a painting, or a piece of furniture), ideas (a formula, or a business plan), or behaviors (a dance routine, or a keynote speech).

Originality and Meaningfulness

When we talk about everyday creativity, we are implying that at least two qualities are present: originality and meaningfulness. These stand at the core of creativity across many different fields and types of concerns, and are common denominators of many formal definitions of creativity. The awe-inspiring and fundamental essence of originality, in particular, is well expressed by psychologist and researcher Frank Barron, in *Creative Person and Creative Process,* who helped formulate these criteria in his studies of eminent persons:

"The sense of the mystery surrounding creation is close to a universal sentiment, and certainly it may be found in the breasts of even the most scientific of psychologists as they approach the phenomenon of psychic creativity. Creativity may be defined, quite simply, as the ability to bring something new into existence. The archetype of the creator is the Divine Being; Aristotle defined the principle of generation of the universe as nous poietikos, the poetic or creative reason."

Do we, as mere mortals, exist so far below this magnificent plane we can only taste faintly of its magic? Or are we somehow heir to the magic by our very existence? This we may well wish to keep in mind.

Below, we look more carefully at originality and meaningfulness, and then apply these to three examples of people and their actual everyday activities. One important goal is to increase our sensitivity to the many forms of "creation" that are happening in the world around us. These are not always obvious.

I myself have certainly benefitted from this exercise. For some years, I studied everyday creativity along with psychologist Dennis Kinney, and other colleagues at Harvard Medical School and McLean Hospital. We had all previously done one or another thing in our own lives which we considered "creative," and we thought we knew the scope of the phenomenon. Yet we ended up seeing activities as creative that we would hardly have noticed at the beginning. All manner of preconception had been getting in the way, including biases toward certain types of activities (especially in the arts), special skills (such as musical or mathematical ability), or activity that had somehow been recognized by society—say, trumpeted from a stage, or published in a periodical. Yet when you hunker down to look for just plain originality, without any of these limitations, new vistas start to open.

Beyond this, one may reasonably wonder if two criteria for everyday creativity are enough. Here, after all, we may be talking about the most complex and remarkable forms of human activity in existence. Are we to write these off with only two qualities to look for? It does indeed depend why one is looking, as we shall see. Here we shall consider three other criteria for creativity—ones which are often used. These are certainly useful, but we, at least, won't require them. Where the first set tends to open things up, the second seems more to close them off. For everyday creativity, we want to cast a very broad net.
First, the two core criteria:

(1) Originality: Here we seek something original, new, unique, or different, about the creative product. Consider some dictionary definitions: "belonging to the origin or beginning of something," "a primary form or type from which other varieties are derived," "an original work or writing, as opposed to any copy or imitation."(*Random House Dictionary*). Fair enough, perhaps, but how much of the product must be original? And compared to what? Can "unusual" sometimes count? Etcetera. All this, again, will depend upon our purpose. We will get to such questions.

Yet how not to miss some important instances of originality? An aesthetic attraction may help us find what is special—bringing us subtle signals from our deepest minds. We sense something new; we turn to see it. A warmth in our thoughts holds our attention. It is good, it is "right." We are glad to keep attending, to record the moment, and add it to our conscious experience not merely through some idle notation, but through an indelible mark in our mental map of our world. This aesthetic moment can, in theory, influence every other thought we will ever have. Here is no isolated sensory event, but a personal transformation.

This is what Frank Barron has called the "rather subtle additional property... of 'esthetic fit' or 'elegance.'" Here, too, is John Dewey's vital new balance, the critical life juncture, bringing new awareness of one's world and oneself in it. Here too, from an evolutionary perspective, is an opening of conscious awareness and our ability to act (either now or in the future) to a new and positive part of life's landscape. This is a happy call, without fear, anxiety, anger, or pain.

The aesthetic message is to be savored—that sense of beauty, elegance, rightness or fit. You look at the painting and it "moves" you. The presentation is "crisp and startling." The new design is "just right. If you don't have to think about this reaction, even though it may involve a complex mixture of emotion and reason. There it is—it awakens you. We all have good instincts for this, or at least can develop this potential. If survival is truly at stake, we each surely have some measure of this right now.

(2) Meaningfulness: It is not enough to be original. One must also "make sure that the original work or behavior makes sense that it isn't someone's delirious ravings, or an accidental production. A test of meaningfulness is that it communicates to others. Consider the keynote speech example; one wouldn't have with the speech, but one should at least understand it. The meaningful ness of a public speech is typically guaranteed. Its whole point is to communicate. The issue comes up more with the likes of Jackson Pollack's "drip" paintings— with semi-planned accidents that end up being called "creative." You or I could do something new and original without even thinking by dropping a pot of coffee on the floor. But would that be creative? More like an unhappy accident. What about a thousand monkeys typing for a thousand years on a thousand typewriters. One of them types a clever maxim by sheer accident; is this creative?

These accidents are far from the deliberate constructions of a fertile imagination; they are results of chance or idiosyncrasy.

An extra step is needed if such a product is to be called creative. For instance, if you dropped the coffee on the floor, thought the brown splashes and broken glass made some interesting abstract patterns, and took a photo of these, you might be creative indeed. Indeed, a lot of creativity may start this way.

But what about something that doesn't look "meaningful" because people don't yet understand it; it is, as they say, "ahead of its time." We'll get to this and other assessment errors.

Casting the Broad Net

Before moving to the three criteria for creativity we will not require, some initial comments and biases:

First, there is no single right answer to what is creative and what is not. Creativity is a construct, an idea we have made up, in informal committee in a sense. Creativity is not a thing one can collect in buckets and put in storage. Nor is it an unambiguous quality such as "breathing." The whole nature of a creative work is unpredictable; it will be different from anything which has come before.

What we want is a word to summarize a collection of "innovative" behaviors or products that we find significant—significant in a particular context. If our goal was to award a Nobel Prize in chemistry, we might have a great many criteria, very detailed and stringent. We would limit our search, to be sure, to people doing chemistry, and ultimately pick one person, or perhaps two or three. This is one alternative approach, and a valid enough one (we may hope) for its purpose.

By contrast, our purpose in studying everyday creativity is to look at ourselves across the vast expanse of day to day life, to learn more about when, how, and why we do things in new ways. (We're not asking much.) This time, everything that is new and innovative, must "count." We therefore go light on the number of criteria for creativity, keeping our scope very wide (criterion of originality), but hopefully not inappropriately so (criterion of meaningfulness).

We look beyond certain accomplishments, say in the "traditionally creative" fields of the arts and sciences, to all possible fields, and jobs, and further yet, to what people do outside of work in their homes, and in their spare time, with their families, friends, and by themselves. Originality can come in as many ways as we are human, across the whole spectrum of human experience. If its function is, in part, one of survival, we would expect it to be no less than ubiquitous. If we looked only at, say, chemistry—or if we only let the sciences "count"—we would be missing a vast portion of human ingenuity.

We would also be harming people. Calling some people creative, and other people not so creative, and meanwhile missing the talent of the second group entirely. This through our own error, our own omission, while blithely insisting we were seeing everything. This is one of our many areas of "blindness." For a start, just consider the effect of this on the performance, self-esteem, and confidence of certain students in school.

Three Compelling Criteria We Won't Use Here

These three added criteria for creative works can be clarifying and helpful. Yet they don't always apply. (Likewise with some other criteria we won't consider here.) We can certainly look for such qualities, but we won't require that they be present, so as to keep our vision broad.

(1) Filling a need. In many cases, this is an excellent criterion, especially where the creative "need" or "goal" is clear, and of importance. Finding the fastest way to work, resolving a fight with one's spouse, getting twice the product shipped out in a given time period. Winning a prize at the Science Fair. We'll also see that, of three examples which will follow, that two of them evolve significantly beyond the original purpose.

It also seems possible that at times our natural urge, and pleasure—most truly is often to just keep on doing it, to keep creating for its own sake. At the very least, we don't want to rule out this important possibility. Such a creative urge may be similar to play, which is partly its forerunner, in any case (See Chapter 7, "One's Own Path").

Underneath all this, as we've said, our curiosity and creative activity may be fueling a larger and more connected evolution. This is the cultural evolution of which we spoke—the "evolution of information" rather than DNA—at the personal, subcultural, and full-culture levels. The webs of new ideas and products we spin, each in our own little space, may be useful in their linked entirety in the cultural long run. Perhaps we even have some intuitive sense of this. It may well be that, only if enough of us keep spinning them, will we all together, somewhere or another, end up with what we need.

Within a framework of diversity, psychologist Robert Albert, author of *Genius and Eminence,* has spoken to the added social need to educate broadly and educate well, so that each person's potential may flower. Here truly is a blind investment in the future, since we don't know what each person will do with his or her education—or will do at all. From a social standpoint, we can just hope that enough people will be in the right place at the right time:

The social and biological premium for human survival is upon diversity, selecting and training all persons who might show any potential.... It is to the advantage of all societies to identify and educate the broadest range of their members for at least two practical reasons: There are far more types of talents among a population than exist in any one group of members in a culture; furthermore, whatever its particular make-up, any form of giftedness and talent early on is only a potential until an environment acts on it.

(2) Finding "optimum form." This criterion goes even further in requiring that a creation, in essence, do a job as well as possible. There is a sense of fit, appropriateness, and special value.

We won't require this criterion, first, because to apply it, we must be "filling a need," if we are to assess how optimal the result is. But there's another reason. We may often be operating from incomplete information, working by approximations. We muddle through and do the best we can. In everyday life, perfection is not the least bit reasonable as a goal.

One may imagine a theoretical "fitness landscape" for our potential ideas. Picture this as a graphic terrain of hills and valleys in an imaginary "idea-space." Our minds are looking for a stable (deep) place to settle—for that "good idea, "or an answer to a problem. The valleys represent possible creative solutions, and we are out there mentally, travelling about the terrain, doing our search. Some ideas might work better than others—hence the corresponding valleys are deeper -- but we really can't get around to every place on the map. We might not, in the end, come up with the best solution for all time—or arrive graphically at the best place to come to rest (the deepest valley). Indeed this is unlikely. We may end up instead somewhere on the south quadrant, say, in a lesser dip (or a "local minimum").

But no matter. From our own personal perspective (not knowing, after all, what all the other possible outcomes may be), we might not be doing a bad job at all of our creating. When viewed from our own local idea-neighborhood, things may look rather good. The idea we have fits, the solution "works." And that may be good enough.

Furthermore, interactive as we are with each other, our own creative contributions will leave their own marks in the fitness landscape (for instance, in what appears or remains for "others to find"). This theoretical idea-landscape may elevate a bit here, sag a bit there, generate a few more theoretical possibilities, erase others, and—if we have done something truly insightful—it may perhaps even buckle and re-conform as a totality, changing the way things are seen in general (Also see Chapter Five).

Finally, if we have somehow erred, the rest of the fitness "landscape" may perhaps reconfigure itself, to take up the slack. (example: when there is a generic "miswiring"). In the long run, it's the cumulative effect of ideas that will count.

One should recall that we are talking wildly about imaginary landscapes of ideas, ideas of the future, known only in theory to an all-knowing mind. Who among us can know what all the possibilities are anyway? Who is to judge? No matter how hard we work and how hard we try, each of us can only do so much. Yet this is fine. To be everyday "creative," in the present view, one need only be original, and not race around chasing some phantom of "the best."

(3) Advancing a Personal or Social Good. We do not require this criterion either, as much as one might wish for it. There are no moral qualifying tests for the use of our creativity, any more than for the use of our "intelligence."

History is replete with examples of terrorism, massacres, sneaky plots and counterplots, that ooze with successful creativity. There are certainly plentiful parallels as well on the personal level, of abusive and destructive situations.

Because we are tying everyday creativity to evolutionary considerations, we cannot decide to look at only part of the picture. Everything a human being does is important, whether it's beautiful or ugly, kindly or hostile. Everything potentially counts. Yet we will also argue that a flexible creative upbringing—or even key creative transformations as an adult—may make a caring and principled use of one's creativity much more likely.

Interestingly, some of these same conditions may advance both psychological wellbeing and physical health. It wouldn't be at all unreasonable for these to be tied together -- health and positive use of creativity from a survival point of view. We shall indeed return to this aspect of creativity in later chapters on creativity and personal adversity, and confronting global threats. Now let's try these criteria.

Is Creativity Present?

Although this is a *yes* or *no* question, it can be hard enough. Consider several examples.

More and Less Creative Analogues

Here is someone who paints an original landscape; rearranges furniture in new ways to improve space, light, and office morale; improvises a beautiful new song; helps a neighbor find effective solutions to personal problems; designs a valuable research project; makes up a series of new games which excite and entertain children; designs and builds customized furniture; makes up clever jokes which amuse friends. Again, just knowing what was done may not be enough; the creativity may be in how it was done.

Now here are examples which are roughly parallel, but less clearly innovative: painting a landscape "by the numbers"; arranging furniture as shown in a book (although the choosing of the model might show original thinking); humming a well-known song (although it might potentially be creative if the delivery or rendition involves original elements) ; listening impassively to a TV discussion of people's personal problems; performing in a routine manner on a task in a research project; playing a standard game with children; assembling furniture "by the book" from prefabricated parts (a mechanical analog of "painting by the numbers"); reciting jokes heard at work verbatim.

Originality isn't as obvious, even though certain examples—for instance, painting, and scientific research—are in areas classically considered creative. Also, note that certain accomplishments may involve considerable skill, for instance, in "word working" or painting. Yet these are not clearly original or creative. It's not that skill isn't important. But it's not the "core" of creativity. It is one thing to copy a Rembrandt painting, but another thing entirely to be Rembrandt.

Examples of Creative Outcomes—and Notes on Process

Here are three somewhat more extended examples. Each includes a creative product, and also some background on the creative person and the reason for their being creative. Descriptions are based on actual study subjects (disguised sufficiently for privacy). We consider what to "count" as creative. Ways to tell. And why.

Don: Unusual auto repair approach. Don is an auto mechanic, and owner of an auto shop, who developed or modified some of the tools he used for doing auto repairs. These tools fit better in Don's hands and worked better for his purposes -- a sleeker wrench for certain foreign cars, some extra-long pliers, a flexible tool-and-flashlight combination. Don was not trying to shape great sculpture, invent new equipment, or for that matter, get any credit at all. The product was its own reward and, in fact, Don ended up taking a shop class to learn more about what he could create. Whereas most people would have somehow "made do" with the equipment from their local automotive store, Don went a step further.

Nan: Home-designed and fashioned clothing. Nan, the mother of a large family, got started making clothes for the family because of a tight budget. She did this from whatever she could find, afford, or recycle, first making only standard shirts, skirts, or pants from store-bought patterns. As she got more involved, Nan started modifying these patterns, then making her own, and also began fashioning some unusual novelty items, like a clown like patchwork jumpsuit. This penny-pinching move became less of a chore, and finally an enthusiasm. Nan combed the flea markets for new materials and ideas, using old curtains, bedspreads, strange beads for buttons, whatever would work. She did turn out a number of standard items and re-runs of older clothing with a few colorful new touches. But she also increasingly tried experiments in design and in fabric combination. Finally, Nan began selling some of her clothes at the flea market, and finally through a local shop in town.

Helen and Auguste: War resistance effort. This was a courageous smuggling operation. No concrete "creative" product was produced, or official credit ever given. Yet human lives that might otherwise have been lost were saved. Helen and Auguste were a respectable couple who ran a small manufacturing business during the Second World War. Undercover, however, they were secretly smuggling individuals in a dangerous underground war resistance movement, as part of a human chain, across land and across water. They would organize the movement of refugees to secret locations and hide them until transport was available.

The work was dangerous, the penalties extreme, and the conditions constantly changing. On a particular night, sources might report that a particular storefront would be deserted and a good waystation for getting people closer to the waterfront and a midnight boat departure from the country. It was important to create believable movements of people in advance, also making sure the refugees were properly provisioned, prepared, and encouraged. On they went, organizing, leading, and modeling the courage that was needed. Fortunately, neither Helen nor Auguste were ever caught.

Originality and meaningfulness. We can think of these instances using the two "core" criteria for creativity. Originality is the central focus. The meaningfulness of Don's modified tools and their use, Nan's clothing for her family, and Helen and Auguste's saving of human lives is fairly clear. Some questions:

"What is your "sense of it?" Answer this question quickly if you can, with a "gut" or intuitive impression. Do the examples carry a flavor of newness? Of rightness, fitness, perhaps elegance?

Were you focused on the ideas (new tools, makeshift clothing, flexible escape plans), or final products or behaviors (actual tools, clothes fashioned, successfully enacted escape scenarios), or both? There are many possible levels of focus.

How strong is the intuitive or "gut" feeling? This reaction involves the aesthetic we've proposed, involving elegant new forms of all sorts. An intuitive sense of this "startling newness" can be vital, in pinpointing creativity. It may naturally be present, and precisely as a spur to awareness. It may take various forms. "Hmm," one thinks, perhaps about Don's decision to modify tools, "that's a little different." Or, "what a good idea!" Or, "wonder if I could do that?" Any of these sorts of things. Here is a clue, a way in, to a creative work's real effect on you. (This sense may also be particularly important where the actual evidence of creativity isn't available in front of you.)

Are you looking only at the creative end-product, of do other factors enter? With intuitive feelings, there may be a useful blurring of creative product, process, and person. The everyday creative product exists for a reason, in the real world -- as with Nan's trying to save money by sewing, or most certainly in Helen and Auguste's helping refugees. Someone else might have responded differently, or not at all. As John Dewey suggested, we may need to know the whole picture to appreciate the meaning of a creative work.

Finally, does it seem that "creativity breeds creativity"? It is worth becoming more sensitive to a certain branching, growing process, that can occur within the creative endeavor itself. Creativity can often build on itself in a dynamic way -- and this dynamic is worthy of separate note.

If we want, we can still judge the individual object or act on its own as more or less original, or creative. But we must always ask, "compared to what?" and "for what purpose?" With everyday creativity, especially, the live situation that gave birth to an accomplishment may help us answer these questions. Hence we return to an analysis of our three examples, including a bit about their dynamics.

We ask questions such as: What about it is original? What is the reference group? And, finally, with a nod to process and the person, Was the creator's original purpose served, and did any further purpose develop? The latter is always a possibility with an opening-up process that admits alternatives. As we said before, "creativity breeds creativity."

Don. What was original here? More than one thing. First, there were the actual tools Don developed. Then, looking further, there was the attitude toward life they imply. Don didn't feel he had to stick with auto repair equipment he could purchase; he could develop his own. This reframing of the situation is really quite unusual -- to think that one isn't stuck with the standard equipment one can purchase at the usual store. It also meant that Don could modify and streamline his methods of diagnosis and repair, using his personal equipment. The total complex of behaviors, Don's unique "approach to auto repair" could then also be viewed as the creative product, and as such, as a sort of flexible dance or improvisation in craftsmanship, in adapting to a situation. Looking into the future, as new problems or ideas arose, Don could again be expected to be more flexible than someone else might be in dealing with them.

What specifically is original? Tools, and methods of use, to begin with. What reference group? This is for us to decide. There were no other tools like this in the town, or in the state. "Other garages in the state" might make one arbitrary reference point. But because Don's goal involved greater personal ease and efficiency at work, his originality might best be assessed from a "personal best" standpoint, as the term is used in sports. It's the situation now vs. the situation then, how much better a situation has become over time, be it doing the 100-yard dash or auto repairs. Don's goal was met, efficiency and ease improved, and Don was also able, as it turned out, to increase both his enjoyment at work and in his leisure time.

A brief digression about "Personal Best." We may often actively create to improve something in our lives. All that matters to us is "now vs. then." It may be irrelevant how a neighbor measures up on this issue, or anybody else. Further, it can be dangerous if we just knee-jerk react to any creativity assessment with a competitive "who's better than whom" mentality. This is a common practice in many schools. We'll deal with this in the next chapter.

The "zero sum game" principle (for every winner there is a loser), is a very unfortunate in situations where everyone could actually win together. To underscore the importance of "personal best," we add one additional example, from personal encounters, not our research.

Holly and Louise: Here are two preteenagers, who invented their own version of the semaphore, a precursor of the telegraph. It's a way of signaling with visual signs that can be seen over long distances. This device was actually invented in 1791 in France by Claude Chappe and his older brother over 200 years ago. But so what? These modern young people weren't trying to transform communication practices across the world. They just wanted to signal each other from their bedroom windows, which they had been thrilled to find were in visual contact. And they want to have some fun.

The preteens decided to set up a large clock face at each window, each one with two brightly colored arms. These could be put in different positions, like the hands of a clock. The pair figured out a code, using these positions, for all the letters of the alphabet, and also a for "space" or a "period." They each memorized this code with glee, and started sending each other messages. They even figured out a way to do this after hours, when they were supposed to be in bed. Goal achieved. The fact is, Holly and Louise also learned a lot about communication devices, codes and language, the process of invention, and their own ability to act in, and change events in, the greater world around them. All of which might be "counted" as part of their personal creativity.

We return to the last two examples, with a note about "reference group." Nan's fashioned clothing might be compared with local store bought products. But with wartime resistance work, we would suggest an absolute criterion: the saving of a life. Route A or Route B? It really doesn't matter unless it works.

Nan. Here, a lot of creativity happened from small beginnings. Let's start with what was original. Certain items of clothing had a novel design, or, at least, involved twists on prevailing styles. These clothes could logically be compared to similar items in local stores -- a reasonable reference group, because that's exactly the alternative Nan had. To make her own clothes or buy them. Certainly, one could compare Nan's clothing designs to other designs throughout all time and space, but one might be hard pressed to justify this.

Looking further to process, Nan's originality grew organically from an original need, until her innovative activities were more complex and multifaceted. Many of the clothes she made from odds and ends turned out to be unusual, by virtue of these choices. She had to solve the jigsaw puzzle of piecing these together. In addition, Nan's search methods for obtaining fabric became increasingly more unusual.

This situation also meant Nan was looking at the world through new eyes—now every piece of cloth from the fabric on a car seat to the tablecloth at a weekend picnic was "game" for her uses. And so were pieces of clothing she might modify, and materials for this. Plain skirts and blouses. Unusual buttons, braids, beads, belts. When Nan started combing the flea markets for "raw" materials, she found even more ideas, more ways to pursue her interests, and finally set up her small cottage industry, with its own organizational as well as product demands—all original products of the same evolving process.

What then is the scope of the originality? There is much—including new clothing patterns and the actual fashioned items, innovative strategies for finding and using materials, and creation and management of a new business. What is our reference group? For the actual clothing, perhaps the community, since Nan wanted her family to look well dressed and to stand out a bit. What goals were met? Certainly Nan's original penny-pinching goals, but also along the way Nan developed new enthusiasm, a new hobby, and ultimately a new occupation.

Helen and Auguste. With this World War II resistance underground, there was constant originality. New dangers, new strategies in response. Escape routes, hiding places, land or sea, sources of information, trusted collaborators. Awareness was at an extreme, every movement, every sound was noticed. Everything was interpreted in a dozen different ways. No danger could be missed because lives were at stake. The original product was perhaps this ever-flexible process of response to an emergency. For Helen and Auguste, at home or out on the streets, lives were all that mattered. No pattern of response was fixed, although a plan that worked could be used indefinitely. But it could also be abandoned if necessary in a second.

Perhaps, if anything, the constant awareness, change and courage were the original product. The plans and their enactment. Here, the frame of reference is perhaps absolute: it worked -- the lives were saved. One could compare resistance efforts by other people, their extent or riskiness, and so forth, but the bottom line is essentially the same. Finally, Auguste and Janet didn't spin this work out into a range of other activities; their hands were full enough as it was.

Oops -- We Made a Mistake

So far, we've only asked if something is "creative or not." Yet it's not too early to think about mistakes. We have the so-called "false positives" (you think it's creative, it isn't) and "false negatives" (you miss the creativity that's really there). These errors sometimes stand out most obviously at the public or eminent level of creativity. Yet the issues have analogues at other levels.

Of course, it's all still "relative"; someone else may disagree with you! One part of this, we suggest, is whether the work truly dialogues with you, and is able to move you (to make you aware, through aesthetic response) and change you (create your own original response), affecting you, or your life.

False positives

Consider for instance the composer who is returning to vogue. Or the internationally known rock star who disappears overnight. At times the original appeal was superficial. At times public "taste" has just changed. What's called "creative" can be a matter of opinion, a social judgment, made at a given time, and for a given purpose.

Consider Will Rogers' renditions of "American values of common sense and decency," eagerly grasped by many during the Great Depression. Yet, as Neal Gabler put it, author of Winchell: Gossip, Poet, and the Culture of Celebrity, in the *The New York Times Book Review*, Rogers' "aw-shucks" style seemed corny just a few years after his death.

In his prime, Walter Winchell, the focus of Gabler's study, with his crisp staccato voice and the latest back room low-down on many well-known public figures, reached an amazing two out of three Americans through his gossip column and radio show. His style was new, informal, and controversial, and a clear contrast to more formal and carefully researched journalism. Nonetheless, Winchell as a person was little known 25 years after his death. The trends he spearheaded certainly were, however. And Winchell may yet resurface, at least as a symbol, thanks to Gabler, and renewed interest in the nature of reporting, and what makes notoriety, news, and fame in our own time.

Creativity is an interaction. The work we notice has potential to move us, and to change our lives. Thus, the originality it continues to generate, is not in the work itself, but in our own heads. If the work is "alive," it will keep on interacting with us. Its meanings and importance keep evolving.

Certainly, some creative works may catch on at first for reasons other than creative merit. These include luck, influence, sheer volume of the author's other output, topicality at the moment, notoriety, and the like. The goal of the producer, in addition, may not be primarily creative strength, or human betterment, but some other bottom line, such as book sales, or theater lines. Hence, other promotional come-ons may be brought to bear. But their power will fade. Consider certain film(s) on the lives of once famous pop heroes, the tell-all memoirs of a famous Hollywood actress, or the unauthorized biography of a member of a prominent royal family.

In some instances, work may in fact move us, but will not really change us. The effect is the expected one, and in the worst cases, somewhat like a drug "fix." What "moves" us may not be primarily aesthetic.

Some short-lived hits may be quick to satisfy a need—one that feels even as intense as a strong thirst be it a need for novelty, romance, or adventure. It's the quick fix: the popular sitcom, the formula mystery. The *National Enquirer* is, after all, the nation's most widely read newspaper. Breadth over depth. Visual excitement. Here is a great time for the creative "couch potato." One can settle back with a bowl of popcorn and a soft drink and do minimal work to "appreciate" the messages. Looking for the subtleties of human nature and motivation? Maybe look somewhere else.

Then there are the works that may, for a time, astound and move us, but don't ultimately change our lives, for another reason: because they were wrong! Here we turn to an example from science.

Remember "cold fusion," the near revolution in energy production that could have solved many of the world's problems? It promised to provide cheap energy, which could be made available throughout the world, even in poor economies, without high tech equipment. Furthermore, it promised to be safe energy. Whatever more could one wish for? Unfortunately, that the original "cold fusion" experiments could never be duplicated.

False Negatives

The false negatives for creativity include the achievements that go unappreciated in their own time. Consider the many poets and authors who submitted their work repeatedly for publication before success, Emily Dickinson being a notable one of them. Not the quick fix at all, this situation sometimes reflects profound messages that appear ahead of their time. At such times, originality may be less the issue than meaningfulness." They just don't understand," says the artist, "what I'm trying to say."

Certainly, unless a work is meaningful, is able to communicate, the viewer cannot be moved, never mind changed. One might as well be speaking a strange foreign language. Consider visual artists like Vincent Van Gogh, who sold only one of his daring paintings during his lifetime. He is now widely revered and a household name, with paintings which at auction, have brought almost 40 million dollars. One can only wonder what Van Gogh might say now— this gentleman who struggled so hard at the time against poverty and mental illness—if he could see all of the posters and reproductions of his ignored-at-the-time work, now adorning the walls of people's homes, offices, and dormitory rooms.

Lastly, when the influence of a work is lasting, when it attains a kind of "tenure" in the cultural world, its ongoing power is a living and universal one. There is an ongoing dynamic; the work continues to change the world, and the people in it. It is part of the life flow, continually affecting things, and being redefined in turn by these new contexts. Shakespeare's writing deals with powerful and universal themes including love, death, greed, power, status, jealousy, friendship. This work continues to alert, advise, and enlighten us. It will surely continue to do so.

The Creatively Aware Observer in Us All

Can we decide what is creative, even when the "experts" can make such mistakes? If not us, then who? It is us, after all, who seek to be moved and to be changed.

Presumably, at the gut level, we "can all do it," we can all learn to sense the presence of a creative work or contribution. With everyday creativity, in particular, developing this capacity seems essential, a part of reclaiming our creative birthright.

We carry an inborn intuitive sense of what's new in our world, what is changing -- we do need to know this! -- even if parts of this sense are a bit underdeveloped in our society. What else would one expect in evaluating innovations that may, at times, include survival level information? In a crisis, who has time to ask an expert?

Not that the experts, the critics, and our gifted teachers, aren't important. Often, an expert or authority can help us see something we missed—and sometimes even the big one, the originality. They can draw from a wealth of background and experience, to reveal underlying structures and meaning. They can reveal the vocabulary and language of a field; they can place a work in a broader context.

One also mustn't forget other resources—books, computer search services, TV and radio, for instance. They all count. There is a world of "study aids" at our service. But that is all they need to be. They can function as learned consultants to our own tastes and opinions." The experts," after all, have their own biases, preference, and agendas. At base, only we can really know what moves us.

Consider a love sonnet by Shakespeare which helps us to savor subtleties of feelings we only vaguely knew. When this happens, we can sense it—perhaps with a start from the gut, or a chill down our spine. Our own inner worlds suddenly reform with new visions of romances of our own, glances and conversations, and new views of those rooms, gardens, and sites of our encounters with those universal feelings of love, passion, jealousy, or longing.

Again, we have been changed.

This again is our own creativity, our part of the dance. We bring our own aesthetic vision, our originality in seeing, whether the seeing is in words, pictures, bodily feelings, or of another sort. To receive the message—be it a startling research finding, a revelation of a friend, or a love sonnet -- means we must do our own innovating. We must collude in creativity, and agree to alter how we think about things. We will if necessary "try on" some new ideas, and at times even jettison some cherished beliefs.

The artist helps us to do this by communicating with us directly, at both an emotional and intellectual level. But we must first receive the message directly, and not just delegate it to a critic, who will act like a member of Congress and carry the decision back to us. It seems crazy. We don't need ranks of experts standing between us and the world, telling us what books to read and what they mean, how to decorate our homes, how to speak to each other, how to organize our day, and where to go on vacation. This is our own pleasure, and part of reclaiming our creative birthright.

CHAPTER 3

THE GENIUS AND THE EVERYDAY CREATOR

"… not that you won or lost but how you played the game."
--GRANTLAND RICE

Who is more creative than whom? Who is most creative? At times we ask these sorts of questions. But now, we step back to wonder why we are asking. The very act of asking can open up options for us, or devalue the creativity of ourselves and others, and narrow our view of the world. We begin with a story.

I recently saw the movie, *Searching For Bobby Fischer*, with what my daughter calls "happy-sad" tears in my eyes. I kept pointing out the lessons to my daughter, who at one point came and hugged me, and said she didn't know why. Forgive me if this account isn't true to every detail of the movie. But this is what was so moving to me.

Here is little Josh looking, in an innocent eyed, winning way, like a friend of mine must have also looked at age seven. Josh is an undiscovered chess genius. He has been watching the guys down at Washington Square, in New York City, playing chess under the trees, Josh himself watching from behind a tree, when one day the little boy is given his own chance. He is seven and suddenly he is making brilliant chess playing moves. A combination piece attack, and at age seven. Bobby Fischer! says an onlooker. And Josh's insightful mother sees what's happening.

So soon does father, a sportswriter, who gets Josh (this is a true story, which father wrote) connected up with a revered grandmaster chess teacher. The teacher is quickly riveted by Josh, for nowhere outside of Bobby Fischer himself has he seen this talent, not in all the champions and famous players he introduced to father. These masters all had tremendous knowledge, enormous skill. They were amazing. But the "true successor to Bobby Fischer," he told father, "… is home right now, sleeping in your son's bedroom." The others all lacked the fire and daring and the unsuspected. The true *art* of the game.

This teacher had all but retired, at least until he saw Josh making his moves. Bobby Fischer! The dream, the hopes of glory, of something larger than life, which he could help bring to life (along with a chance to replay some of his own issues), now drew this teacher out of his retreat.

Suddenly, "Bobby Fischer" and all he represented, became greater than Josh, the little boy.

Josh's whole life turned increasingly toward chess, his hobbies getting dropped, his field trips with father focused on chess matches only. The White House? The Lincoln Memorial? We didn't have time for those, father explained to Josh's classroom teacher. Now Josh gets switched by father to another school, this despite Josh's real regret (and mother's knowing glance), because the new school will value chess a lot more than the old one.

Now at match after match, we see parents, usually fathers, hovering, talking, worrying, biting their figurative finger nails. Will their child win? Who will *win*. Josh is doing a lot of winning. Finally, at a match, an interviewer points out to Josh's father, half-laughing, that, because his son is so successful, "every other parent hates you." Josh's teacher tells him the same thing, but more seriously: that the other kids, his competitors, are hating him too.

The better Josh is, the more they will hate him. And so, of course, Josh's teacher tells him, you've got to hate them back. Bobby Fischer knew he was better than they were. He knew he could win. He went around with "contempt." "That's part of winning, "Josh is told, "contempt for your opponents."

Josh wasn't so sure about this. As his mother emphasized, Josh "has 'a good heart'." Josh was particularly torn at the suggestions he and mother had so far resisted that he stop seeing his older chess-playing buddies at Washington Square. These good natured men, who joshed and played with him and each other in noisy rapid-fire timed matches, were good humored competitors who were fueled by their caring for each other, as well as the chemical rush of their fast-paced competition.

Josh's particular friend, Vinnie, tall, bold, voluble, African-American, and supercool with orange vest, bald head, sculpted mustache and beard, was a fast and fierce player and a warm human being. He wanted Josh to win, and for no particular personal reason." Come on," he'd say, "come on and beat me.... Now you're playing chess! Beat me!"

We play the person, explained Vinnie later, and not the chessboard. And we play to win, not to avoid losing. His game was a dare, a thrill, a moment for its own sake. "You've gotta risk everything, go to the edge of defeat. That's where you've gotta be..." This was his pleasure. There was joy and humor in the advance of each flying piece.

But the grandmaster teacher teacher finally convinced parents and Josh that his Washington Square friends were off limits. They'd lead Josh to bad chess playing habits. And Josh's job was to win.

Now Josh lost his will to play. He threw a match, and wondered why his father stood so far away from him afterward. Josh's teacher hardened, mocked him about his longed-for grandmaster's certificate, the symbol of excellence that Josh coveted, saying over and over again, and brutally, that this wasn't it, this wasn't it. Josh was on his way to greatness. He must do nothing, say nothing, think nothing, that wasn't along this road. Kid X, another super-competitor, whom Josh would surely meet in the finals, was certainly not wasting his time with fishing, friends, and, by no means whatsoever, with bad chess playing habits.

Intuitive and gentle mother overheard all of this, and in a wonderful moment, threw the revered chess grandmaster teacher out of her house.

Every good chess player is trying to please their father, someone had said. As if there were no other way to connect with a father. To win your father's love.

Father listened to Josh, and finally heard. The wisdom of his son broke through. Josh went back to playing with Vinnie in Washington Square, with father seen grinning on the sidelines. The big tournament was coming, the one in Chicago. Kid X was spending every moment practicing, they all knew this, but Josh went off with his father on a fishing trip. Two weeks without a rook or a bishop. (A little hard to believe actually—but Josh had also become expert in mental chess.)

Still, Josh had flipped his priorities. It was the whole of life, connection with the world, that had come back into focus, with Josh's chess as one part of all this. Albeit a very special part. And Josh knew that his father loved him.

Frankly, at this point, I was a little afraid that Josh would give up his chess ambitions, finding that a more homogenous life was preferable. That you can't excel and have friends. That you can't push yourself to the limit without inner self-doubts and a neurotic relationship to your parent. The conclusion might therefore be to give up on excellence. But happily that was not to be! It was on to the national chess finals in Chicago.

Now Josh knew more than ever that chess was his. It was important to him.

Vinnie came to the tournament, as proud as could be. And Josh's father came. And his mother. The family had hoped Josh's grandmaster teacher would also come to this crucial contest; he had been so important to Josh. Could he now give Josh some support? Nope, he had said, prior to the event.

Yet right before the key round, the teacher not only appeared, abashed, informed, and more connected with his own issues, but presented Josh with a magnificently adorned grandmaster's chess certificate, a personalized version of the one he had denied Josh before. And he movingly said to Josh, "I've never been so proud of anyone in my life." The circle of transformation was complete.

The match was incredible. Josh, of course, cared. He loved chess loved *chess*, much more than winning at it. He looked across the large room of competitors at a friend (yes he still had some friends there) and exchanged a special sign of mutual good luck. Josh looked with curiosity at Kid X. Kid X was soon glaring at Josh. Poor Josh. Poor Kid X.

Then round after round of play, narrowing it down. Finally, it's Josh vs. Kid X. Suddenly Jason starts playing the Washington Square way. Look at your competitor, psych him out. Play the *person*. Josh does this, bold moves, fast moves, out with his queen, much sooner than his teacher would have wished, always with an eye to Kid X's reaction. He's doing great. "I showed him that!" shouts Vinnie.

The play reaches a new plateau. Kid X makes a mistake. Now the clock slows, the time expands and there's a hush. Suddenly, we see the face of Josh's grandmaster teacher, the fire in his eyes. "Look deep Josh. It's twelve moves away—but it's there, you got him." He thinks this fervently across the large playing room, he wishes, whispers, and quietly tells father. "Play it in your head. Don't move until you can see it. Don't—move until you can see it."

Josh is distracted, looks down but doesn't see, sadly thinks, "I'm sorry Dad." But then he stops, complies, and looks, settles down now to really look, chin on his hand, time clock still running. "Play it in your head..." Kid X is confused, thinks he is winning, and smirks. But Josh is now in his own world, his own mode, and now his other teacher's mode too, for it's come time to shift, to do it the other way, it is all there together in the totality of Josh's mind, laced together with fishing trips, the enthusiasm of his father, and his mother's deepest trust. Here is creativity as an *art*, chess as an art, drawing on everything in one's total experience—and drawing on all the people who have shared it. Bobby Fischer himself is present, through the grandmaster teacher who has learned his every move. And so Josh hunkers down to think.

Suddenly Josh smiles the tiniest of smiles. "He sees it!" the teacher exclaims. And Josh slowly looks up, up at arrogant Kid X, and across the table Josh offers his hand. What is this? asks the kid. A draw, offers Josh. Take it, and we can both be champion. Refuse it, and you'll lose.

Kid X can't believe it. "Look at the board," he says. Josh offers his hand, and offers again. Josh empathizes with the kid. It's a horrible life. To win and to lose. To lose even meaning to die, to lose love, to lose yourself. We can win together says Josh. Don't do this to yourself, don't let this happen. "Take my hand," he says in effect, once again. But the kid refuses.

Fair enough. In a flurry of moves, Josh now brings it all home. Kid's pawn makes a queen, Josh's pawn makes a queen—which I'll take, thinks kid, but now Josh says "check," and the kid has missed it. He sees the inevitable, tips over his king in concession, and walks sadly away, while the joyous crowds converge on Josh. How quickly Kid X, the "loser," and a spectacular chess player, is forgotten.

"My man, I knew you could do it!" says Vinnie, joined by Josh's father, and grandmaster teacher, all proud teachers converging to celebrate. And here is the happy confident face of Josh's mother who, in a remarkable moment, has seen the ultimate victory: the fusion of Josh's extraordinary talent with his "good heart."

As for the rest of the kids, for the "losers," we see Kid X's teacher instructing him behind closed doors, and another kid's father, the dad of Josh's friend in fact, berating him openly for "bringing out your queen too soon" (the same thing that Josh had done). "Didn't he say anything else to you?" Josh asks his friend later. "No," says the hapless kid. Talk about love on a contingency basis. But Josh, at least, says something very supportive to his friend, and they walk away together, while Josh's dad watches misty eyed from a window. Lesson learned.

So much is here. But we'll focus now on this one: Why compare Why seek the No.1 superlative chess player?

Here, for one, may enter our mystique of the genius, the one who stands alone, who can do something no one else can do. This extraordinary person is unconquerable, almost inhuman; this person can move ahead where we cannot, can save us where we would otherwise fail. This can also be embroidered with the mystique of the hero the one who forges forth, who takes the hero's journey, and returns to share the results, to help us, and to do good. This splendid person who stands apart is also our benefactor.

Who is Bobby Fischer? In the abstract, he is a world chess champion, showing us an epitome of human possibility. And he also takes us even further, into realms we feel we cannot ever possibly travel.

Yet here is precisely the problem. For it need not be so.

In Josh's world, there were any number of superlative young chess players. Give or take five minutes sleep or a lucky break, any of a number of others in the tournament might have taken first place. Most certainly including Kid X. Josh won, but he did not stand alone among competitors. He stood at the apex of a constantly shifting pyramid of young chess players, who were having good or bad days, or luck. At that instant, at least, Josh shone supreme. But as such, Josh stood there as a symbol—he represented the excellence of all the young persons present, as well as a point to which they might aspire. He did not by any means stand alone.

Josh's offer of a "draw" acknowledged this fact, as well as his comfort with it. "We are both good," it seemed to say. It is all the same.

Yet look what happened instead. Seconds after the critical play, the one boy was a hero, and the other was forgotten. Indeed, every child in that room was a finalist at a national chess tournament. Why should so many have had to leave disappointed, devastated, even in disgrace?

A Touch of Genius

First, we ask how often this excellent hero does truly stand alone. A very key point.

Are the qualities of genius unique? It is beyond the scope of this book to go into the many complex debates about "genius," and there are some excellent books available. But two types of points should be noted, before one concludes that a person of genius is in in no way at all like the rest of us.

First, the notion of "genius" is being viewed more and more as a social construction, and less a term describing an isolated human being who is fundamentally different from everybody else. Some of this specialness may not derive from the "person" at all, or at least from the person in isolation. It may represent a more complicated equation of personal traits, fortunate circumstances, a historical period that can make it bloom, and finally, one that is able to recognize it publicly.

A work of genius is first, a very rare attainment, and then one which is so appropriate and well-timed that it affects a lot of people.

Plus it affects people in a way that they are pleased about. Why else would they (or a professional field of endeavor) pay so much attention? Was Salk's polio vaccine a good idea? You bet. Sigmund Freud's stunning proposal of an "unconscious mind" explained or seemed to explain, many previous mysteries of human experience, and even offered possible ways to intervene.

Yet a person who, in the basement, untangled some ultimate mysteries of consciousness and never shared them with anyone would never be designated a genius.

Secondly, with exceptional mental strategies, researchers are finding, increasingly, many similarities between creators at vastly different levels of sophistication. Psychologist David Perkins summed this up: "These same resources of selection explain masterly and more ordinary creating. The master will notice more, remember more, exercise better critical judgment, and so on, but the processes involved are the same in kind."

Think about it. Sometimes a person can be just a little more expert than we are at something, and we are blown away. We are amazed. We could never do that! But our lack of understanding can magnify the discrepancy; we are not really in a position to judge. As Perkins says, one should also keep in mind the interesting human tendency to rate something higher that we don't understand than something we do. Once the trick is explained, it may seem less meritorious than it was before.

Here is a thought experiment. Imagine that Bobby Fischer explained the logic behind a breathtakingly mystifying sequence of chess moves. Assume the explanation made perfectly good common sense. Can one imagine now valuing the strategy at least a tiny bit less? Recall that it is still the exact same strategy. Did we think he did it by "magic"? Did we hope so? We'll return to this interesting situation.

Discontinuities?—"Major" and "Minor" Creativity

This position seems rather amusing, when one takes it literally. It holds that there are two types of creativity: major and minor. The major kind requires a massive change in one's conceptual framework. (A clear example is, "The world is round, and not flat.") In the minor kind, one applies the same old strategies to new tasks ("How far can one see across the ocean before the world's curvature makes it impossible?" And "what if the waves are so-and-so tall and far apart what's the farthest one can see?")

Few people would argue that Pasteur, who developed the germ theory of disease, changed completely how we think about infection. Most people would say this was more creative than the—nonetheless very difficult and important—job of finding new antibiotics. But the real question is whether these forms of creativity are so completely different from each other that one cannot possible shade into the other. Are they like apples and oranges. One creative process uses the green neurons in the brain, and the other the red neurons? And if so, why are there just two levels of creativity, and not three, four, or five?

They Came Close

In parallel with the "pyramid" of chess masters, with a "winner" on top, it seems possible that for every person who gets "crowned" with the title of "genius," there are a great many more who are near, and not so near, misses.

Here are the people who didn't quite have enough money, enough free time, enough exposure, sufficient encouragement, confidence, adequate training, they chose the wrong major in college, got severely ill, and so on. We propose that the genius in general, as with the chess master specifically, may be more a symbol for all the like-minded others who came close -- and not so close.

Turning to science, one may thus understand how two people may simultaneously make the same scientific discovery. The "time may be right." It's in the air. A number of people have similar interests, training, devotion to the field, and are working within the same basic information network, within their scientific field. They are reading the same journals, going to the same conferences, talking with the same people -- and they are all closing in on the answer. For instance, even as James Watson, Francis Crick, and Rosalind Franklin, in England, were converging on the double-helix model of DNA, Linus Pauling, in California, was developing his own triple-helix model. The basic concepts were similar. Of course, only the former discovery was correct, and received the Nobel Prize. (Important as well to note discussions on how Rosalind Franklin deserved the Nobel Prize, along with Watson and Crick.)

Scaling The Pyramids of Potentiality

This discussion is not to detract in the least from the exceptionality of certain creative people. They are extraordinary in the breadth of their vision, and complexity of their thought. Yet, taking specific qualities, such as, say, spatial ability, they may be more quantitatively different from others than qualitatively different. They essentially have "more of" a spatial ability, rather than some qualitatively unique spatial capacity (say, a capacity to sense a mythical fourth dimension).

Or they may have some highly rare interaction of "ordinary" spatial ability with something else you rarely see with it.

When one specifies combination of certain qualities, one can get rather steep pyramids of potentiality—for that particular activity—even if the individual ingredients aren't that rare. Level of spatial ability already forms one continuum. Now add relevant logical abilities, basic chess-playing knowledge, and a lot of experience. Already very few people are at the pinnacle of this mountain.

Now add an extra large dose of enthusiasm, persistence, and frustration tolerance. Plus the originality and risk-taking to try some unusual and nonstandard moves, rather than "go by the book." Now for good measure, add an excellent visual memory—make it photographic—and finally the potential to play and replay 20 moves over and over in one's head. If you go out on the street corner and wait, you won't meet too many of these people walking by.

In other words, some exceptional people may display rare and startling interactions of qualities. The qualities in themselves may not be all that unusual. But the combination they create is vanishingly rare.

Yet even here, the person at the apex of a particular pyramid of potential doesn't stand there alone in the wind. The mountain is crowded with all the other folks who "just missed." They didn't present precisely that combination of qualities, but were "off" just a little bit (for this purpose, at least), in one direction or the other, and on one variable or another.

Pyramids of Potentiality -- For Us All

But there are a lot of other pyramids of potentiality, if you will. And we all have our own pyramids, our own mountains where we stand on top. We are all unique in our own ways—in our own combinations of enthusiasms, abilities, resources, and experiences. This is another way of saying we are all individuals.

Take an analogy. You'd have to throw a hundred thousand dice, say, and have the whole hundred thousand come out "just so," to get one particular combination of interests and skills and experience. Think for instance of the complex logical, spatial, strategic, mnemonic, and other capacities, enthusiasms, motivations and opportunities necessary for developing that exceptional chess player.

This reconstruction would not be easy to do after the fact, if you wanted just a certain type of person. You'd have to do an incredible amount of dice throwing. In truth, you probably would not live long enough.

But what our immense world is doing, though, with the rich variety of people we all represent, is throwing those dice a great many times, and all at once. We are each of us the product of a unique throw, and also together represent a rich tapestry of multiple possibilities. Then we develop our possibilities further in our life choices and experiences, choosing from a true infinity of paths. For who knows what exactly is be needed?

This discussion is truly about much more than chess playing. Or about genius. How hungry we'd all be, how cold, how little we'd have to see or do or read or wish for, and how few people we would find to help us, if all that we did, each and every one of us, was play games of chess.

We might just as well be speaking of a range of difficult things we would each of us like to achieve. Such as finding the "right" mate (the failure rate is phenomenal). Or the right work situation (how many are unhappy). Or the right living community (how many are lonely). And so on. It can be hard for each of us to discover those situations in the wider world that resonate with the special combinations of qualities we bring. How hard it can sometimes be "to find our place."

Our grandmaster "genius" of chess just happened to represent the right throw of the dice—of personal qualities and circumstances—that society needed, at that particular moment, amongst the many other people and possibilities that existed. This among the incredible range of roles available in society. For chess. This is why we hear of this person, and not the many others whose "throws of the dice, "if you will, were one number off, in one direction or another. Off, that is, for chess. But not for the writing of poetry, or the raising of a family on a Midwestern farm.

Some Myths and Beliefs About Genius

At what great cost we may idealize the lone hero—who has now become superhero. Untouchable. Unknowable. While we, the admirers, who might really like to attain some of this expertise ourselves, can only trail behind passively in the dust, pretending it's "not for us." We can end up not only devaluing our own potential, but amputating it completely.

Talk about our lack of awareness of the creativity around us. Certain high points—the "winners"—may stand out, like islands rising out of the ocean; the rest disappear completely under the surface. And, it gets worse. For someone else may even have made the call for us: the awarders of the prize, the designers of the contest. They designated Person Number One as creative and bestowed great honors; they perhaps gave Number Two and Three a nod, but number 4, 5, 6 and all the rest were consigned to oblivion the moment they didn't get the recognition.

We mention a few other potential factors that may (incorrectly) help distance us further from the creative genius. They come under the rubric of potential myths and beliefs about genius.

1) Creative insight—that rare and special gift. Not so rare at all, as we'll see. We all can have insights. But the ancient belief was that only certain persons were blessed with this vision. As Plato wrote of poets, "... it is not they who utter these words of great price when they are out of their wits, but that it is God himself who speaks and addresses us through them." There is the related belief that one must wait patiently for one's muse (in whatever form this muse takes), or court that muse through the right actions and ablutions.

2) The freedom to create—which one must have in abundance. This involves both a conceptual and temporal freedom, a freedom of thought and an expanse of time to seek those sometimes fickle insights, and develop those special thoughts. There is much to be said for such freedom. But at its extreme, only an elite population with wealth and leisure would be able to participate. The well- to-do artist (or the starving yet free artist), or the advantaged scientist could participate. The 9-to-5 person seeking everyday creativity on the job would be at a disadvantage by definition. Or the artistic hobbyist who works only when there is a little time. This will necessarily be "second best" if it even "counts." However one can have creative experiences at many odd times, and during other activities. Women, in particular, have had occasion to report this.

3) The strange, weird, and possessed—being inescapably peculiar. Einstein, with hair in disarray, has become one symbol of the eccentricity of genius. As if Einstein were so preoccupied or inspired that he couldn't possibly find time to comb his hair. Or that it wouldn't have mattered anyway. That he dwelt in a different realm where this wasn't important. The belief returns us once again to the notion of the creator as "possessed" and hence totally different that we are. Certainly highly creative people may be nonconformist and different, but this belief is at an entirely different level, and erects fences between exceptional creativity and us.

4) Mood disorders and creativity—illness is part of it. John Dryden wrote "Great wits are sure to madness near allied/And thin partitions do their bounds divide." How can this person be anything like the everyday creator ? Well, in fact, there is some basis to the fabled connections between mood disorders and creativity, as our work and the work of others has shown. But mood disorders certainly do not explain all creativity, and the patterns are, in any

case, complex. This link between creativity and mood disorders occurs not only within the same person, but across persons in the same family. Interestingly, the fully psychiatrically normal relatives of manic-depressives may show advantages for original everyday creativity that other normal individuals may lack. The issue is not necessarily about illness, and there is much here that we all can learn, mood disordered or not.

5) Suffering--all real creativity must involve this. This view fits with the notion that creators are different, strange, disordered or ill, and also with the observation that many artistic works do arise out of profound suffering and dissatisfaction. One may indeed use one's craft to overcome great personal difficulty (ultimately moving in the direction of health). But difficulty and pain aren't absolute requirements, particularly outside of the arts, and with everyday creativity. And, as we'll see, whatever its origins, creativity ultimately tends to work in the service of health.

The Fruits of Competition

Another factor may distance some people even further from the person of genius, leaving them unable to identify with the achievement, and devaluing their own potential. Oddly enough, an unconscious self-destruct could even be part of the purpose.

There are serious risks of "playing the game" in our highly competitive society. Consider, for instance, chess masters such as Josh and Kid X, or, for that matter, Bobby Fischer:

* If idealized and distanced from ourselves, these chess masters cannot be in direct competition with us. They are in a world by themselves. Apart. Furthermore, we may be able to benefit directly from their sparkling expertise, indeed as a consumer might do (in reading a book on their strategies), as well as obtain some reflected glory ("our country's chess champion"); but

* If not idealized, these exceptional players might be recast as our rivals, or at least potential rivals, who might someday, somehow, end up in a chess competition with us. Then (as in the case of Josh and Kid X) there is the potential to lose (that is, lose "everything"), never mind encounter the window-dressing of an unpleasant contest in which an opponent may be de-idealized, and even devalued, and hated.

Alternatives: "Making the Grade" or "Personal Best"

Josh, the young boy, wasn't into this winner-take-all competition. His interest was in a Grandmaster Certificate? A player, we were told, earns this recognition by slowly accumulating points for particular learnings and accomplishments. Josh was delighted when his teacher started giving him some points.

This is not a zero-sum game, a "you win, I lose" situation. Josh and Kid X could each get a certificate—the two of them could excel together, indeed along with many other people. By contrast, only one person could win the tournament. The rest would be "losers."

The Grandmaster's Certificate is a form of "criterion-referenced" evaluation. Whoever meets the criterion—whoever can do the job—makes the grade. It can be one person or even everyone. Josh's getting the award wouldn't mean Kid X would automatically be denied it. There is a "personal best" aspect as well to Josh's Grandmaster quest, the term we used in the last chapter. The concern: self-improvement. Doing better than you did before; the standard is your own performance. Josh and his friend at the tournament could work together toward such a goal. In theory, so could Josh and Kid X.

In this situation, one young person need not automatically view the other as some sort of enemy or foe. Nor need they feel smug, arrogant, contemptuous, hateful or afraid of the other, who is, after all, only a kid like oneself with a strongly shared passion.

Yet be that as it may, we still need to deal with the blood and guts of a "zero-sum" competition. And how this may affect questions of why and how we assess creativity.

Competition vs. Cooperation

One point of view is that competition is always destructive, no matter what the context. That competition is aggression. Period. There can't be winners without losers. Others will therefore become the enemy. And competition is bad for self-esteem. For someone's self-esteem. Never mind that competition can be bad for the activity itself, which can become tainted with bad feelings, and can lose its intrinsic challenge. That indeed there are better ways to challenge and to improve oneself than at someone else's expense.

There is indeed research suggesting that cooperative learning can accomplish more than competition, and can be more fun. Think of six college students who combine their efforts for an oral report about a particular country. They each choose a separate focus—government, technology, the environment, the arts, education, and social organization—but they also share and work together. They end up doing a humorous play about why the Summer Olympics should be located in this country, stopping at six different points for asides on their special areas of expertise.

At its best, working together has the potential to be more fun, more motivating, can lower anxiety about "how one is doing," and can keep the focus on track—namely, on the real learning, and not on a quest for "being number one," or sniffing out the weaknesses of someone you're "trying to beat." It can also capitalize on the unique offerings of different people.

As in the group report, working together can also build trust, sensitivity, communication, and the ability to take another's viewpoint. The solid competitor, by contrast, may not want to trust anyone too much or to share information that might give an "opponent" an advantage. What a training in process! In addition, learning to be sensitive, and taking another's viewpoint might payoff best where one could second guess the opponent and "get the drop on him."

Competition When You Least Expect It?

There is certainly merit to this view against competition, and we could perhaps do away with much of the competition we've got. For how subtly we may pit ourselves one against the other. Consider this provoking example from Alfie Kohn, author of the excellent book, *No Contest.* This sort of thing happens all the time.

A woman and two little boys are headed toward a pool, and she asks, "... who's going to jump into the pool fastest?"

"We both are!" the kids responded, refusing to play the game.

But, wondered Alfie Kohn, "How long can they hold out?"

I've done it too. And you? I for one plead guilty to issuing this sort of challenge. The goal has usually been to get some kids from point A to point B without too much delay. Yet one could say instead, "Let's see if you can both get there in 10 seconds," or any number of other things that challenge the kids without pitting one against the other.

Again with kids, and on a perhaps more ominous note, I am reminded of a brochure I saw, sent to applicants for a private kindergarten, in a school that goes up to the 12th grade. Do we see images of happy little children learning to play and study together? Only in part.

This introductory brochure also includes the average SAT (Scholastic Aptitude Test) verbal and numerical scores of the graduating seniors from that same private school. For *Kindergarten*? Should this really be one of a parent's first concerns: How much more brightly a child at this school may outshine his or her college bound peers—not even in general, but on two numbers, a popular duo of "aptitude" measures—which will be measured more than a decade down the road?

Wouldn't it be better to focus on the child's own interests, self-esteem, sense of competency, love of learning, and connection with peers?

Is Competition Sometimes Helpful?

By contrast, what about the "playing for fun" that was portrayed in *Searching for Bobby Fischer* with the Washington Square chess playing crowd? Here one person wins one day, another person presumably the next day. Cheerful competitors seem to "push" each other in a collegial way toward peak performance. In theory, they are as interested in the process, in the "playing," in the fun of the struggle, than in each particular outcome. With the Washington Square crowd, one might think, it is "all in the game."

In this portrayal, it's the game and not the ego that is up for grabs. The jugular is not permanently severed. For how many people is this realistic?

Here is a similar model that emphasizes competition and cooperation, described by Olympic athlete and Pentathlon champion Marilyn King. She defines competition as "using your environment... to help extract your 'best self.'" And she continues, "I was not particularly a gifted or talented athlete.... I knew that the reason I would compete at the highest levels of my sport was how I thought about things..."

Ms. King tells of an experience in the 1976 Olympic Trials: "... in the trials my primary competitor was a woman who placed first most of the year that I competed. She was a taller, stronger, bigger, better athlete than I and she usually beat me. But she began to miss her high jumps.... I went across the field to her and said, 'Jane, what are you doing? You left me here by myself.... What am I going to do? I need you in order to jump higher!'"

This all sounds great, and quite sincere. But one must also wonder if Jane, who was missing her jumps, felt the same way at that point about the competition.

Ms. King feels the problem is not in the competition per se, but in the context in which it takes place. She was profoundly struck by how the winners were crowned and the losers often forgotten. As in Josh's chess championship, you win or you are nothing.

King noted the day that both Carl Lewis and Ben Johnson broke the record for the 100-meter dash. The media emphasized only the winner. Both men had run faster in that race than any person in history. Too bad. The fascination with the winner was so overshadowing of this triumph of human potential, that it too was lost in the wake.

Ms. King also told how at age 19, she was incredibly proud to be in the Olympics at 11, in Munich. This was enough (indeed). But on her return, and after hearing she had attended, the next thing people would ask was, "Did you win a medal?"

"When I said I didn't win a medal, they didn't have anything else to say—that was the end of the conversation. And as a 19-year old, I was pretty devastated by that."

Like it or not, in real- life, there are a great many situations in which one person will be compared to another. For starters, a Presidential election. From job selection to choosing a mate, people are always mixing and matching. Thus it makes sense to have some good ways to do it, ones that are valid and fair. And for creativity too. At times it is largely a question of "fit." But at times, there is more than one qualified candidate for the job, or job for the candidate.
The destructive effects of competition can at least be minimized. Here are a few examples of what can be changed:

1) Improving oneself. Avoiding a sense of a contest primarily to beat out an "opponent"-- who can therefore become the enemy -rather than to improve oneself.

2) Seeing that many outcomes "count." Rejecting the notion that only a few outcomes are worthy: only "first place" and not second, for instance, a total absurdity, or only victories in sports, or in math, or... rather than in the myriad of complex roles in society. We are all at the head of another pyramid of potential, with a "fit" in one setting or another.

3) Many routes to excellence. Valuing the myriad of abilities and qualities of human beings, rather than thinking that a few mere honors or figures tell the whole story or are the only worthy outcomes (e.g., a chess championship; high verbal and numerical SAT's).

4) An ongoing process. Seeing oneself as a process in motion, with dynamic skills that are growing and changing. Hence one is advancing up the "pyramid" of a chosen endeavor in order to seek a "personal best." The people at the top are not so much rivals, as positive role models of what one may ultimately achieve—and, indeed, will achieve in one's own way.

5) Creative uniqueness. Recognizing that one's own creative signature marks everything. With very few exceptions, one's achievements in a particular area will reflect who one is, and no one else. As we shall further see, very few things can be measured all at once on the same single ruler (or pyramid). The many flavors of ourselves are complex in the extreme.

CHAPTER 4

FINDING THE CHILD IN YOU

*The majority of people go little by little to the prosaic side of practical life,
conceal the dreams of their youth, consider love a chimera...*

--LEV VYGOTSKY, *Imagination and Creativity in Childhood*

Premise: As children, we learn to think in some wondrous ways. These are not just steps on the road to something better but, in one sense at least, are as good as they will ever get. The trick, as we get older, is first consciously to hold on to these colorful modes of thinking, and then to weave them integrally into our so-called "mature" styles of thought. This could happen more often than it does. Yet to do so involves building mental bridges, so we can go back and forth readily. It also requires comfort with the sometimes startling arrival of these "primitive" thoughts when we don't expect them, and a comfort with just how far these can take us. This is not the equilibrium of rational conceptual thought, but a path toward disequilibrium and, at times, even massive destabilization. It's a zap to a new dimension, a new viewpoint.

We turn now to some rich qualities of the creative process and some of their possible early origins. This is summarized in the premise, above.

This premise sounds fine, perhaps, but we are not here to romanticize whatever a young child wants to do—nor, for that matter, to give free rein to our own latent childish selves. This is, after all, reality. Nonetheless, there is much we can learn from children, both about originality and awareness. This is "the freshness of childhood" people are sometimes trying to recapture. Along with a few other things.

But now here you are one morning as the hassled parent (personal story here), on the way to work, late (of course) as you exit the door, and bringing in tow this delightful little preschooler who wants to stop and look at everything, and do everything, with total absorption, and not a care in the world. Never mind the realities of schedules, school times, work obligations. You perhaps threaten a bit with a timeworn, "I'm going to count to three..."or, "if you don't get in the car..."You begin to feel like a drill sergeant, a mistreater of children.

And now this child is wandering off across the back yard lawn, in irregular absentminded steps -- a little dreamwalker, a hypnotizee.

"Where's that bird going in the grass? I'm going to follow it. Look, there's a hole in the fence. What's behind that hole in the fence? *What is behind that hold in the fence?* I've got to know. It could be anything. I've never seen out there before. I can look through that hole. Then I can see it. I've got to see it. Maybe it's scary, maybe it's a dinosaur! Maybe it's a baby T. Rex, a meat eater. It's going to be kicking and trying to get out of there. I'm going to go see it and I'll tell it *Hi*. Then I'll run in the house and say mommy mommy."

Here is a mystery, an obsession, even some veritable magic—and it is the most important problem in the world. The entreaties of the parent are heard far in the distance.

Now what does a parent do? The focus here isn't on setting limits, but let's face it, a child simply can't do whatever she or he wants.

Yet at a more subtle level, when you look at this kind of scene, do you sometimes feel just a twinge of discomfort, just a bit at times, that in a different way, things are going too far? That the thinking of this child is just a little too odd, or uncontrolled, or out of touch with reality? And do you ever fear, in an instant about face, that maybe it's you who are missing the boat? That there's something magical going on here that you have forgotten how to see?

Where Did It Go?

How a child thinks—and how an adult thinks. You might think that we, as adults, could do all the things a child can do, and then some. We'd logically have all the more ways then to be, to experience, and create. We could use the various child modes with an adult's sophistication. Yet it often doesn't work this way. We look first at originality in the context of how kids, and adults, form concepts. Then, in the next chapter, we look at the awareness of childhood, the freshness of thought, which adult habituation and preoccupation can erase. (In later chapters, we will deal specifically with questions of early education to preserve and enhance the creative thinking of childhood.)

Originality and Child Thought

A preschooler may say a broomstick is a horse, or a couch is an airplane. These fantasies are fixed to the concrete objects. The broom is an important part of the ride. In fact, if someone pulls away the broomstick, the child's ride is probably over. This is an example of symbolic play. Certain images or objects are taken to stand for something else. A broomstick is a horse. The magical transformation takes place in the child's imagination. The developmental psychologist Jean Piaget summarized this process in terms of two now widely touted terms which he introduced. In symbolic play, Piaget said, there is a primacy of *assimilation* to *accommodation*.

Assimilation

Something means what one wants it to mean. Assimilation, in this case, pertains to the broomstick becoming a horse. The new information is assimilated to what is already happening in the child's head. For a young child, this is no problem whatsoever. The child makes the new input (in this case, the broomstick) work with whatever's going on (wanting to ride a horse). And it doesn't matter a bit whether the broom has bristles, no legs, can't whinny, and the like.

This is a game for the child, and a mind-expanding one too. In the end, the broom will go back to being a broom. And the child will know it.

But let's take a mind-contracting option, and use an adult for the example. An adult can sometimes bend external reality, even through a full U-turn, in defiance of reality, to forcefully maintain a blind belief about something. One truly stays "blind" to reality, and closes off other options, even in their perception. The "real evidence" may not make a dent.

Here, assimilation (and we're including wishful thinking and psychological defense) can be abetted by our tendency to habituation. A situation seems so familiar to us hardened creatures that we can revert to autopilot and slip in the old "schemas"—those thought and behavior patterns that always seemed to work before.

We may do this unconsciously—how often we do—if no change in our world wakes us up. Some people have been known to prejudge members of certain reference groups without knowing a thing about them, not a bad example of the phenomenon at all.

By contrast, the process of accommodation involves bending and adjusting to new data, to an external reality. This time one notices "the evidence" and changes one's thinking accordingly. For the child, the broomstick doesn't really have four legs, in fact it doesn't have any. "Maybe I'll fly a rocket ship," thinks the child instead, deciding to take an even faster ride. (Obviously, this choice of vehicles still involves a lot of assimilation.)

When we talk about creativity, we are invoking the first type of assimilation and not the second. The broadening type, and not the constricting type.

Accommodation

The extreme of accommodation involves automatically bending to new input without testing it at all against inner experience. In this way, one might buy "the Brooklyn Bridge" from a person on the street. One word for this is *gullibility*.

Little kids may go too far at times in believing their parents or other authority figures, and can sometimes get woefully misled. By adolescence, however, they are probably beginning to reverse this balance. To be sure, some young people will no longer believe anything a parent tells them! We should probably be applauding this trend more than we do (even as we are wringing our hands at our teenagers). For we as adults still have a lot to learn. And we may still ourselves bend blindly to authority.

Even in the best of cases, few of us have gotten things all figured out. Indeed, we may barely even perceive them to begin with, through our veil of expectations and perceptual filters. Hence, except for an impossibly closed-minded and preprogrammed person, we're all going to keep on accommodating to the world. We'll keep changing a little bit, from time to time, whether we like it or not.

The Balance of Thought Processes -- An Adult Ideal?

Someone comes up to you and says that "the house is falling down and needs rebuilding from the ground up." You don't necessarily believe it, and you wouldn't rush out to renovate the house. Or they announce "the school curriculum needs a total overhaul." You don't scrap everything you've been teaching. But you will probably give some thought to what has been said. This evolving balance between information that arrives from the outside, and what you already know, the balance of assimilation and accommodation, is a condition for adaptation, a key, in Piaget's view, to healthy mature mental functioning.

In the child, the functions of assimilation and accommodation are not yet in balance, as they are said to be in the mature adult, according to Piaget. This later equilibrium is a key to maturity. It is a happy metabolism of old information interfacing with the new, representing an ongoing dialectic and process of mental compromise. There will be some flexibility, but also some resistance to change.

With a few ongoing jigs and jags around the hypothetical center, this process leads to some stability. This is a process and not a state. A way of life. The information keeps coming in from the outside and getting processed in a realistic way. One is neither swept away by an inner fantasy, not blown over by an opinion from the outside.

This ongoing rubbing of one's inner world against the outer one brings a clearer picture of the world and oneself in it. In the example above, one will learn much more about the strengths and weaknesses of one's "house," if one gets a warning about it, whether or not one decides to tear it down. One's mental map becomes elaborated through this new input. Because, whether it's true or false, the healthy adult will deal with it.

Nonetheless, for creativity in adults, we're not going to buy this ideal completely, as one shall see.

"Primitive" and Imbalanced Thought Processes—Another Ideal?

For kids, things can be enjoyably self-centered and wish fulfilling. For the child riding the "horse," the "broomstickness" of the object counts very little -- at least compared to how fast it will go!

Things are way off from the equilibrium point, here in the assimilation direction. Fantasy clearly reigns. From an adult point of view, things may be way out of kilter.

Even for the child that can sometimes be true. It can be hard to put brakes on one's imagination. In play, the child willingly makes the object whatever is wished. But the child's wishes and fears can take on their own reality. Think of the young child who fears a "shark" in the bathroom or a "monster" under the bed. You talk about it. You show the children. And they are still convinced that the monster will reappear, if not now, at the very moment you leave the room.

Later, kids will learn that these fears are unfounded. They're nonsense. But right now, they don't have the equipment. They are terrified.

Later, kids will learn more about the "reality" of concrete objects (having some consensual, agreed upon properties), and can "reality-test" what exactly they have found before them. Later still, they will learn to think abstractly, and to manipulate this reality logically and reversibly in a "what if" kind of way. They can imagine unlimited scenarios, without the need for props and concrete aids. If it's drama they want, they can figure out "what happens next," in many dozens of alternative ways, imagining all consequences. Their mental maps and their worlds of possibilities have blossomed. (These are Jean Piaget's stages of "concrete" and "formal" operations.)

But what about when "a broomstick is a horse"—what of these early, concrete, self-centered, and imagination-driven ties between things? Are we now just too grown up to think that way anymore? Now that we've finally gotten assimilation and accommodation under control? Many schools seem to operate under this assumption.

It's hard to believe nature would be that wasteful of young kids' efforts. How much more sensible to design a training ground for some special capabilities.

Perhaps these early modes aren't just early mental push-ups, in preparation for the "real thing" later on. Or ways of "passing the time" while some more advanced neurons in the brain get wired up. These more "primitive" thoughts may have laid their own foundation for some new, and perhaps happily disruptive types of adult thinking, that may help to kick us out of our ruts.

But Is It Creative?

There are actually people who debate whether "true" creativity can occur in very young children, says psychologist Mark Runco while arguing the opposite. We too would suggest that this imaginative play is surely creative; it is original and meaningful.

The child is no fool and knows just what is intended in mocking-up a broomstick horse. She or he didn't make a horse out of a lampshade or a pair of shoes. A broomstick made more sense. And the play the horse inspires, the ride, the chase, the exploration of a dangerous canyon, for instance, is a joyous exercise of a creative imagination chosen when the child could just as easily have reproduced a drama from a storybook.

Or imagine a child building a "castle" out of standard building blocks, and elaborating a tale. Surely this too is original.

And it is typically meaningful, it communicates, sometimes in more than one way. Sometimes there is a clear story line or purpose. Sometimes kids are also communicating with each other through subtle forms of child-child awareness, of which we may only be dimly aware; as psychologist Sandra Russ and others have shown, play has a stronger social function than was once thought. Sometimes, the meaning may reside in the process of exploration and what we see may be fragmented and changing. It's certainly not a clear story line. But no matter. It's not the point.

Say a child is building some odd thing with blocks, yet he just keeps switching the parts around. Next he's knocking them over on purpose, and just going back and forth. There doesn't seem to be much of a goal." Is this a kid in trouble?" some worried parent might ask. "Destructive, unfocused, showing signs of an attention deficit disorder?"

Let's give this kid a break. The world is new to her or him, and this child has never had the chance to stack and res tack and knock about blocks like this before. What a thrill.

Here the perceptive adult may instead see a child "hard at work," doing a set of developmental push-ups, as it were, exercising a range of mental and physical skills, in exploration, manipulation, imagination, and so on. As with physical adult push-ups -- which may look pretty strange to certain kids—there can be a real pleasure for kids in this exercise. It is, after all, play.

Kids are not adults. We might indeed be surprised if our next door neighbor, age 36, was often riding around on a broomstick-horse. But it's a different question whether adults completely "grow out of" children's modes of thinking. And whether they must.

Example of Insight

Below, we will consider the possibility that more "primitive thoughts" can be used by adults for a little shaking of the system. A little accent, a sprinkling here, a sprinkling there, a source of insight when one might otherwise be stuck. This time, however, these thoughts will ultimately be juggled around by a more "mature" processing system. They will finally need to prove themselves, to show their "meaningfulness," on a more adult stage.

There is a famous story in organic chemistry. Friedrich August Kekulé dreamt that he was a snake biting his tail, which led to discovery of the benzene ring, a central concept in organic chemistry. This ring is six carbon atoms linked in a special way in a loop.

When Kekulé processed this notion, he did not really think he was a snake. Nor did he think that a benzene ring had a tail. But the fact of Kekule's being long, and the snake being long, was for the moment enough. In fact, in the dream, Kekule was a snake. And the snake's being circular (biting its tail), and the benzene ring's being circular, were also enough. The identity was established.

Kekule didn't get hung up on all the other properties of these objects. Did the snake have venom? What would the snake-Kekule do with his arms? Kekule's primitive combination of images -- linked together without a lot of irrelevant clutter -- led to a key chemical insight at the highest level of abstraction.

Keys to Insight? -- Strange Concepts

Just what is a "broomstick" anyway? Young children form concepts in their own characteristic ways. But we should remember that we, as adults, have all come the childhood route. One should see if these forms still produce a glimmer of recognition.

According to Jean Piaget, from when kids first start using symbols until about four or five years of age, they form preconcepts. These aren't anything near abstractions or classes. They're doing pretty well if they can find a "match" between just two things.

Think about a pile of hard candies, of different shapes, in wrappers of different colors. A very young child wouldn't particularly think "candies," and take it all in. Here she is, liking this red one, or this blue one. Now let's say you take a candy out, a round sour ball in a yellow wrapper, twisted at the top, with orange crosshatches to make it look like a pineapple. (This is how you see it -- one of the group of candies, wrapped to look like a pineapple.) The child isn't even thinking candy, perhaps, and certainly not linking it back to the others where "it belongs."

She may just focus on the crinkly paper at the top. Or some other thing. "It" may even keep magically changing in identity from one moment to the next, because the child's attention keeps jumping to different aspects. Now it's a yellow thing. Now it's something to throw. Now it's something to unwrap. (Underneath, there's probably some tiny conditioned response that has to do with "eating" it.)

The candy has neither general qualities shared with other objects ("candies"), nor individual ones that don't change (e.g., yellow wrapper) no matter what else is going on around it. This is the world the kids see! It may be hard for us to imagine.

Assimilation and Accommodation -- A Shaky Balance

Both assimilation and accommodation are on the job in shaky ways. For instance, another yellow candy could be assimilated (read "accepted") into the pile, because it looks like the yellow "pineapple" one. It now "belongs" to the whole set! But let's say, instead of candies, some other objects were also there, such as a seashell, a butterfly, or a pair of scissors. Even the flying broomstick could be there. The yellow candy would still belong. It matches the other yellow candy -- and that's good enough for the child. It's all she can deal with.

Accommodation, too, can work in this shaky way, taking a limited focus. Let's say another broomstick arrives. The child matches this to the first broomstick, amidst the hodge-podge of sweets and assorted objects, which now all become identified with Broomstick. (Forget the seashell, butterfly, and all the candies.) Gullible? Fickle, at any rate.

But kids, as they approach adolescence, do learn, and their concepts come to look more and more like our own concepts, and more and more like each other's. "Candies," "broomsticks," "seashells," the abstractions are slowly getting laid in concrete. This prepackaging has its disadvantages too, as we've said. But now we can really communicate; these concepts increasingly serve a social and cultural function. The earlier and more "primitive" modes of thinking may seem to disappear, or at least to be driven underground.

Keys to Insight? -- Thinking in "Family Names"

We can see the picture a little more clearly when we turn to the "Father of Russian psychology," Lev Vygotsky. His experiments with children showed five stages of what he called thinking in family names (or thinking in complexes). Here is an even closer look at "primitive" grouping, as with the candies above. In considering these, do keep in mind Kekule's snake, and his insight about the carbon ring. Possibly a couple of these thinking strategies will ring a kind of bell. Vygotsky found, for young kids, that a group of objects could take on an overall umbrella identity. Call this a TGR, GUK, or LKO. (He used nonsense syllables.) But this putting- together was done two by two, based only on ties between individual members. There didn't have to be any unity connecting all the members. Indeed, there often wasn't.

This is a bit like people in a real human family who seem, overall, to have very little in common—they all look very different from each other, and have few common interests but they are all "Smiths" or "Joneses." There were five stages of this.

Notice the first and third strategies. The first involves multiple associations (think of the bond between each daisy petal and the center of the flower). The second involves chain associations (picture an ongoing sequence of links in a chain, link to link to link). There are "creative thinking tests" that have people doing tasks like this, as we've seen.

I. Association by similarity. All links are with one "nuclear" object. But the reasons for links keep changing A red block is the first nucleus, a "parent," perhaps, in the family metaphor. Tied to it are: a blue block ("blackness" is held in common), a striped block, red pencil, red ball, red paperclip.

II. Association by contrast All links are with the nuclear object, but involve being not like it: not red, not block like, etcetera).

III. Chain complex. An ongoing linking of one object to the next, a chaining of items in free association, with "rules" that can constantly change: Red block, green block, green ball, ball that is yellow.

IV. Diffuse complex. The rules or criteria keep shifting, but a little less so, and finally a tenuous connecting pattern is starting to emerge: triangles change to squares, for instance, or oranges merge into reds.

V. Pseudoconcept. All items link with each other, but only by accident. This is truly a "fake concept." From the outside, it looks just like a concept, but was still formed pair by pair. Example: all red objects. This time, the criterion stays the same -- red and new blocks, cylinders, and so on, kept getting matched to the nuclear triangle one by one. It just so happens that all the objects match each other too.

Let's take two more examples, moving from blocks to some delightful and ideas of young children. Here, after a fashion, are what we have called multiple association and free association.

Multiple Association. Consider a toddler who thought a chain saw was a cow (it made the right noise). A cow was also a black- and white patterned fish at the aquarium (it had the right colorings). Finally, a cow was the familiar farm animal that gives milk.

Free Association. This time a child starts with a black and white figure of a cow and begins to find things that "go together." Now here's a cow that's all black, and a horse that's black, and a little boy who sits on the horse, and another figure, a little girl this time, and here's a house (and now the figures go inside, but the child bumps the house in doing this), and here's some shaking of the house (this time the child rattles it on purpose), and now the chimney falls off, but here's a block that's the same shape as the chimney (the child puts it in the house for safekeeping, along with the chimney), and claps his hands. There! he says, delighted.

There are elements here of what's called a thematic, or story telling grouping, as well, so this is not a pure example. Plus we don't want to force-fit the following point. But we shall keep in mind the similarity of some of these primitive conceptual schemes to patterns discussed in the next chapter:

1. The fluency, flexibility, and originality measured in tests of creative thinking ability.
2. The unusual associations, and the over inclusive thinking characteristic of highly creative people.
3. The unusual associations and overinclusion increased in any of us by mild mood elevation and, as we'll see in a later chapter...
4. ... also in people who are manic, or hypomanic, have other specific conditions, or are at risk for a bipolar mood disorder—all conditions which have been linked with heightened creativity.

Keys to Insight? -- Adult "Thinking in Family Names"

Now, we no longer have a struggling child, whose best effort is to think "in family names." Here's an adult who chooses to do it. And who, in addition, can call on the powerhouse of "mature" adult thought. This adult can use the new insight in a way that is original and meaningful. Interestingly, one point of a program such as William Gordon's Synectics is precisely to generate startling new insights through the use of unlikely juxtapositions and analogies.

There is evidence in fact that "primitive" modes of thought can stick around, lying latent in the older person. And that they can be reactivated, when the schools, or other structures show interest in this, and not just in logico-deductive skills. Indeed, the highly creative person tends to "have it all." As I said in a 1981 monograph on relations between creativity and psychopathology (Note: it is more about health!) here is a "flexible access to conceptual styles of different developmental origin."

The creative person can pick and choose, and weave all of these thinking styles together. By adolescence, in the best case, according to Vygotsky: "... imagination has become a higher mental function as a result of the influence of inner speech, and collaborates with thinking in concepts to form a psychological system that organizes creative thinking."

Trying It Oneself

Let's say one wants to try out this thinking. How does one as an adult "get there"? Interestingly, states of mind that seem to facilitate such free-flowing thought include mild mood elevation (as above), relaxed states of lowered arousal, and states of defocused attention, here where one lets one's mind run free. Depending on what you call "normal consciousness," these might be called "altered states of consciousness." One could perhaps try to hook into these.

But it may not be all so complicated. We may have run into these states of mind routinely as a child; they were part of our status quo, back then, in our world of creative play. They may also return more often than we thin. The various bodily changes of mood, relaxation, broadened attention may not be all that strange and "altered" when we look at our personal history.

In addition, such states may be the effects of creativity as well as a facilitators. Think of the people who may start out in a negative mood, and who say creativity can help to bring them out of these depths, back alive, more relaxed, and positive again (see Ch. 5, Abnormality and Normality). In this model: Creative response creates conditions for creativity creating more creative response creating conditions for creativity. And on and on the ball may roll.

One can try this out oneself, can essentially force-fit the result, by doing one of the "creative thinking" exercises mentioned earlier. (Example: "Think of as many 'round things' as you can." A sample set of responses follows.) But you must make yourself get started, no matter how hard. Then keep on stretching yourself more and more, get to the wilder and wilder possibilities, don't for heaven's sake stop and edit, judge, or criticize yourself, and you may find that the bodily changes come all on their own. They are not perhaps the point anyway. An obvious point is seen in a sample:

> Round things: wheels, tires, marbles,...,eyeballs, cheeks, noses, and certain
> ears, dishes, plates, coffee mugs,..., merry-go-rounds, gears, gyroscopes,
> planets, orbits, galaxies, eternity.

"Eternity?" Is this a touch of humor, or a reality? Either way, if the respondent wasn't having fun with this, he or she probably wouldn't have said it.

Not Piaget's Equilibrium

This playfulness may be far indeed from Piaget's perfect equilibrium of formal conceptual thought, with its balance of assimilation and accommodation. Of mental operations that are logical, reversible, universal, and consensually understood. Of the mind in equilibrium.

Here a little chaos may often reign -- or more likely, one holds court at a metaphorical "edge-of-chaos." Here is bizarreness and idiosyncrasy, egocentricity, assimilation over accommodation, and a direction that can't necessarily even be imagined, never mind reversed.

If one is in fact on the road to a mental "edge-of- chaos," there may be an exquisite sensitivity to initial conditions. A mental puff of air may destabilize and reorganize whole mental substructures of belief, which were perched precariously on a shaky assumption. Think of Copernicus's conclusion, "The earth is round." Indeed, one's ship will no longer seem at risk of falling off the edge of the world. But beyond this, there are profound and complex scientific, historical, religious, and philosophical consequences. Or consider the quantum mechanical puzzle, "a photon of light can be both a particle and a wave at the same time." The implications are staggering.

When the whole mental house of cards falls down in a new and insightful combination, it will not be particularly fruitful to try to put it back where it was. Like it or not, one is now in a new place. And this is the whole point of creative insight. One will never see the world in the same way again.

Following our Memories: In the Forest

One may watch one's own thoughts in another sort of armchair experiment: the way one remembers things.

Our memories, after all, aren't organized according to strict rules of logic. Mentally, we live in a richly interconnected world of associations. It is a dense neural forest, an ecology of thought and memory. Here, each new exposure can reverberate deeply within one's prior experience.

Let's stay with the forest a minute, and material I also presented for *New Directions in Child Development,* written while imagining a redwood forest. This is a particular place, in Northern California, tall sequoias to the heavens, dense ground beneath, cool, wet, stray beams of sunlight flickering through tall boughs, hanging moss, the ground matted with needles, cones, brush, ground ferns, trails of soft slimy creatures. You stop, you listen to the silence. Not even the distant traffic is heard, so usual that its absence is thundering. The song of a bird, the drop of high moisture, and then it's still. One is enclosed, enwombed, in a forest that exceeds one's own scale even to imagine, one's mightiest parent, so comforting and natural that, indeed, one might always have been there.

Associating Through A Forest -- The Content

How does one see this forest? It's not a sensory snapshot, taken verbatim, to be filed away. It is processed by its own creative process, in conjunction with everything related and remembered in one's past. It is linked to a web of prior experience by its most salient subjective points in a way that is richly complex, and that can be accessed later in any number of different ways.

There are the stories about the forest you once heard, the summer trip with your family, the drives with your grandfather, the walks with your mother, the picture books, the postcards from a friend, the last segment of Star Wars, a two-week summer camp, the smell of special soap from a dear friend, one night as a teen with a special person. You may not consciously summon up all this history. You may not even summon up its feelings. You might not even be able to remember it consciously if you wanted to. But, somehow, it is all there.

Perhaps even deeper longings join as well, ones common to us all as a species, and which also lie latent in our mental structures. E.O. Wilson asks why we go to such trouble to plant those trees in the yard, to visit the forests and National Parks and stand and gaze in wonder. Why would so many of us go to so much trouble? Perhaps because this fulfills an ancient yearning, a "biophilia, "a need to connect with the rest of organic nature, and to be "home."

Associating Through a Forest -- The Process

Now look at how these associations have formed, even below our awareness in the depths of the mind. We've gone beyond concepts and logic. We are swimming from oceans to grandmas to camping trips and walking slowly down a sunlit lane. These memories are borne on the tides of our feelings, and on the links of the most primitive of types of complexes and syncretic ties. Yet somehow these all connect, and so intimately and well.

One can indeed regress to an earlier level of development, and indeed to an altered state of consciousness, and mentally swim most freely amongst the myriad content that is there. In this way, one can forge new connections that might never have arisen if one had stayed on the road and taken the well-travelled highways of concepts and structures and topic outlines.

Down here, in the primordial soup, one sees the snake bite its tail, and there is Kekule's concept of the carbon ring—six carbon atoms in a ring like structure—shining through one's dream and heralding the basis for all of organic chemistry.

CHAPTER 5

ABNORMALITY AND NORMALITY

"The lunatic, the lover, and the poet,
Are of imagination all compact."
--WILLIAM SHAKESPEARE

The sources of the creative process draw so widely from our experiences and our many modes of thought that some people end up equating creative "difference" with "pathology." This problem is made worse by the ever-critical forces of conformity. This can be a problem indeed.

Once, I was complimented by a total stranger, to my amazement, for daring to wear the socks I had on. These are the shade of tennis-ball yellow, that bright neon-looking greenish yellow, that will show up through the fog and rain during a tennis match. I had not actually bought these socks because I like tennis-ball yellow, but because the socks were on sale for $1.99 at a pharmacy I frequented. Yet, truthfully, ever since that comment—and please note that I still put these socks on just as often—I have always asked myself, just where will I be going with these socks? And what will people think?

According to Victoria Jones, a British-born radio personality, and long-time U.S. resident, this is not surprising. The U.S. can be a particularly tough place to differ from the norm. Tongue-in-cheek, she compares the U.K.:

"The U.K. encourages eccentricity in its citizens—always has—it's quite acceptable to be odd, different, slightly batty. Here in the U.S., we encourage people to be 'regular' -- just look at how many TV ads want people to... be just like everybody else.... in business, the most eccentric thing you can do as a man is to wear a bow tie, and that makes you suspect."

On a more ominous note is the story of a young boy, who was as nice as could be, an attractive brown-eyed blond, with an open manner and winning smile. He was also bright, capable, and had always done well at school. But he'd been ostracized at one time by many of the kids, because he was a little different. Stuart had had a slight speech impediment. One didn't notice it at all at times. But at other times, and especially when Stuart was flustered, he could be extremely hard to understand.

Why should Stuart's acceptance have been such an issue? And so contingent on this one area of difference?

We, as sympathetic people, are surely happy to hear that Stuart ultimately did much better. With speech therapy, patience, and understanding, he overcame most of his problem during grade school, and regained the acceptance of his peers. And—how important indeed—Stuart now could communicate with ease. But watch out!—for we are also colluding. How subtle that feeling of confirmation we may get, that falling back again into line, and acting like all the others, is the answer.

We finally should say, in Stuart's case, he had not only been ostracized by the kids, but by some of the parents as well. One of Stuart's first teachers recalled certain parents' comments with clarity. One mother, for instance, had asked pointedly, "Why is Stuart in this class?" Another had specifically stated that she did not want Stuart riding in the same car with her child during class field trips, or assigned to her own car if she were one of the drivers.

The teacher was quite upset, both about this little boy, and the forces of conformity in general. It was one thing with the kids, she said—a phase to get over and to learn from—but another entirely with the parents. She asked, "What can you be passing on to your children with that negative kind of attitude, that closed kind of attitude. It's awful, just thinking about it. "But," she concluded sadly, "it's out there."

"Abnormality" as a threat.

Think of the potential pressures on certain creative people who choose to share unusual ideas, including ones that people don't particularly want to hear. There is always some risk of being censured just for being different. Particularly if the statements are unsolicited, shocking, and come out of no particular context, from a person without institutional backing or another structure to give social support. "He is a weird one," you might hear someone say. "He says some of the oddest things." And so forth. What a reception for the birth of new ideas—of new memes—in our world.

Indeed, how does the word "abnormal" sound to you? Is it neutral in tone, or negative? (Surely not positive.) Some usual connotations of "abnormal" are indeed negative. Among potential reasons for this, we suggest two powerful ones. The first involves fear of strangers (xenophobia), and the second a fear of mental illness (and more accurately, a fear of the less-than- logical thought processes we all share).

First, speaking now in geological time periods, we humans are creatures sprung recently from our environment of evolution, prior to the development of agriculture, about 10,000 years ago. In our small groups of hunters and gatherers, we fought to preserve the viability of our tight "bands" or communities. We knew every person in our little band—we were all in it together—and we were loyal to each other and wary of outsiders. When someone different, someone unfamiliar, rose up on the horizon, we were startled and afraid. Our awareness of difference was potentially, and instantaneously, an awareness of danger, the stranger, the enemy, the attacker. And similarly, in modern times. It's abnormal—and it's frightening. Our first awareness may be far removed from the beauty of a difference. Of the new possibilities for growth, for creativity, and improvement in the lives of all of us. It is a reaction of fear.

Yet as seekers of creativity, we need to keep in mind that first, creativity means being different. Secondly, and this should be underlined and bold-typed in red: being abnormal means no more than being unusual, or different from the norm. As with creativity, this deviance can be an incredibly positive quality. It doesn't imply being sick, pathological, or harmful or harmed in any way. Indeed, why should it?

When Is It "Thought Disordered"?

Here is the second clue. For sometimes the abnormal which is innocuous, and the abnormal which is pathological (that is, which is truly harmful to a person or others) may superficially look very much alike. Yet in other ways, in intent, meaning, context, and integration, just to name a few, they may be far apart. Yet to the casual observer, "that kid is so-o-o-o weird!"

One possibility: Certain usefully "deviant" thoughts represent no more than the creative adult's return to the thought patterns of childhood; these were "normal" processes, in fact, for all of us. A loose association here, a primitive concept there, and this thinker comes up with a powerful new adult metaphor and entirely different point of view. Yet, utter this material at the wrong time, and the adult may get targeted as being abnormal, deviant, and sometimes even psychotic.

In this connection, see what you make of the following three picture interpretations: Two potatoes with eyes and a mouth trying to climb up some kind of pipe or pole.

A witch on a broom stick. And it looked like an electric broom stick or something... gas powered because she had a cloud of smoke.

"It's black, dark, darkness, lovemaking."

These colorful responses were made by psychiatric patients to a measure called The Thought Disorder Index. They are descriptions of what these people saw in Rorschach Test inkblots. The task may be hard for you to assess, since you are not seeing the actual inkblots. But be aware that, by one set of rules at least, these responses were considered "thought disordered." The Rorschach is the type of "projective" test where you use your imagination to interpret what you see in a rather vague stimulus, in this case, an inkblot. You therefore "project" what it might suggest to you. This kind of blot is made by putting ink on a page and folding the paper down the middle, giving a symmetrical smeared-out image. As with clouds in the sky, you can imagine many things in such patterns.

But where, one might ask, in the responses above, is the "disorder"?

Once again, it's not what one says necessarily, but why one says it. There is a fanciful quality present here which might be appealing, in a different context. Take "it's black, dark, darkness, lovemaking." This phrase might be alarming if blurted out in a business meeting. But what about in a line of poetry?

These phrases are examples of types of thought disorder that have been linked with clinical mania, the extreme form of mood elevation found in manic-depressive illness. In fact, there is some truth to the reputed association between "bipolar disorders" such as manic-depressive illness, and creativity, particularly in the arts. Referring to the creativity of eminent creative artists, psychologist Kay Redfield Jamison notes: "It would be wrong to label anyone who is unusually accomplished, energetic, intense, moody or eccentric as manic-depressive. All the same, recent studies indicate that a high number of established artists—far more than could be expected by chance—meet the diagnostic criteria for manic-depression or major depression.... In fact, it seems that these diseases can sometimes enhance or otherwise contribute to creativity in some people."

The complex and fascinating underpinnings of an association between everyday creativity and bipolar mood disorders are documented further in the references, and will be treated in depth in a future book. The interested reader is also referred to a more academic book being coedited by Mark Runco and myself, *Eminent Creativity, Everyday Creativity, and Health.*

What is critical, however, is this association may be more about *health.* Those who are *better functioning,* either in general or when manifesting their creativity, show the association.

Three further things should be noted here: First, that treatment for mood disorders can be highly effective; a great many people are suffering unnecessarily. Secondly, that our work at McLean Hospital and Harvard Medical School and the work of others suggests that treating a mood disorder can both reduce great suffering, and at the same time may *enhance* creative potential. Think of the tragedy of the people who refuse help, who put themselves at risk, and meanwhile voluntarily shackle their creativity.

Thirdly, related to this, is the notion that great pain and suffering aren't necessary ingredients for creativity—either among the mood disordered or the rest of us. In fact, we have found that some psychiatrically normal relatives of manic-depressive and bipolar individuals also show advantages for creativity. The phenomena may be subtle indeed. Among other things, there may be mild predilections for "thought disorder"—if it is truly that—and we continue this discussion below.

Even "Normal" Relatives May Seem "Thought Disordered"

Now we look more broadly beyond individuals with major psychiatric disorders, to their much broader group of relatives indeed a large segment of society. Interestingly, it also turns out that some of the psychiatrically normal relatives of patients with various forms of thought disorder (including but not limited to persons with manic-depressive or bipolar disorder), can show similar patterns of thinking to their ill relatives. The main difference is that this occurs in a more dilute form. The "black, dark, darkness..."example for instance illustrates looseness of association. Specifically, according to Solovay and associates, a "loss of cognitive focus.... ideas that seem either unrelated or arbitrarily or tangentially related." Not a bad thing for a creative writer, perhaps. Ask James Joyce.

The witch on a broomstick illustrates a "playful confabulation." In the world of thought disorder, this is an example of going too far, of elaborating a response beyond the qualities of the inkblot, but in a playful storytelling way, that is not considered too "extreme." However, some odd things can get brought together.

Interestingly, books have been written on the importance of doing this deliberately in the service of creativity -- bringing together previously unrelated ideas. This relates to what Arthur Koestler, in the *Act of Creation*, called "bisociation," as we mentioned previously. So again, we may need to look at one's intent in exercising such thought. (Furthermore, if a witch can actually find an electric broomstick, all the more power to her!)

But where things can get malignant is when a person, who is thinking in unusual ways for creative reasons, starts getting diagnosed and labelled.

Not to Romanticize Thought Disorder—or Disown It Ourselves

Some important words of caution -- for we do not want to romanticize thought disorder, or the painful conditions which can produce it. This very important. For not every disordered thought is creative. Not at all. In addition, these disordered thoughts are very often painful. True disordered thinking, which can occur in a number of different psychiatric conditions, and take a number of different forms, can reflect degrees of being "out of touch with reality." Such thought is not produced or sought volitionally, does not carry automatic pleasure, and can feel quite the opposite. One should note well that treatment with medication can be incredibly helpful in relieving the pain and restoring good adaptive function.

It helps in understanding, perhaps, to know we have all had the experience of distorted thinking to some degree. We all carry about our little mini-delusions, and definite blind spots (for instance, views of certain friends or romantic interests). We can also be unrealistically hard on ourselves ("I can't do this problem... I just can't do anything," and the like.) We may also have some consensual delusions, as a society—for instance, that there is plenty of space, plenty of trees, and science will solve all of our environmental problems. We shall deal with such issues later.

Beyond this, specifically, the notion of one's very thoughts leaving one's control, is terribly frightening to many people. No doubt this is one reason for a fear and rejection of a bizarre thinking, and often the thinker, no matter what the source. This can be scary stuff. The fact that creativity may partake a bit of this process—of uncertainty, unpredictability, and eruption of new ideas through "creative insight"—can indeed be off-putting.

Creativity and "Abnormality" on Psychological Tests

Indeed there are a number of ways in which creative people have shown up as "abnormal"(that is, unusual), when they are not necessarily "ill" (or maladapted) on standard tests of personality or psychopathology. Take, for instance, psychologist David Schuldberg's finding that creative college students tend to have more unusual perceptual experiences and beliefs.

The links with creativity were fairly weak, but were still statistically significant. Here are the top four questionnaire items, found with over 600 regular college students, and linked with a complex (factor) measure of creative problem solving and cognitive complexity:

* feeling that a TV/radio broadcaster knew I was listening.

* special powers of numbers like 13 and 7

* could learn to read others' minds

* people make me aware of them by thinking about me.

Now let's look at another variable, "psychoticism, "a dimension of personality, according to psychologist Hans Eysenck. You don't either "have" psychoticism, or not. We all can get some score on a psychoticism scale, even as we would get a score on Eysenck's introversion-extraversion scale. The issue is whether our score is high, low, or intermediate. Those people who score at high levels seem to be those at most risk of becoming psychotic—that is, out of touch with reality, and unable to meet the ordinary demands of life. Low scorers appear to be highly socialized and conventional people.

And where do the highly creative people fit? According to Eysenck, in the middle. With a sufficient touch of psychoticism to be interesting, but not highly dysfunctional or out of touch with reality. Interestingly enough, these people also show higher levels of overinclusion; Eysenck feels this is one of the common factors in both psychoticism and creativity. It is discussed further below.

Look too at what Frank Barron, Donald MacKinnon, and associates found when they gave a major measure of mental disturbance, the Minnesota Multiphasic Personality Inventory

(MMPI), to renowned creative persons, including writers, and architects, in a major series of studies at the University of California, Berkeley.

The MMPI is a standard multiple-choice measure for psychopathology. It has scales for qualities such as Depression, Hypochondriasis, Paranoia, Schizophrenia, Hypomania, and Hysteria. Being high in one of these diagnostic areas doesn't mean you "have it," but it does mean that you have answered questions in ways similar to people who do carry that diagnosis. What was notable was not just that creative persons scored high on a number of these scales, but that the average architect was in at least the top third of the general population on every measure of psychopathology and the average creative writer in the top 15%. We're speaking of your average writer in the group, now, and not the more unusual members. The finding is remarkable.

What was equally remarkable was that these writers and architects also scored very high on a measures of "ego-strength." Ego-strength, a Freudian psychoanalytic term, involves the ability to stay in touch with and deal with reality. This implies, at the same time, managing one's more primitive urges and instincts (the Freudian "id") and also dealing with one's internalized prohibitions, from parents or society (Freudian superego). Ego-strength, in other words, involves functioning well in the real world, and "keeping it all together."

Generally speaking, if scores are high on scales such as Schizophrenia, Hysteria, and Hypochondriasis, on the MMPI, scores on ego-strength are the opposite, they are low. The pathology is in the forefront, presumably, and may dominate a person more than one's adaptation to reality. Their ego can't quite manage the burden. Yet the creators flipped this typical pattern. All kinds of strange thoughts could flit in and out, but the creator, ultimately, was in control.

In Dr. Schuldberg's study too, creative college students' ego strength was high. If the creators' thoughts seemed bizarre to some people, these creators were also in control of them. Frank Barron attributed this in part to a greater "psychological openness," rather than pathology. Creators were more in touch with their inner experience, whatever it might be. As such, these creators were painting with a fuller palette.

Although there are still a few twists to this story, the crucial point is that we are seeing a broader and more complex picture of the normal range of human functioning.

Comparing Creative Thinking Test Results

The point can be highlighted by comparing two sets of answers to a creative thinking test item, "List all the uses you can think of for a pencil." One person says the pencil can be used for writing a letter, a note, a postcard, an essay. A second person says it can be used for a backscratcher, a potting stake, kindling for a fire, a rolling pin for baking, a toy for a woodpecker, or a small boat for a cricket. The second person gets higher points for a score called originality.

Now this is a popular type of creativity test, developed initially by J.P. Guilford and colleagues, as described in *The Nature of Human Intelligence*—but not developed in order to measure creative accomplishment. It is aimed instead at identifying types of thinking which may help people be more creative. There is actually some controversy about just how predictive these tests really are, although one can imagine that doing them might be good "practice" for thinking up original ideas. Scores include fluency, flexibility, and originality, where fluency has to do with the total number of answers a person comes up with. Presumably, if you can think of many uses for a pencil, you're more apt to come up with a good use than someone who can only think of one or two ideas.

On the other hand, if you're not very flexible, you still might not do much better. The person who gave these uses: writing a letter, note, postcard, essay, etcetera, wouldn't get very far. All the uses are about writing, writing this or writing that. Flexibility: limited. But look at: a potting stake, kindling, rolling pin... Now we're seeing the pencil from many perspectives. Flexibility: good. And the ultimate point of all this? Presumably, it's originality. To generate a lot of possibilities to finally pick a winner.

But—"small boat for a cricket?" Isn't this getting rather far-fetched? Yes indeed. This too is part of the plan in idea generation. For instance, in the popular practice of brainstorming, used extensively in business and industry, for instance, people get together in groups and generate as many ideas as they can, however crazy, each triggering the next person to higher levels of nonsense or improbability. "Suspending judgment" is a cardinal rule of brainstorming. For once you turn that internal censor on, the flow of ideas is likely to slow, and maybe even to stop. This is a great way to generate a mental "block."

But you finally do turn it on -- but much later -- at a whole separate phase in the process of creation. You look at all your ideas and, with some particular goal in mind, decide which one you now like best. There's certainly no penalty for the ones that are thrown out. Indeed, they may come in handy another time. (Plus you have exercised those mental muscles, so there's an inner benefit as well.)

But just watch out who you tell about the ideas you've had. In the wrong context, a "boat for a cricket" might be a good candidate for "thought disorder."

Overinclusion

There is certainly a place in creativity for loose, fanciful, and sometimes bizarre thinking. We will refocus now on the quality of cognitive style called overinclusion, and see how this concept relates.

Because we will also be looking at the stage of "creative insight, "we will first step back and look at one model of the creative process, and where insight fits into the picture.
Four steps to Creativity

Creative insight. The Aha! experience. Insight is what Archimedes reportedly had when he jumped from the bath, yelling "Eureka!," suddenly knowing that a submerged object displaced its own volume. "Eureka," he yelled, meaning "I have found it," in Greek. Yet just a moment before this, he had not.

What might creative insight have to do with overinclusion? This we shall see.

But first let's put insight into its place in the creative process. Walla (1926) talked about four stages of creation: preparation, incubation, illumination, and verification. Life may not be quite so simple, but a division into four stages is useful. Let's say you're writing a short story. In the preparation phase, you play with a plot, you make up histories for your characters, you look up background information and so on.

During the incubation phase, you might think on your project only in passing, go for a walk, wash the dishes, forget about the whole thing for a week. The presumption is that whatever you are doing, your mind, below the level of consciousness, keeps working on the story. All that information you fed in is still there, and being jostled around in various ways. Until suddenly... Eureka! Illumination. You rapidly see how the plot will develop. In fact, other little insights may cascade from the original one, alternating with further preparation, and so on. Creativity rarely proceeds in four simple steps.

Finally, step number four: Verification. Now you check it out, develop the insight, do the mopping up work. This stage may be quite different for science and the arts. But there it is. The Four steps.

Finding One's Cognitive Style

Cognitive style involves ongoing modes or patterns of thinking that are consistent with our basic personality characteristics. Some people tend to be more clipped, specific, and factual. Some are more long-winded, and may tend to wander and embroider their stories. That sort of thing.

Most of us, it should be added, can also manage more than one style generally within an overall umbrella of characteristic patterns depending upon the circumstance. We can flip in different schemas, or patterns of reacting, as it were, for different occasions. Say you are talking to a friend, for instance, or an immediate supervisor, or to a curious young child. An acquaintance who overheard the conversation would probably know it was "you," but might also be able to guess to whom you were speaking.

Conceptual Styles

Within cognitive style, we now look at conceptual styles, or how one puts concepts together. Unlike the last chapter, we are now at the adult level of capability. The concept of "teacher," for instance, allows us to group together under one label or name, various individuals who may help us to learn something. College, high school, elementary school teachers. They all have jobs, they all get paid.

But what about unpaid instructors? What about peer teachers, the students that teach each other? What about our children when they (as they so often do) instruct us. One person's concept of "teacher" will not be precisely the same as another's. This is how we get differences in adult conceptual style.

And we must not forget the immature concepts and preconcepts of young children discussed earlier. For these can be intertwined with the others. Here is where it gets interesting.

Now, with the conceptual style of overinclusion, we can talk about both quantity and quality. This lends itself to comparison with measures of fluency and originality, in test of creative thinking ability. With quantity, we ask how many instances one tends to put together into a category (someone who gave 18 different types of teachers in the example above would be over inclusive). With quality, we ask what the rules or reasons were used for including these items (let's say that a young man cussing out a friend could very loosely be called a teacher). With overinclusion, some rules may be more vague, or distant, or developmentally primitive.

Another example of overinclusion might be this list of responses to "List things with wheels": a car, truck, a bicycle, a unicycle,... watch parts, earth on its axis, wheels within wheels, Wheel of Fortune, wheeling and dealing, a wagon wheel used as a table,...

There are plenty of things "with wheels" here (quantity) even in this abbreviated list. And the basis for their inclusion (quality aspect) isn't just the formal notion of a rotating weight bearing device used on vehicles of conveyance. "Wheels within wheels"? That's surely a new take on the question.

Perhaps some people will find surprising the research results of Nancy Andreasen and colleagues. They found that both creative writers and manic patients (but not schizophrenics), showed high levels of overinclusion, involving both quantity and quality. In this way, at least, the writers and the manics were similar. This does not automatically make patients who are manic into writers, of course, nor the writers into mood-disordered manics (although the frequency of mood disorders among eminent writers is certainly of interest, as we'll see.)

Important differences were found too. Creative writers were much stronger than manics on abstract and cohesive thinking. Once again, the creative group could think in unusual ways, and could also "pull it all together."

A Good Mood Can Bring On Overinclusion

Overinclusion can be made to work for each of us, and one can try this right now, mood disordered or not. We are able to set our conceptual thermostats for more overinclusion!

The thermostat is a good metaphor. For it turns out that, people who are put into even a subtle good mood, are more apt to show this over inclusive thinking than people who aren't feeling as positive. (A full manic mood elevation is hardly required and would likely be counterproductive.) The good mood you're in today may bring a more ready flow of ideas than the bad mood you had yesterday. The good mood of today may in a sense heat up the neurons so that the ideas flow more easily.

It also appears that a good mood—just a tinge of a good mood, in fact—can increase how unusual one's word associations are. Cat-Dog, Cat--Rat, Cat--Halloween, Cat--Nap, Cat--Nip. Now we are talking about originality. And a good mood also seems directly to increase creative problem solving, as shown in certain research tasks. One example is the problem of how to attach a candle to a wall (a corkboard) so that it doesn't drip on the floor, using a cardboard box, some tacks, and a book of matches.

There is also more direct evidence of unusual associations and of overinclusion in connection with creativity. This helps complete the circle. Conclusion: Mood, creative thinking, and over inclusive thinking all have something to do with each other.

Altered States?

But what does this mean? At one descriptive level, one could talk about a mood-produced "altered state of consciousness," a distinct state such as dreaming, but quite a bit less obvious.

Under the influence of one's emotions, one's style of thinking, or style of processing information, can shift. It is a mixed cognitive affective (intellectual and emotional) state, and a transformation. When we talk about people for whom "overinclusion" is more the ongoing norm, we then talk about a distinct cognitive style, a habitual way of thinking consistent with ongoing personality trends.

And it does turns out that an over inclusive style may at times be a particularly creative one.

Consider the methods of Alice Isen and associates. These researchers "induce" a good mood in their subjects by the likes of showing a short comedy film. There is a lot of literature, and discussion, actually, on mood induction, and what it means compared to a "naturally occurring" mood.

One explanation of the "good mood" effect is that it helps bring about "low cortical arousal" and "defocused attention." It helps the mind relax and let things emerge from deeper levels of the mind for conscious use. Plus, many more thoughts are tied to good moods than foul —we seek these and try to escape the other kind. Hence the available webwork of associations (the good-mood network) one may travel is more complex. This also can help a creator enter this more diffuse mental state. Likewise for people who are quite comfortable with emotion and feeling—they'll have this more extensive mental library to use.

It's important to note that an artificial chemical method, such as a stimulant drug, would not work. It would increase arousal, and this is just the opposite of what is desired. Creative response becomes less likely. We do not want to imply that watching an evening sitcom, or hearing some good jokes from a friend will help one's creativity. But it might.

Toward Creative Modes of Being

We've discussed an over inclusive cognitive style. This person prefers to link ideas, many ideas, together in unusual, wide-ranging, diverse, and sometimes primitive, ways. We also see in highly creative persons a preferred style of thinking called "integrative complexity."

This is not a static quality, but is a process, and one which might in theory be taught, and toward which one (if one is so inclined) might aim. This person, according to Dean Simonton: "perceives the world in a multidimensional and flexible manner, simultaneously considers diverse viewpoints, and yet manages to integrate all these inputs into a single perspective."

This preference for doing it the hard way involves a kind of deferred gratification— because the last thing this person would wish to do is jump to conclusions.

One instead prefers to wait, to learn a little more, to juggle some ideas around a bit longer, to bring in all kinds of peripheral information, and to relish and embrace this disorder. The disorder is not valued in itself as some random or chaotic sort of experience, but as a means to an end. A step toward an ultimate new, elegant, and aesthetic order or solution: namely, one's creation. To do this, one must have ultimate faith in oneself, one's creative imagination, and in the future. It must be worth the wait.

According to psychologist Frank Barron, this enthusiastically sought state of disorder, is: "... simply the possibility of a future order whose principle of organization cannot now be told."

An ultimate faith shines out of this statement.

Some ongoing traits of highly creative people have also been reported often enough that they have been grouped together as "core" personality traits associated with creativity. One can perhaps see how they fit with the cognitive style of overinclusion, and indeed with other qualities discussed in this and the previous chapter. Interestingly, Barron and associates found these traits across fields as different as creative writing, architecture, science, and mathematics. The creative people were carefully chosen through a stringent procedure of professional nomination.

In view of the style of "integrative complexity," one quality which almost goes without saying is a tolerance for ambiguity. If things seem a little muddy, it's really OK. Another is a preference for complexity. A person who is a simplifier, or who needs to quickly settle on an answer, will not stick around for this exercise in idea juggling. Indeed, a liking of integrative complexity implies, by its nature, a liking for the process.

There is also rejection of suppression as a mechanism; this person accepts whatever comes to mind, and takes a look at it, rather than quickly trying to banish it. Many primitive thoughts would stay buried otherwise. The system is aided by a psychological mindedness, an interest in the mind and its workings. There is definite help from courage and ego-strength, because who knows what can come to mind! And if one is open to all the strange currents of one's childhood, as well as adulthood, not only the joys, but the demons and the dangers can further proliferate.

Some other "core" qualities that may seem unsurprising include independence of judgment, self-confidence, intuitiveness, flexibility, introversion, and lack of concern with society's constraints.

We potentially have before us a creative person who takes off mentally on his or her own, fully in flight, confident and unhindered by what others say. This person is thinking flexibly and with all fibers of one's being, including the intuitive (and the aesthetic) ones.

Creative Traits, states of Mind, and Moments of Insight

Finally, this person is not a fait accompli, whom we either resemble of not. These traits give us another lens on a lifestyle, representing still shots of one aspect or another. One problem with traits -- like talkativeness is they are nouns. She is talkative, he is quiet, and so on. As if they always were, always will be.

We all have some tendency to keep doing the same thing. But life is a process, and so is creativity. It is not hard to see how certain of the so-called "core" creative personality traits might make it easier to do creative work. But a person who starts doing more and more original things might also find they were shifting on some of these ways of being.

Another issue. We've been talking about people's differences, and respecting these about all the ways in which a creative person may deviate from the norm. It may seem curious that we now turn around to produce a list of similarities.

But these are similarities with a twist. They act by opening up options, and letting people go their own ways. They ultimately lead to greater diversity—of personal style and outcome. The common core involves a temporary disorder, a state of change, and a liking of this state of affairs.

I t seems possible that a preference, not only for complexity, but for a metaphorical edge-of-chaos, might be part of this picture of a creative person. This may also give us new perspectives on our sometimes fickle muse, and the "mystery" of creative insight.

CHAPTER 6

GROWING UP DIFFERENT

"Variety's the very spice of life."
--WILLIAM COWPER

Nurturing one's creative potential can be hard in a society that is focused on the conventional, and on preparing people for certain groups and roles. How often, in fact, do you think creatively inclined students feel "understood" in school or in the workplace? Things may be worse than you think.

The creative person is, by definition, a person with a difference; he or she will do things unpredictably. Not every school is set up to handle this. Embracing the quirks of a person bursting with creative energy can be a challenge indeed, particularly in a crowded classroom. All the worse when the students aren't that accepting themselves of "difference." And kids can be quite cruel.

We turn again to qualities of the creative person, and look at "true and false differences." In the "true" case, we consider individuality which is suppressed, unrecognized, or undervalued. We use a school situation as an example. We then turn around and look at "false" differences which, by contrast, people can embrace all too readily. These include stereotypes we may all carry (even at times when we think we've shed them) as part of our automatic and unaware way of reacting to the world. These limit both us and the other person, creatively and in general.

"True" Differences: The Creative Young Person in School

Now here is a teacher who says, "OK, I'm a nice and tolerant person, and I'll somehow deal with this 'different' kid."

That's still not enough. There's a whole added step in the positive valuing of this divergence. This includes valuing the range of styles in our society: the many ways in which people can choose to behave and learn—not only people who are creatively inclined, but everyone. This is also a way we can value ourselves.

Fears of Difference

Yet how early the fears of "differences" begin. Already in preschool, children are making distinctions. Here is a little child, sweet and bright, but who walks with a limp, and the kids are saying he can't come to their birthday party. Here is someone who looks distinctively of a different ethnic origin, and so they too are treated differently. Here is someone who is very "out of it," as far as the latest superheroes are concerned, and a number of other things as well. They're just not "cool," not cool at all. So they are excluded.

Here is someone who has terrible allergies; she is just too different. Someone who is so bright he seems to know all the answers and is obnoxious enough to say so. Here is that creative upstart, who may be constantly disrupting the atmosphere, or at times just so "out to lunch" with an idea, that she reacts with irritation when interrupted.

Finally, here are some boys who won't play with the girls, no matter who they are. And some girls won't play with the boys, at least when they're playing rough. And some other girls who would like to play with the boys, but the boys won't let them. "Boys aren't supposed to play with girls," one of them intones.

How early it starts. "You are my friend, you are not my friend, you are not coming to my birthday party." This is what they are saying to each other, even before kindergarten. Some of these attitudes may come from parents, some from peers, indeed some may have been ingrained as one-time adaptive xenophobic reactions down though many lifetimes of evolution.

Being "different," one may come to believe, is potentially dangerous; it becomes important to "fit in." Fitting in may mean to conform. Our friends will therefore be like us. Let us take two examples.

"Too Quiet and Aloof"?

Here is twelve year old Bobby, and the teacher is saying that he is just not fitting in with the other kids. He gets into working on something and it just doesn't matter to him if the period is over, if other kids are going outside, if they're organizing into groups to play, or whatever. He just can't put aside that project. He just can't put down that book. He is fascinated with biology. The teacher thinks it's rather odd that what he especially likes is to study is snakes.

Sometimes Bobby takes a book outside during a free period and sits in the corner of the playground where the building makes an "L, " oblivious to everyone, unless a ball rolls up to him. Bobby is just too much in his own world. And when he does play, he tends to do so only with his friend Chris. Chris is a loner too, the teacher adds. (Wait a minute, aren't they playing together?)

With Sharon, the teacher continues, things are different. She is just as fascinated by biology, and Sharon also gets just as involved at times. Plus Sharon does hate to stop an activity, but she can still fit in better with a group, and can work along with other kids on a project. She also comes to class and tells about the nature outings she went on with her family, as well as other ways she works with her "hobby." Sharon shares her enthusiasm. The teacher says there will be some special project groups organized, later in the year. Maybe she can put Bobby with some other kids who will help him "come out of himself. After all," she explains, "that's a lot of what we're trying to do here."

Now wait a minute. Is Bobby unhappy? Is Bobby without friends? Is he begging for some help so he can socialize more, and can stop channeling all that energy into his studies? Is his good concentration a bad habit?

Surely, at times, such patterns are symptomatic, but at others they can also be a healthy expression of a learning difference. Of a style of learning and of relating that works for a child. Properly handled, it is also an opportunity for class members to learn about and to value -- the range of stylistic differences. To be more open minded about others and themselves. This is not necessarily easy for a teacher to accomplish. For instance, one doesn't want to single out a nonconforming young person. One is still moving against the powerful tides of conformity. But that is precisely the point.

"Too Noisy and Disruptive"?

Then we have Norma. She was a ten year old girl who at the time lived down my street. Norma was one of the more talkative, friendly, and creative kids in the neighborhood.

Most neighbors knew Norma well because this appealing child would come up to them on the street, at one time or another, and start asking them a lot of eager questions. Norma was funny and spontaneous, and she would also sometimes round up a child or two and improvise a crazy skit. Once, with her younger sister and some cohorts, including my delighted daughter, Norma moved all of my backyard furniture around to make a boat. The kids then sailed away, enacting a drama about sharks and dolphins.

At one point, I asked Norma how she was liking school that year. The fifth grade. The young girl sighed, and said, "School is something to be gotten through." This was not what I'd expected to hear.

"What?" I asked. "What do you mean?"

"That's what my dad says," Norma explained. I don't like school very much. But he says that school is sometimes just something to be gotten through."

As it turned out, Norma's large classes weren't very flexible in dealing with her creativity—with her sudden ideas, her wish to jump up and to try something. She could also come across as disruptive to the teacher, unable to wait or listen to others. In fact, It had not always been so; in fact, even the year before had been much better. But now it was getting worse. Nor, let us add, was this just Norma's problem; such patterns and others below can be seen with creative kids, as writings of Runco, Torrance, and others show.

With Norma's handpicked friends, at least, her boisterous and enthusiastic style was fine. But some of her other classmates found her too talkative, too intrusive with her own ideas, and too apt to make gratuitous wisecracks or clown around to get attention. They would put her down or ignore her.

Norma was now trying harder to be quiet in class rather than keep interrupting. And things were starting to go a little better. But Norma was also learning to withdraw—to emotionally disconnect from the classroom and the people there. So much of what she wanted to offer was getting smothered. Norma's goal was now to sit as patiently as possible, in her same-for-everyone structured lessons and somehow "get through it." Except for when she couldn't resist a wisecrack or two.

Valuing True Differences

Now no one is saying that Norma, or kids similar to her, would be easy to deal with. Or that one wouldn't sometimes feel a bona fide frustration. But Norma's style is not unusual for creative kids, and the school just wasn't connecting with this. Norma blossomed much more easily in the less structured atmosphere of afterschool play.

Bobby's style represented another alternative you sometimes see. The quiet and aloof young person. And potentially a youth, from the teacher's point of view, who might seem "harder to reach." At least, along the lines of some of the teacher's goals. But if one met Bobby at the level of his own intrinsic interests, say snakes and wildlife, it might be a different story.

Difficult and Different?

In research on creative young people, there are many reports of how such kids may seem problematic. Some are difficult, disruptive in class, headstrong at home, in conflict with parents, class clowns or jokesters, or isolative or withdrawn. It isn't always easy to be different in this society, to go against the flow.

What actually happens depends on the particular teacher; some teachers place a high priority upon creativity and make allowances f or it. These allowances must be serious and committed ones not a little lip service to creativity. This may be difficult to do, and especially in large classes.

Psychologist Mark Runco and associates asked an important question: Do teachers who say they care about creativity really *mean* it? The answer turned out to be no. Frequently, teachers state they value creativity, yet, when the question is posed differently, show they don't value the various nonconforming behaviors that go along with it. The message for all of us as facilitators of creativity is: You can't just say that you value creativity. You must be prepared to work for it. There will be a certain degree of unpredictability and even trouble.

An even more rejecting view of creativity by teachers is typified by a classic and influential study in the Chicago area, reported back in the early sixties, by Getzels & Jackson. They found, that secondary level teachers preferred adolescents who were of lower creativity, and higher IQ, relatively speaking, compared to students with higher creativity, and lower IQ.

(The kids in this particular school all had rather high measured IQ scores, so the IQ variation was less likely a factor than creativity.)

Alert, bright, agreeable, cooperative, dutiful, assignments in on time, sit quietly in class, model student, good citizen? Along these general lines, there was strong positive similarity between the high IQ adolescents' rankings of personal traits preferred they preferred and a list of traits they believed teachers preferred. They and their teachers were on the same wavelength. But, for high creative students, the picture was different altogether: the two lists were switched enough around from each other that the correlation was negative.

In other words, what the teachers seemed to prefer, in the students' view, what not what the creative adolescents themselves represented. Not at all. And what the creative students wanted for themselves had very little to do with what the teachers appeared to value. This was tough luck, in particular, for the highly creative students. For in their school, it was their teachers, and not these creative students, who were making up the rules.

Increasing One's Options

This discussion is not to imply that a young person shouldn't learn some "rules" for getting along flexibly in one setting or another. For instance, at home. Or that a young person should just breezily do whatever she or he pleases. There are times to go along with a group—indeed to prefer this—and when one's preference on one's own might be entirely different. To see a greater good. To compromise. To work with others. And times to stop doing something when told. Or to start. Or to make an effort to speak up, when silence seems more comfortable. Or to stop talking, and to listen to others.

Learning social skills, and learning how to manage oneself, are very important, and are separate issues from creativity. Nor are they incompatible at all with creativity! Yet, even as with creativity, these should be in the service of increasing one's options for living in the world, and not restricting them.

What seems particularly unfortunate is when a teacher or parent who actively values creative expression, unknowingly devalues the varied creative styles of learning that actually generate or go along with it. The adult can unwittingly become a standard bearer for the status quo. The motives can certainly be good. "These kids must 'fit in' now," the adult may reason, "or how will they get along in middle school, or high school, when kids are even tougher on each other?" Or "when the teachers start getting really hard and demanding." Or "when they are getting a lot of lecturing." Or when "the class size gets much larger." Sometimes, the norms of this higher level school -- be it middle school, high school, or college -- and the norms of the peer group of the future, can become an unassailable standard.

Uprooting False Differences

We turn fully around in a circle to look at what might seem the opposite situation: The valuing of false differences, rather than the valuing of people's true differences.

Actually, this is the same issue suppression of the richness of who we really are. It's ironic that this process may give the illusion of even greater variation between groups of people. For instance, when people play the "in-group" game, and find many ways that others are not "like me." (The others are also, potentially, not "as good as" the in-group.)

There may well be an evolutionary component to this process. And sometimes an aggressive edge. But these days it isn't working. in a shrinking world, we need a much deeper awareness of the similarities across groups, not the differences between them. To work better together, not "beat the other guy."

There are endless ways of packaging and limiting real people, through the creation of artificial boundaries and expectations. This can stunt both the packager and the packagee. The examples include ethnic and cultural differences, differences of geography, means, education, so-called "breeding," etcetera. Recognizing this, we take only one example, and only briefly.

Men, Women, Culture and Creativity

What does gender have to do with creativity? More than one might think. It turns out that the more highly creative people get, the more certain culturally-induced stereotypes will fade. This, by the way, is not the same as eliminating sex differences.

We do live in an unfortunate world and time in which boys, more than girls, are taught that feelings can be "weak." And where "thinking like a girl" can be taken as an insult. Rationality is one ideal. And so is action.

"Don't be a wimp—just do it," some boys are told. In the extreme stereotype, men are strong, and women are weak. Action becomes more of a "masculine" type of outlet—which, at one unfortunate pole, can even lead to acting out and abuse. How sad to have one's other expressive outlets seem so much less available. Relatively speaking, the world of feelings has been delegated to women, along with the primary responsibility of caring for others. Caring and women. Empathy, mutuality, sensitivity, intuition.

Until very recently, men of "feelings" have been widely devalued. And even now, the "Alan Alda" syndrome, the "sensitive male," can draw a kind of half-smile. Yet men who buy fully into a gender stereotype game, can be accepting a kind of emotional lobotomy. (Women who buy into the female counterpart can have their own kind of lobotomy.)

This situation is all the worse because authentic emotional connection with others can actually improve one's health, one's resistance to stress, and one's psychological wellbeing in general. Is it only coincidental that women live longer than men, and that men with women live longer than men without?

But the women certainly lose too, when gender differences are overplayed. And, in addition, some of the acceptable "female" functions are devalued and stifled. Are sensitivity, empathy, and mutuality taught in school? Are they found on the SAT's? What does it feel like to hear one man insult another by saying, "Don't act like a girl."

And how well, after all, can women and men connect with each other, if each is suppressing a part of herself or himself, pushing them further and further apart. The popular books one can find on how women and men communicate—or how they don't communicate—attest to such patterns.

The woman: "I just want him to know how I feel. If he would only listen to me. That's all I care about."

The man: "I feel so inadequate if I can't do something about her problem. I want to be able to solve it. I don't like these discussions."

For women, in addition, as important as caring may be, what if one comes to feel responsible for everyone. Imagine feeling, at the extreme, that one must care for everyone -- except perhaps for oneself.

And what if, as the keeper of caring, one also becomes loath to express feelings of anger, frustration, and conflict, to not upset others, to always be "nice." In this routine, to excel professionally might also be seen by some as not nice, the so-called woman's "fear of success." Is it sensible to think that one must always make others happy, even at one's own expense. (And that to not do so is selfish, which is of course also bad.)

This is the crisis that can peak for adolescent girls—to feel that to mature as a woman, to find a place, and to find a mate, may mean to give up part of oneself, to stifle many true and valid emotions and capabilities. Yet to "be oneself" may be to risk loneliness and extrusion. A nice double bind.

What then does this have to do with creativity? Everything. Such role restrictions for both males and females stifle the whole person. Creativity is naturally stifled as a part of this. The creative male—notwithstanding the particular area of interest, be it in technical fields, say, or in the arts—is not so reluctant about sensitivity, intuition, emotional expression. And where, indeed, would creativity be without these? The creative female is not so reluctant about dominance, assertion, and forceful independent action. One would be hard pressed to challenge the status quo without them. Creative men and women can each "have it all."

With creativity, the gender stereotypes soften and can even fall away, and the creative person can draw much more widely than another might do, from all parts of her or his personality.

Here then are people who are truly "much more themselves." This enriched identity has been called "androgyny." This term is reasonable for the common core of what is shared. But it is also not to abolish the distinctions. Such creative men and women, may at various times choose to do things that just happen to be more "stereotypically masculine," or "feminine," and why after all should they not? Having the choice is truly the essence of "having it all."

Hence, we underline, once again, the importance of our real differences: these are our riches, our creative fortunes. The real differences open up alternatives. They enrich both our potential to think creatively, and our motivation to think creatively—to break from the past and the usual norms. The false differences, such as stereotypes and conformist self-limitations, are what constrict and stifle who we really are. Then our creativity must emerge in whatever watered down form it is able, despite them.

We now return to specific abuses of the real world. The world (and each of us in it) is often doing its job of perpetuating these sex-role stereotypes, even for kids at the earliest ages. An awareness of how we do this is, of course, the first step. I will start with myself.

I was with another mother, my daughter and her son, at a local playground. The boy had run off right away for a tall and imposing slide that spiraled down, at a very steep slope, from a great height.

In a flash, Nolan was up at the top, waving madly and ready to zoom down its course. I shouted, "Great, Nolan!" And the conquering hero conquered. At the same time, my daughter was hurrying off toward another part of the playground, and I shouted, "be careful." She turned around uncertainly, wondering perhaps what the problem was that I didn't think she could handle.

I realized immediately what I had done—I had encouraged strength and fearlessness in the boy and weakness and fearfulness in the girl." Well, at least," my friend had reassured me, "you were aware of it." Yeah.

We can't always be so sure we are aware of it. Imagine being a fifth-grade teacher—this is a real person and story—who is getting ready to be filmed for national TV, for NBC's "Dateline." Jane Pauley was anchoring a show about subtle sexist messages in children's classrooms, and how girls don't therefore don't receive the same education as boys. The whole country would be seeing this feature.

The teacher knew these films of her teaching would be scoured by NBC staffers for any little hint of unconscious bias. Knowing this, the teacher had agreed to take part.

This story is told by Myra and David Sadker, in their important book *Failing at Fairness: How America's Schools Cheat Girls.* The "Dateline" feature was about the Sadker's startling discoveries in the classroom. The authors were sure that this video would show some bias. The story gets more interesting, because, next thing they knew, two "Dateline" staffers were calling up in frustration after poring over the film, again and again. "The teacher is terrific. There's no bias in her teaching. Come watch."

The Sadkers did. And terrific the teacher was, but despite her best efforts, she was more terrific for the boys, and the staffers had missed it as well. One segment that "Dateline" showed was a math group, with, as it turned out, boys on the right, girls on the left. The teacher gave the text to a girl to hold open to a particular page, and then turned to the boys and proceeded actively to teach them. She did turn occasionally to the girls, but only to read the examples in the book. A lectern would have done as well.

Personally, I hear such examples with the double consciousness of a woman who in fact did go ahead and get a degree in physics with distinction (and with a math minor), and who then went on to do graduate work in biophysics, before turning to medicine and the social sciences. Some people always looked at me a little oddly for having made these choices. Physics! For a girl? Why ever, they wondered, would she be doing that? To get a husband? (No kidding.) And if I said I thought that doing physics was fun, then they really began to wonder.

Along those lines, the Sadkers tell a moving story about their elder daughter, who was evidently at risk of being tracked into a slower junior high school math group. The teacher tried to reassure them. "Robin is adorable, such a pretty girl. But she just can't do math. Don't worry about it. A lot of girls have that problem." But the Sadkers did worry about it. It turned out that Robin could do math just fine. And Robin is now in medical school.

But this discussion isn't just about a particular realm of study, say math or science, or about a particular type of teacher response. In schools in general, boys tend to be called on much more than girls, and their responses tend to be taken more seriously.

Later, as professionals, women's work can be devalued compared to men's. Years ago, a colleague, Lenny Glick, sent out a psychology paper for review to a number of professional reviewers, as part of a research study—the very same identical paper—except that half the copies had a woman as author (e.g., Jane Doe) and the other half had a man (John Doe). What do you think? Did Jane and John get equal treatment? Well, guess again.

Let us look for a minute at outcomes for girls and boys in Lewis Terman's famous study of gifted children. Out of a quarter of a million California public school students, Terman chose just those youth with exceptionally high IQ's, and followed them to see, among other things, how many would show exceptional achievement.

The girls showed such overpowering differences in circumstances that Terman ended up studying them separately from the boys. Consider this: their superior "intelligence" was comparable to the boys, and the girls equaled or excelled the men at school from the first grade through college. Yet Terman said of the girls, that later on: "If they do not marry at once, they accept whatever kind of respectable employment is at hand. After marriage they fall into the domestic role and only in exceptional cases seek other outlets for their talents. The woman who is a potential poet, novelist, lawyer, physician or scientist usually gives up any professional ambition.... My data strongly suggest that this loss must be debited to motivational causes and to limitations of opportunity rather than to lack of ability."

If the creativity of women is to prosper, there needs clearly to be equality of treatment and opportunity. But we mustn't forget that men lose too. We all lose, whenever people are artificially divided up, assigned certain qualities, and denied others.

In this particular instance, men may come out better on some conventional indices of training and success. But we all lose big, both in the external world, and within ourselves. We all become little part-people, struggling in a world that needs full and holistic thinkers—holistic people—to cope with a shifting and complex future.

Understanding as the First step in Valuing

Children are incredibly malleable and this, again, is probably no evolutionary accident. Thus it is important to start valuing true human difference and diversity as early as possible. Two examples follow where preschool children learned to understand people who seemed "different" under the guidance of creative and sensitive adults. This led to greater valuing of others as individuals, greater closeness, and increased flexibility and openness in the children themselves.

Daniel, Teacher's Aid

Daniel was a young adult who had suffered from cerebral palsy. He was intuitive and talented with young children, and had gotten a job as a preschool teacher's aide. But Daniel's face, in particular, looked different from most people's, and some of the kids could mock him, intentionally or unintentionally. Sitting in a circle with Daniel they might say, as kids do, "What is wrong with your face?" Or more ominously, "Why did they let you work here?" (In this case, one suspects the not too light touch of a conformist parent, passing on biases to yet another generation.)

But Daniel, good natured as he was, had heard this sort of thing before. And he was buoyed by the school's administration, which had wanted both to give Daniel this chance, and to teach the kids about the different ways that people can be--can be, and can be delightful to know.

The teacher openly allowed the children to ask questions about Daniel, privately and in their group. They asked her, and then they asked Daniel directly. He told them about his cerebral palsy. He said told them what it felt like. It didn't hurt. He could eat just like they could. He liked to play baseball and go to the movies. It was hard sometimes to have people treat him differently. He also told the kids about other people like him. All these exchanges were matter of fact and natural.

And what a difference. At the beginning of the year, the kids had held back a little and made their comments. By the end, when Daniel carne through the gate, the kids delightedly squealed "Daniel!" and ran to meet him. Daniel had become an individual—and a beloved person.

How Opposite is the Opposite Sex?

This experiment in a preschool first looked like it wasn't going to succeed. This was a preschool where four year old girls tended to play with girls, and boys with boys. Furthermore, there was a male dominance hierarchy with one clear person who was "top boy." First, these little girls and little boys were separately asked questions about the opposite sex such as, "What do you like about boys/girls?"

The boys had said things like, "They always play with me and help me with things." And the girls, "We like kissing and hugging boys."

If this sounds more like stereotyping and silliness than mutual understanding, one would not be surprised next to see girls and boys sitting facing each other on the floor, with some boys fidgeting visibly, and not paying much attention to the girls.

Suddenly, the little girls got started telling a story together, different children adding on new lines. The story was about a wicked baby sitter and how one little girl had tricked her. The wandering boys became fascinated, and seemed to connect.

The next event seemed like a throwback. The girls were asked, "When you play a game with the boys, who goes first?"

One little girl said, "Boys go first!" She giggled, looked at the other girls, and then started to chant this statement as a refrain. Soon all the little girls were chanting together: "Boys go first, boys go first, boys go first."

The picture that this suggests, of relatively unformed little four year olds, already trapped in these expectations and able only to vent in this way, strikes me as incredibly sad. The researchers themselves were taken aback.

But somehow, this little ritual may have pulled a stereotype way up and made it visible -- high enough even to be smashed. In the free play period that followed, the astonished teacher said, "I've never seen this before!" The little girls and boys were now playing together, some running around in little groups holding hands. And the hierarchical patterns of the boys had completely disappeared, with the powerful "top boy" pretty much off by himself, and no one paying much attention to him.

The Sooner the Better

Broadening our awareness and understanding—this is the point. And now is the time to do it, while the children are still young and the patterns are mobile. An understanding of others is the door to a much truer valuing and caring, as well as a valuing of the best in ourselves. Yet it's not that easy. We have, all of us, gone through so much packaging and stereotyping of ourselves and our world that we are still doing it even when we think we're not (I speak for myself again). Yet we have everything to gain when we meet each other afresh, and understand each other as complex and feeling individuals. Finally, the children who surround us will never again be as open to doing this. This openness was described poignantly, by Maureen Chambers, a preschool teacher of 3 and 4 year olds, including my daughter, Lauren, at the *Duck's Nest Preschool,* in Berkeley, California:

"At the preschool age," Maureen said, "children live in the present. "They do not have a grasp on the concept of time. They can be furious one minute, and then laughing again before the angry tears have even been wiped away. They have not learned to put on the masks that adults wear. They are intense and forgiving. That is why it's so important to let them feel and think and create now, because at some point, later in life, the walls will go up."

CHAPTER 7

ONE'S OWN PATH

One day through the primeval wood

A calf walked home as good calves should;

But left a trail all bent askew,

A crooked trail as calves all do.

A dog took up the trail next day.

A bear, too, went along the way.

And then a wise bellwether sheep

Pursued the trail o'er vale and steep....

And soon the central street was this

Of a renowned metropolis.

A hundred thousand men were led

By one calf near three centuries dead.

For men are prone to go it blind

Along the calf paths of the mind

And work away from sun to sun

To do what other men have done.

They keep the path a sacred groove

Along which all their lives they move;

But how the wise wood gods laugh

Who saw the first primeval calf.

--SAM WALTER FOSS

But now here comes a young person who dares to be different. Thousands of years of tradition, and millions of years of genetic programming converge to tell her or him: stop! That is wrong! Join the rest! This is not how it's supposed to be! Stop, or you will never succeed! You will never get into college! And your parents will never be proud of you! Just how often will this child give in, and get back on the path?

We look here at a few ways to make things worse—and a great many more ways to make things better. We focus this on the schooling of young children. But the principles also apply to parenting, and to working with others in a range of job and personal situations.

Creativity, Play, and Freedom

If there ever was an antidote, it is creativity, and if there ever was a time for it, it's in the play of the youngest children. This is where children can first discover that there are many paths, and that the ones they can find in themselves are incredibly special.

How interesting it is, indeed, that children who do a lot of make believe, who can fantasize and make up their own little worlds, can be both happier and more flexible when new situations in their lives arise. These children, in fact, can be happier in general.

Miriam de Uriarte, Director of the Berkeley Child Art Institute, says just this, based on over 25 years of helping young children express themselves creatively. She puts what she does a little differently, however: "I give them the materials and let them develop their own ways of expressing themselves."

In fact, here are preschool age children running back and forth to a central table where they are joyously dipping their hands in pots of paint, red and yellow and orange and blue and so on, carrying the paint quickly to the wall before it drips too much, and applying it with their hands, however they wish, on large white pieces of paper t aped to the wall. These papers are almost as big as the children are. The pictures are wild abstract patterns, in general, and one is entirely bright yellow." This is not what most kids are allowed to do at home!" laughs Miriam, who is a fun loving woman, with a twinkle in her eye." They are definitely going to do some exploring here."

The Berkeley Child Art Studio is a world apart, of walls dripping with layer upon layer of multicolored ribbons of paint, the signatures of kids down through the years. The floors, too, are a mosaic of color. Then there are high shelves, everywhere, piled with bottles and colors, and brushes, and rolled up paper and canvas, and a range of other materials. The smell is heavily one of "art," of paint and solvent, of creativity in motion. This is not your world of "everything in its exact place" (although it's really quite organized), and there is a sense of freedom, and of anything goes.

Miriam also does teacher training at the studio, and she gets teachers to do many of the same things the kids do. One preschool teacher told me, "It was an amazingly freeing experience. She had us all running around a table covered with butcher paper, making whatever marks we wanted as we whizzed by. It makes you see how we get into such set patterns."

Although Miriam doesn't tell the kids what to do, she does encourage them to avoid set formulas—such as the time-honored blue stripe at the top of a page for the sky—and instead to tryout their own images and expressions. Plus, she encourages them to explore different ways of doing the same things. The focus is not on some final "perfect" product, but on the trying, the exploration, the process. The goal is to take off in interesting directions, and on the fun of being able to do this. To see the world in many different ways. In fact, the more diversity there is in what they create," she says, "the more the children seem to enjoy it."

Very touchingly, young children in particular may express themselves wholeheartedly with the integrated creativity of their being. Happily, they haven't yet learned they're supposed to do art today, writing tomorrow, and movement the next day. These kids may make up stories about a picture, spontaneously doing this, or dance to an image, or sing while they're working -- without making all the distinctions of medium and expression that adults can get into." To them, it's all one thing," says Miriam, "it's all creativity."

"Play, the Cornerstone of Imagination"

It's surprising how many people still think that children at play are just fooling around, just passing the time, or indulging their various fancies—although kids may certainly at times be doing this too.

But children don't just play by accident. This is a laboratory for life, for learning about other people, the world, and the worlds one can create, through fantasy and the power of one's imagination. Play is as much a gymnasium for the mind—and the heart—as the gymnasium on the schoolyard is for the body.

Play has been called "the child's work," and "the cornerstone of imagination." According to Sandra Russ, it is, after all, one place where a primary importance is given to curiosity and exploration. Play helps kids to take chances, to look at things in more than one way, and to value the importance of finding multiple solutions to a problem. Play can also teach children to attend to each other, to resolve differences, and to work together. Play at its best can help children learn to learn, and to learn together, so they can make their way more flexibly in a confusing world, and a world for which we adults certainly don't have all the answers. But let us now look at an example of something that was billed as creative play, and which didn't exactly work.

Conformity Plus

Here is a classroom in a preschool I found rather frightening, particularly since it was presented as being "creative." "We are eclectic," said the teacher proudly, "we use things from a lot of different traditions." She also proudly displayed a poster from a "creativity workshop II she had recently attended. I left truly worried about how these kids would turn out if they had no other influences in their lives. We powerful adults can have such a deep effect.

I was informally visiting this classroom with a creative colleague, my brother Dexter Richards (known as Rick). The very nice preschool teacher encouraged us to look at all the materials and talk with the children. We dove right in, perhaps deeper than expected. Please note this is not a critique of any particular program, materials or their potential uses, but of a particular process and some hidden messages, as we observed them at one point in time.

First, Rick and I started watching two little girls, about three to four years old, who were playing with counting rods. These rods were constructed in alternating segments of red and blue, so as to graphically show how long the rods were. A rod of two units length was painted half red, and half blue. (It looked like two blocks put together, one of each color.) A rod of length four was first colored red, then blue, then red, then blue, with each portion indicating an additional unit of length. A clever idea.

These little girls decided to make a tree. They were all excited about this idea. They started with a block of length two, put a "three" right under it, then a "four," and so on. They were very careful to keep finding the block of the next highest length, and were

Really happy about the alternating colors of red and blue that was emerging, making a kind of patchwork, pattern, a very "pretty tree," they said, as they continued.

Then out of nowhere, and I kid you not, the teacher came over and criticized these girls. They were doing it all wrong! She wanted us, the observers, to know, that the correct way to proceed was to line all the rods up from a left-hand margin, first the "two, then the "three," then the "four," and so on, so that you could see how each rod was one unit longer than the ones before.

That was the right way. The little girls' way was therefore the wrong way.

The girls were taken aback, and looked over their shoulders at Rick and at me, since we had been so openly enthusiastic—we had not been quiet observers at all—about what they had been doing. So I told the teacher I liked the girls' tree. And the teacher decided to let the girls continue (whew).

Next, one little girl ran to a shelf in a totally different part of the room and brought back a bucket of beads. The pair started putting the beads on the multicolored branches of the tree. One bead for each colored space. Some beads looked like flowers, some balls, and some barrels. There was a scattering of pretty shapes. From a math point of view, they were placing these tokens in 1-to-1 correspondence with the colored patches, an excellent exercise. Pl us now the girls' attractive tree had been elaborated to become a Christmas tree. The creativity was organically bursting out from their original project. And the girls were having a great time.

Yet, at this point, the teacher got quite upset." The beads go over there!" she said." They're for another project—we don't want to mix them up." Not a word, I might mention, about the work that the two girls had done. Not a word, except to criticize. (And this was with observers, after a prologue about creative learning.)

I asked the teacher what she would do, then, if a child wanted to decorate a construction such as this one. She said that there were, in a back room, beads and buttons for just such a purpose. All a child had to do was ask. With three and four year olds? I couldn't realistically see this happening.

Well, things got worse before they got better, because now one little girl had taken some rods off the tree the pair had been making, and was setting up an enclosure or corral. She was herding all the beads inside the walls she had made, talking to them as if they were living animals. "Come here," she said, "go inside," and the like.

This was such a departure from the original (the "right") use of the materials that the teacher was dumbstruck. Yet she was now becoming aware of our reaction. I, in turn, was—and this is telling—beginning to feel like a "bad child, "a troublemaker, for stirring things up and encouraging the children to do the "wrong things" in the classroom. Rick later said he felt the same way.

By now, some of the other kids had gathered around, because Rick and I and these girls were having such a good time. When we went off to another part of the room, they followed us, followed Rick actually, as if he were the Pied Piper.

There, Rick proceeded to ask what some kids were doing who were seated around a little table. They were pouring tiny little plastic figures of animals, very cute, in pastel colors, from one small vase to another. A tricky business, but they were doing it very well, and enjoying it. Exercising their small motor skills.

Rick watched this for a bit and then had an idea. A creative idea. "What," he said, "if you do this instead: Put the tops of two of the vases together," (he took one child's materials to demonstrate), "and then just flip the whole thing over." Rick turned the setup end for end, the way one would reverse an hourglass.

The kids were fascinated and they all started trying this, with varying degrees of success. The teacher was quick to the rescue. "No, stop, he's doing it wrong," she said. "It will only work for him because he has such large hands." And she proceeded to pour the little creatures from vase to vase the "right" way, demonstrating what the children should be doing.

There were a few other incidents of this sort, but you get the picture. A well-meaning teacher, who clearly cared for the children, and thought she was stimulating them creatively by letting them work and discover on their own, was in fact indoctrinating them in a range of unfortunate lessons. These included, "there's a right way and a wrong way to do everything," and saddest of all, that "your way is the wrong way."

When it came time for me and Rick to end our visit, the kids were finishing up "circle time," where they were gathered together, for discussion, stories, and sharing. They were sad to see us go and at the teacher's urging said a wonderful, loud, and resounding "goodbye." But then some of the kids decided to say a second and" then a third "goodbye." We left this little embryonic environment of learning to the sound of this teacher saying, "Now children, one 'goodbye' is fine; but more than one is too many."

Creativity and the Unexpected

Freedom, self-discovery, discovery of world, and one's ability to act in it. What we often think we want.

But there is another side to the picture, when one is encouraging—or expressing—creativity. Paint dripping on the floor, a gleeful messing up of materials, this may be only the beginning. The nature of creativity is to be different, to do the unexpected. These young creators won't always behave in ways an adult might predict or prefer. And this is not just true for very young children, but for older kids and, most certainly for adolescents, during their crazy time of self-discovery.

In the example above, my strong sense of being a "bad child, "when I encouraged preschool children who were departing from the teacher's expectations, was a telling sense indeed. How subtle are the norms we may sense almost through a kind of osmosis. And if they are enough to set a visiting adult squirming, what will they do to a creative child?

Yet these classroom situations are not an easy call for a creative teacher, and the more conventional teacher above certainly meant well. There are many issues. What, one might think, if a child gets too bizarre or outrageous, or doesn't separate fantasy from reality? Or if a child uses "being creative" as an excuse for acting out, for misbehavior or wildness, for the pulling of a parent's or a teacher's strings. The question can be much more than "How does one draw the line?" It is sometimes how to see the line in the first place.

We now look at some issues that come up around the creative process and creative products or activities that result. Of course, any school will have its pros and cons. But we will take this inquiry to a preschool that provides one useful model of creative openness, holistic learning, a valuing of diversity, and a stressing of individual and group purpose.

Swimming with the Ducks

We are again at the *Duck's Nest Preschool*, in Berkeley, California, ready to see how some of the staff there handle things. My daughter, Lauren, one should note, loved this preschool.

The Duck's Nest is a multilevel jigsaw complex of redwood buildings, play areas, trees, and little lawns and paths; broken sun shines down through the leaves and branches, onto multicolored flowers in window boxes and planters. You enter through a tall brown fence and gate, into a different world of children's squeals and laughter, set back from the unlikely setting of an industrial street near the waterfront of the San Francisco Bay.

There is an international feel to the school, with a staff which, between them, can use five spoken languages, and American Sign Language. The children too bring a multicultural mix. The goals are play-centered and developmental, focused on kids' social, emotional, and intellectual growth, their connection to each other, and to the earth.

And here, by the way, are the ducks. Two white friendly ones with yellow-orange bills, who love to be fed by the children. Not to mention the bunny, and the chickens. Each morning, the children gather the chickens' eggs, and they feed the animals leftovers from the day before. "We don't want to waste any food," they explain.

The children like learning about the animals, and helping car e for them. Did you know chickens like to eat dried out eggshell? The children know. "For calcium," explains one tiny child, impressively. Here is a laboratory of process and interconnection." The chickens make eggs for us," a girl says. "We give them some food, but they don't like hay." She is reporting on her own experiments. "They do like grass," she offers, and then adds with amazement: "Guess what? If we drop our sandwich in the sand, they still like to eat it!"

And then there's the corn out back, the tomatoes and the radishes. The avocado tree. The herb garden. The children don't just watch these products of nature; they help them grow. They feel responsible—and also needed. Industrial Berkeley now boasts a few chic artist's lofts, cafes, and discount outlets. But this evolving school environment is something else.

Now we are passing a tall flagpole with a large white flag and yellow duck, rising from a climbing structure that looks like the bridge of a ship, connected to earth by marine-type netting, climbing ladders and poles. An adjacent structure has ladders and a slide, and secret in-and-out hiding places, and the whole is surrounded by a sandy play area. This area now boasts a child-made river/lake and beaver dam, the branches, leaves, and mud carefully interwoven by little hands to hold back the water, from one part of the enclosure to the other. It does look a bit like "after the party," though, at this point. The water is now seeping away slowly into the sandy earth.

Finally, we are entering the "Mandarin Duck" room. Here are the seniors, and these four and five-year old "big kids" are proud of it. They are about to have one of the more structured full-class lessons, about a serious, traditional subject: the solar system.

And now here comes Mara Guckian, the teacher and "Creative Program Director" of the school -- or rather, at the moment, Mara in the guise of "Ms. Frizzle," as in the *Magic School Bus* series of books. (This was before the PBS animated television series, with Lily Tomlin speaking the part of Ms. Frizzle.)

"OK, up the boarding ramp," directs Ms. Frizzle, and one child starts checking tickets, as the kids pile into the "rocket ship."

For "solar system month" (other themes have included "ocean" or "forest"), one whole end of this irregular classroom has been turned into a spaceship, going up four stairs and into a second level of the room. The kids slip into various positions, amidst ceiling to wall posters of a multi-windowed space cabin, controls galore, a joystick, and all the planets arrayed about them -- including a large red Jupiter, Saturn with its rings, and the Earth with the Moon. Asteroids too, and cornets (some child made). And stars, stars, stars. Sign on the wall: Our Rocket Ship. There are tables, chairs, radios and headphones, paper and pencils for "charting the course," and "communications."

"We're going to blast off!" says the captain (a five year old), "fasten your seat belts." The kids all count 10-9-8-7-6-5-4-3-2-1-0- BLAST OFF!, getting in a little numbers-work too, as they take up their roles, working together smoothly. The communicators radio to ground, navigators callout course corrections. Space scientists share information about their destination. Faster, faster.

"This is a trip to what planet, today?" asks Ms. Frizzle. She says "today," because the starship has been flying about before this.

A four or five year old navigator responds, "Saturn! "adding something about "rings." The kids recall where they've already been, and now "we're leaving the four inner planets, the rocky planets,..." announces Ms. Frizzle.

The atmosphere is electric. Little space scientists shout out what they've learned as they pass these planets at an incredibly high speed. Hello to our earth, visible off the port side. It's planet number three, as the kids know well. Imaginations are also on "high," and one can almost see these planets whizzing past the spaceship windows.

Now, we pass Jupiter, and count its moons: 1-2-3-4-5-6-7-8-9-10- 11-12. That's a lot of moons. Our earth only has one, you know. And finally, we're at Saturn, "The most beautiful planet in the solar system," says Ms. Frizzle, as per the *Magic School Bus* book. Then she looks puzzled and asks, "but would a bunch of rocks and ice and dust look beautiful?"

The kids look serious as they consider this important aesthetic question and the chemical composition of the rings of Saturn.

"There is something about a ring," Ms. Frizzle finally concludes.

Soon, the class really gets going on, if one can imagine, the density of the planet Saturn. (Jean Piaget, watch out!) "Did you know Saturn would float in a bathtub?" asks Ms. Frizzle.

One child remarks about how big the bathtub would need to be to fit the planet Saturn into it. Ms. Frizzle goes along with this in high spirits, saying "Can you imagine a giant bathtub floating through the solar system, measuring the planets?" The children are laughing and trying to imagine this. (No single child, it would appear, is confusing fantasy and reality.)

"Our spaceship might bump into the bathtub, "laughs one child.

"With this good navigation system," says Ms. Frizzle, with a nod to the navigators, "it's probably big enough to steer away from it."

And so the voyage continues—science, art, wonder, math, imagination, reality, excitement, humor, role playing and drama, and a web of human interactions, all seamlessly interwoven into an integrated learning experience, truly a voyage of discovery—drawing on the diverse talents of the children. It didn't compartmentalize, over intellectualize, or unnecessarily limit. In fact, I learned a lot from this space flight myself. It was a trip to remember.

Of course, every class isn't a rocket ship ride. The "Mandarins" work in smaller groups or on their own a great deal of the time, whether devising space art, their own rockets, Lego space stations, or non-space projects such as self-portraits, sand table or dinosaur dramas, "carving" of modeling clay, building with magnets, designing dioramas, toothpick skeletons, "potato prints," or making real paper (from real pulp, with glitter added to the mix by the children).

Each day in the main room, kids can choose from two such very different projects--these are do-able in the kids' own styles, with their own unique signatures—or they can go to the "listening center," where in cooperative groups of three, they "read along" with popular children's tapes.

Finally, "circle time" on Mondays is a "business meeting." It's the kids' turn. What did they like, and what didn't they like, about the week's activities? Did this work for them -- or should the teacher make some changes? The children are learning to be the final arbiters of their schooling.

We the visitors will now depart this little world at another full-group gathering, a "circle time," where the word "flexible" has just come up.

"Flexible—who knows what that means?" Mara asks the children.

"Being able to do everything you can't do exactly on time," offers a child. Not a bad definition at all. Some other definitions follow.

Mara asks Anna, a five year old, to stand up and be stiff for everyone, to be "inflexible." Grinning, Anna stands board like. Then Mara asks her to be "flexible," and she stumbles about, wiggling arms and legs happily. This is great, I think. They're defining a word, not just in terms of other words, but using children's own movements and their sense of their bodies.

"Now," says Mara, "everyone stand up and be flexible," Hilarity follows, as the whole class wiggles." And now be 'inflexible.'"

What next? Do we use the new word in a sentence?

Instead, Mara asks the children an ultimate question of creativity: "How are you more comfortable—flexible or inflexible?"

"Ask the Teachers"

A nice visit to be sure, but now let's "ask the teachers." I spoke with five of them in depth, along with a creative movement consultant, and the school's innovative founder and Director, Monika von Gierke-Stoltz. I was particularly interested in the fantasy vs. reality question, and asked Mara about that.

"It all depends," she said. "Is it an art project or is it science? If it's science and the class makes ducks, they'll all look the same, with two this, two that; there's a 'right way to do it.' But if it's an art project," and Mara emphasized this, "then it's none of my business.

She continued to tell about one little boy, call him Matt, who wanted a frog to have two legs. Mara said that the frog would die. Matt said it wouldn't—it would have superpowers." I want to respect his story," Mara said. "It's a hard call. Will it push this child emotionally to not respect his expression?"

I'd asked a number of other teachers how often they worry that kids will get "too wild" with their ideas, and how they would set some limits without "turning off the kids' imaginations."

These teachers didn't worry very much or very often. Some responses: "I usually just let them do it, wild or not." And, "just let'em create, if that's what they want. Let's say they're doing 'self-portraits,' and some are self-portraits, and some aren't. It really doesn't matter."

One teacher addressed the risk aspect, saying he'd only stop a child's creative expression, "if it poses a danger to themselves or another person, or risks some permanent damage to an object of value." His answer is particularly interesting because, according to this teacher, if a child temporarily muddied a table, say, or dented a replaceable cardboard box, this wouldn't in itself be a reason to halt the child's creativity.

These are very flexible teachers.

"It's also so hard sometimes to let them do it on their own," said another. "But let that self-esteem grow. And—it just kills me we do need to follow our schedules. But sometimes you see them building a structure with blocks and you think,' what's really more important—for them to follow this schedule right now or to finish?' Sometimes I'll set something aside for a child to finish later."

Kids do need to adapt to rules, the teachers indicated, and to each other. But if we're always pushing them to conform to our schedules, as if nothing else in the world really mattered, what message will we be giving them?

I also asked these teachers the "acting out" question: What if a child who is creating gets particularly "silly or inappropriate."

"Redirect them—they've usually lost interest," was a common response. Or: ignore it, use distraction, deal with it directly. So-called "bathroom words" were a common issue this particular week; kids can love to be shocking. "Everyone has an P or a V, and goes potty," said one teacher. "Talk it out—they can see your reaction." Another stressed finding out why the child was asking. "You don't want them to think they can't say it.... There's no question that's not justifiable, if they're serious."

Openness is the norm—if the kids are serious. They learn that with creativity, anything goes.

These kids include the more adventurous and eager ones. But I also asked about the more reluctant children who just won't "take a risk." Teachers mentioned things like individual attention, modeling, and compliments on what kids do achieve. Always, there's a focus on confidence-building and self-esteem.

One teacher has an interesting plan. Each day, a different child is class "leader" a rotating job the kids love. "It makes them feel special, they are the first in line to go outside, they get to sit in a special chair at 'circle time', pick a friend to help them with chairs after an activity (clean-up chores are special too—e ven enough to share with a friend), to pick an activity for the whole class," and so on. They also get to wear a special "star medal" around their neck a sign of distinction. The "leader" role, the teacher said, helps different children in different ways. More timid and conforming kids can learn to be more comfortable in a prominent position where they take initiative.

"Well, that's a hard one," said another teacher, specifically about children who are nervous about trying out their own ideas in certain activities, and who worry what others will think. "Pull them aside, get 1-on-1, ask them questions... make them feel comfortable, and say it's OK to talk about it (their ideas), and express themselves. It won't work in a group." Said another, about drawing, specifically, "set up the child who is afraid apart from others, maybe with one other, then later compliment the child in 'circle'... it's so important, what they hear there."

Another teacher sometimes tells kids, "'Just look at so and so, you've done it before, look at those lines, those are great, I love the way you made this structure'—but never," she added, "draw on their work. Also it's important to hang pictures up in class, with names on them, and to encourage parents to hang them up at home. Some of them won't take them home," she continued poignantly. "I say you can dispose of them later, but not when the child is looking."

If censoring, correction, tight schedules, and lack of parental interest, or teacher respect, aren't enough, here are some other answers teachers gave to the specific question of how and how often adults might "stunt" a child's creativity:

"All the time, "said one, "anytime you're trying to get 17 kids to do the same thing."

"It's the teachers with one right answer, that's their style – a lot of teachers have their own ideas of how they want things to turn out, interjecting their own ideas into a child's process... this will really turn a child off from creating anything... it's an indirect kind of thing."

Actually, we've already met such a teacher, in the other preschool example. As well-meaning as she was, even the subtle waves of disapproval that issued from her were upsetting.

Creativity, Inhibition, and Movement

I asked similar questions of Judith Sims, a creative movement consultant and coordinator of the preschool program for the Oakland Parks and Recreation Department, who was making a regular visit to *The Duck's Nest*. Judith goes around to area preschools on a regular basis and leads the kids in fun activities.

Judith's sessions are a chance for kids not only to move, but to listen, to watch, to relate to each other, and finally to learn by moving with each other. As part of this, one of Judith's goals is for kids to learn to be free, and to "be silly with your body—there won't be enough chance to do that later."

Yet even now it begins. Judith told about one little girl who came to class in a ballet tutu. Judith figured this girl must know some dance already, and would enjoy the class." But she didn't want to do jumps," Judith continued. This child seemed to feel creative dance 'wasn't grown up enough.'" Already this little girl was editing out, restricting, categorizing. There was a right way, and a wrong way.

The kids I saw, for the most part, loved Judith's program. For instance, Judith had little 3 and 4 year olds follow her in a long single-file line of bouncy little people, doing a snake dance, with each child copying the child directly in front. Meanwhile, Judith, prancing at the head, tapped out a rhythm on a cow bell, winding around and through the classroom, and in and out of the door, and into the schoolyard and back. The children were hopping, skipping, creeping, even rolling!, and always they were listening, listening, and observing.

Later, when they had "warmed up" a little more, the kids did a mirror exercise where kids sat facing each other in pairs, moving again to a rhythm, with one child copying the other in whatever—whatever! The other child did. And then they switched, with the partner becoming the mirror.

Some kids just sat opposite and moved their hands. Others turned around, looked through their legs and the like. Others pulled their hair, made faces, and added silly noises. Whatever they did was fine. As they proceeded, these little people got less and less inhibited. But always, they were listening, watching, and even learning to anticipate their partner.

Some curious kids came up to me later, during a free play period, while I was sitting outside at a picnic table, writing notes. I asked how they liked the dance class, and the kids were enthusiastic. But one little boy felt differently." The snake was embarrassing, "he confided after the other kids had left." I was afraid somebody would laugh at me." This, I might add, was when he was only supposed to be copying someone else, and not even moving on his own. As Judith told me sadly, "already adulthood is reeking into them—of I can't, I can't, I can't."

Yet this little boy in fact did do the snake dance—and was proud that he tried. With another chance, and another, and another, he can still learn it is OK to be himself, and to express himself as he wishes.

Learning *For What?*

Finally I talked with the founder and director of the *Duck's Nest*, German-born Monika von Gierke-Stoltz, who has run this school for eleven years now. She is proud of the diverse and international feel of the staff, which is, of course, not accidental.

According to Monika, "the diversity and unpredictability of human nature supports the child's development.... it can help the child to become just as diverse. However, there needs to be an openness, and a love and acceptance of the child's own individuality, at the same time."

Monika sees the school, on the one hand, as providing times for children to "express themselves with no limit," to free their creative energies, and discover who they are, through a hands-on process of doing (and not the end result).

At the same time, the school introduces "realities, responsibilities, awareness, and patience," as in animal and plant care, and working with each other. The children's foundation for social skills, will include "helping," "feeling important," and acting with "purpose." Monika stressed the "patience," and the great "flexibility," which talented preschool teachers must have, to nurture all of this. These qualities must be a core part of their own creativity.

These qualities are every bit as critical for creative parenting. Monika bemoaned the lack of importance given to this vital -absolutely vital—function, which can shape a child's future or even destroy it. Parent education. Where is that in our schools? Are parents supposed to come upon these talents "naturally"?

This is hardly an isolated complaint, and I quote from, "Our Culture's Oversight," the Preface to Dorothy Corkille Briggs' book *Your Child's Self-Esteem*: "... we parents are not trained for our job. Vast sums are spent to teach academic and vocational skills, but the art of becoming a nurturing parent is left to chance and a few scattered classes. And yet, paradoxically, we regard children as our most important national resource.... We turn freely to the medical and educational professions to check on our children's physical and intellectual progress. But for guidance on nurturing children to emotional health, we are left largely on our own."

The helping of others, caring, nurturing, and stimulating of complex learnings with emotional components, are not, as we have said, activities which bring high status in our society. The relatively low salaries of preschool teachers—or teachers in general—attest to this.

We are speaking of the integrated learnings of emotion and intellect, of one's self along with one's world. A lack of concern with such integral learning can be yet another reflection of the artificial separating, categorizing, assigning to certain groups, and devaluing, of those fully human qualities we all badly need. Indeed, if you ask many adults, their greatest wishes in life include more caring connections, better feelings about themselves, a greater sense of efficacy, and a fuller life experience and purpose.

So here, instead, are many parents of young children, already worried whether the kids are getting the right "pre-K" (pre-Kindergarten) skills -- learning their numbers and letters and words, "the basics." The popular film "Baby Game," with Diane Keaton, jokes that if kids don't get into the "right preschool," they won't get into the "right college." Or consider the comedy film "Parenthood" with Steve Martin, where a preschool age girl is being drilled night and day with flashcards by her neurotic father (Rick Moranis), for fear her life will otherwise be ruined. In real life, there are real tears behind this sort of laughter.

It's time to stop and ask what kids are learning all this information for. And, by the way, whether anyone has noticed that the kids who are storing away the most information -- like little acorns in the autumn -- are also the ones who are learning how and why to learn.

These kids aren't just cataloging away some facts. They are weaving this information into a web of meaning, which is their own developing map of the world, and themselves in it. It is an empowering map as well, for they are including within it ways to question it, and creatively to change it. And, finally, it is a happy map, one of curiosity, exploration, and fun, and as Monika puts it, of "a love of learning intertwined with feeling good about oneself."

We conclude, with all apologies to Sam Walter Foss, with an amended version of his poem from the beginning of the chapter.

One day through the primeval wood
A calf walked home as good calves should;
And left a trail all bent askew,
A crooked trail as calves all do.
The next day came another calf
And cheerfully walked a little left.
Another came a little right.
She frolicked there, and what a sight
For soon there was a web of paths
A happy choice for prancing calves.
Adventuring here, exploring there,
For our world's paths lead everywhere.

CHAPTER 8

DEATH BY AUTOMATISM

Anyone who is able to knit while watching TV,
or listen to the radio while driving,
knows how learned tasks drop out of mind.

--ELLEN J. LANGER

A lot of people are very deeply immersed in their conditioning....
They will live and die as programmed automatons.

--CHARLES A. TART

There are so many ways that we every one of us -- need to wake up, both for creativity and for life in general.

I was especially surprised by Karen, a delightful woman I know, who had always been adventurous, curious, and fun. She had retired three years before from a demanding management job in health care—and she told me those three years had passed like a streak. Where did they go? It was almost as if they had never existed.

Here was someone who, after a busy and restless life, had found a peaceful coastal setting for her retirement. Palm trees, scrub brush, scattered pines and hemlocks, quiet trails winding up the warm and sunny rolling hills, a cloudless sky, bees buzzing over golden poppies in the hot still air, an ocean shining far below, and stretching out miles to the horizon. Friendly neighbors, quiet days of reading and walking, wandering the beach, and resting and enjoying life. At the height of one's frenzy, one might wish fervently for such a site, and for such a life. What more could one want?

Clearly something. For the first two years, Karen had drifted in a kind of stupor through the hot thick days. Then, slowly, she started getting more and more unhappy. She came to feel stuck and helpless, almost immobile at times, and to make matters worse, Karen had started blaming herself for not thriving when she had these many advantages "that other people would be so happy for." Yet these "advantages, "as it turned out, were not what Karen really wanted. What Karen found was missing was the change and challenge, and the sense of purpose. She had become used to the energetic demands of life in a busy corporate office, had even taken these for granted. They were part of the background noise, if not an annoying and negative factor, an ongoing pressure and stress, and something from which she had felt she could finally escape. She had thought retirement would save her. But it didn't.

At first—and this was a bit frightening, in truth—Karen began wrenching herself away from her routine. She saw she needed to reinstate the change and the challenge, this time, on her own terms. Karen joined a local hiking and nature club. She had feared that she was too old for this club, picturing hordes of healthy twenty year olds with tans, backpacks, and unlimited energy. Karen was embarrassed even to dial up the organization, hoping her voice wouldn't betray her age. But she took the risk.

It turned out that people of all ages belonged to this group, and there was even a special group for people who wanted things less strenuous. Karen decided she was not in this category, and chose to go with the regular program. (What, Karen kept thinking, if I had never even called!)

Karen met a number of interesting new people, although this had not been her primary goal. One man was so unusual he had actually built his own airplane! And from a kit, no less. This man flew his plane, too, of course. And one day, Karen finally got up the nerve to go along. Meanwhile, Karen became more and more active in this nature group, helping organize various trips and social functions. She also started doing some personal writing. Karen had always loved to read, but writing was something she had done only at work—on business proposals, letters and memos. Now Karen started writing for pleasure, for herself.

Karen also wrote a few announcements for her organization's newsletter, and after a bit started submitting some short pieces on nature. A few of these, incredibly enough, were run. Here was something Karen personally cared about, and it felt incredibly good. In a way, it was like giving back to nature, having a different and more active kind of relationship with the world around her. And helping others relate to nature a little more fully too.

Next, on the encouragement of people she knew, Karen even started submitting an occasional piece to the local newspaper. At first, she got rejection after rejection -- for this is often the way. Yet at one time, Karen would have been discouraged and given up completely. Karen's friends kept urging her to continue. And her group's newsletter kept printing some of her pieces. Karen kept telling herself, "my writing must be OK, or I wouldn't be getting this response." And she kept working at it. Finally, Karen even got up the nerve to meet with an editor from the local paper and get more pointed feedback. She also found out what the paper really needed. She soon developed an environmental feature that caught on.

Things had become overwhelmingly better, not only on Karen's calendar, but in the journal in Karen's previously slippery mind. Every day was now rich with new events, carrying meaning and challenge. These were engraved deeply in her fond recollections, and would be forgotten only with difficulty. Retirement was not at all relaxed for Karen now -- but this turned out to be exactly what she had needed. And paradoxically, the clock hand which had been zipping around faster and faster in Karen's head, and seemed to be spinning out of control, was now running much more slowly.

Retirement was not the problem here. Nor for that matter was a still and sunny hillside. It was the routine. The lack of novelty. The lack of challenge. And the lack of meaning, in connection with others and through activities of importance to one's truest self. The lack of living landmarks to break up the days in one's memory and experience. Things which demand of us something new, something that contributes to own personal development, or that of others, and thus to our greater survival and wellbeing—hence a demand which can be truly lifegiving -- and which forces us into the efforts of discovery and of growth.

Instead, we may habituate, and the same days pass, the same routines, the breakfast, lunch, and dinner, the drive off to town even the book on the veranda, the rustle of the palm trees, and the walk through the humming hills. Because, before you know it, the palm trees have become all but invisible, except with the most excessive of efforts. The buzzing of bees becomes only a background murmur, no more conscious than the beating of one's heart. The days collapse, and so do the months and years, and the clock runs faster and faster. Until the alarm finally rings.

On Automatic pilot

The price can be heavy indeed when we go on automatic pilot, especially when we don't even know we are doing it. In a certain sense, or in certain ways, we have ceased to be alive. We have most of us felt this way at times.

"On automatic," we have stopped interacting in a changing creative way with the world; we aren't contributing to the evolving process of thought and action, but are more or less riding upon the waves which others have generated. At the worst we may seem like machines someone else has wound up. Because conscious direction is no longer necessary, many repetitive functions may go underground, become non-conscious, and be lost from our awareness, our records of ourselves, and our further ability to act and change things. Time seems to drop away—and this may indeed feel like a sort of death.

We may still be responsive to a little spark here, a surprise there, we may turn to these as if to the popping of popcorn. Plus we remain the putters-out of fires -- we can always respond in an emergency. We may further go out of our way to seek a thrill or two which, in the absence of the rest, can loom large as a mainstay of our awakened "reality"—almost like a kind of drug fix. But these are reactive, rather than mindful, forms of awareness. Meanwhile we miss our chance consciously to appreciate the rich and infinite remainder of the world, which is in continuous flux around us. If this is not a form of death, then it is at least a type of disability.

Waking up can be contrary to many parts of our programming. But our remarkable ability to think about how we think—our conscious evolution—is one of our most shining qualities. This can be furthered by the quality of mindfulness, as presented by spiritual leaders including Vietnamese Zen Master Thich Nhat Hanh, and whether applied to our bodies, thoughts and feelings, or the world around us. Mindfulness involves more than just noticing. We can watch a movie and become completely absorbed in the story. We see everything. And we also believe it. Suddenly we wake up, and we're back to the world where the dishes need washing. The film is over.

Perception by itself, as explained by spiritual teacher Joseph Goldstein... engages us in the content and story of what appears. Mindfulness emerges from within the story and notices the moment-to-moment arising and passing of sense impressions, thoughts, and consciousness itself.

And the story, in this case, is our lives. We can just live our lives, or we can stand back and ask, "What are we doing?"

We look below at some forms of automatisms. This brief discussion certainly doesn't pretend to be comprehensive. Nor does it correspond precisely to Western notions of mindfulness as expounded by Ellen Langer in her excellent book, *Mindfulness*, or to Eastern views as in Thich Nhat Hanh's lovely book *The Miracle of Mindfulness*. Plus it has its own quirks, some of which have already been mentioned. In the happiest spirit of mindfulness, the reader is encouraged to add to challenge, alter, stand on its head, and turn inside out this particular compendium, in accordance with your own experience, best sense, and intuition.

Areas of Automatism

The word "automatic -- consider three definitions: (1) occurring independently of volition or intention, (2) unconsciously mechanical, and (3) an automatic rifle, pistol, etc. (*Random House Dictionary*). Indeed if we ourselves are the automatic rifle or pistol, we'd better watch out who is firing us. And where.

Here are three areas of potential blindness, areas of mental lapse where at times we may not even know what is happening! First, we have problems of perception -- information we may never even perceive initially, due to the way our sensory apparatus is put together. Second come problems of automatic misinterpretation, ways in which we may routinely, and incorrectly or incompletely, interpret new input; these are discussed using Piaget's concepts of assimilation and accommodation (See also Chapter 4). The third area, only touched on here, and to be considered in a later chapter, involves distortions of our awareness, using our ever-handy psychological defenses. In this way, we can come to see what we want to see, in a very selective way, and avoid all the rest of it. We may even pretend that large parts of our experience do not exist. We will discuss such distortion and dissociation, not only for individuals, but for whole societies.

Nonperception: What We Don't Even See

When it just stays there, we may stop seeing it: Monday we see the tree, Tuesday we see the tree, Wednesday we see the tree, and Thursday, we notice the lawn needs mowing. We don't think about the tree.

It may seem strange that we'd stop noticing something simply because it's static in our field of action. But billions of neurons are working away all at once on countless other mental projects. Our conscious awareness can only keep track of a very limited piece of this picture at a time. Our minds are busy keeping us breathing, walking, eating, listening, speaking, hosting a party, dancing, scanning the room, listening for a newcomer at the door, thinking about tomorrow's day at work, and also unconsciously working on why the checkbook didn't balance. Who, after all, has time to keep noticing the tree that is sitting there in the front yard.

As long as we have a good system to interrupt us, to pull a conscious whistle if something worrisome happens—say if the tree falls on the house—then this might seem a pretty good system. Or at least from the perspective of our genes and their goal of continuance. We will do what we need to do to survive. And we will save our energy for doing this.

If, as we have proposed, our "memes" have their own more subtle wake-up calls, including our generalized reactions to "beauty," this response, too, may be most operative if someone is going to do something about it. When one plans to make some change in one's own own information storage, or that of someone else—in the overall evolution of information. Things may be quite different if we're going to paint that glorious tree out front, or photograph it, or describe it to someone in a letter, or invite a friend over to see it. But if we just keep passing it there on the far side of the lawn, on our way to more urgent matters, then that may be the end of it—truly the mental end of that tree. Poof, and it's gone.

We May See It If It's Changing

Yet it does seem a dirty trick for Karen, who looked forward to her retirement, to have her dreamlike retirement view fade before her eyes. She, and we, in general, cannot hold an image constant in our minds, however beautiful or stunning it may be, if it's not acted upon. That's not how we've been built. Our change sensors are where the action takes place. We have cells in our visual cortex literally to detect dark-light edges, when the eye scans from one part of a visual field to another.

And we can readily detect dark and light changes over time, if the transitions are abrupt enough. Indeed, consider if an enemy enters our visual field. Or consider sound. Even the slightest movement, the rustle behind the shrubbery, and we are instantly alert. We are a live to the sudden rustle, the cry or the rumble, detected by the slightest vibratory change in our ears.

But the musical, somniferous, repetitive crashing of the waves, as lulling as a lullaby, may fade into the background, along with the punctuating cries of the flying gulls, as irregular even as the latter accents might be. Here is a random yet familiar pattern, like a scattering of grains among the sand, a pattern in the abstract, which we have come to recognize. Perhaps, as with the dripping of water from a tap, it is a fractal pattern of nature whose disarray we recognize automatically and resonate comfortably with. But of whatever the exact coding may consist, it is precisely what—if all is well—we would expect.

We may indeed have conceptualized the total symphony of oceanic sounds under "waves," the appearance of the beach under "ocean sand," and the gulls' sounds under "bird cries." And then forgotten these as a packaged, conceptual whole. Or the whole experience— including a stiff salt breeze and the slight squinting of our eyes as we walk out toward the water—as the sensation we have personally of "being at the ocean." We need not process this whole complex of information again when we walk down to the beach the next day.

More apt to attract our attention perhaps would be a stronger version of this stiff salt breeze, and a feeling of chill." I should have brought a heavier jacket"-- might be the main response that registers.

Even our pure and heightened emotions, our great initial pleasure at this wondrous scene, may be subject to the same process of habituation, to the fading with time. Once again with our emotions, we become most aware once again when a feeling is vivid or new. Wow! said Karen, the first moment she saw her retirement view. I love it! This is absolutely heaven. All those years I spent in that tiny downtown apartment, looking at the neighbor's window across the street. There was the tiny touch of view way out at an angle if I put my face right up to the glass. But that was the end of it. Now, look at this! I'll be happy to look at this view every day for the rest of my life.

More likely for only a month or two, before parts of it start to fade. And before one must start reminding oneself to look.

Vivid, new. It's even true with our sum-total mood, right now or over a period of time, our summary experiencing of ourselves and our lives. This is our general content or discontent with things. We don't need to feel happy about a retirement situation day after day after day. There is nothing more to be done. The pleasure fades into the background vibration of the underlying personality disposition. So too may the pain, at least if it isn't severe trauma one is facing, and if the mildly unpleasant situation looks likely to persist without change. The budget is tight, the times are hard. But we are coping. Are you optimistic, are you enthusiastic? Weary, cynical? This is what may ultimately come out. Personality is the stable thing, we are seeing, after the rest of the variation in one's mood has faded or been averaged out.

Bad Mood as a Warning

Considering this, it is of great interest that Karen, in her retirement stupor, came to feel depressed, stuck, discouraged, guilty. Although this seems like yet a new wave of bad luck, it may actually have been a piece of good luck—a red flag of warning that somehow broke through to Karen's conscious awareness.

Please note we are not talking here about a major biological depression; this is a critical point. Such a depression can occur without obvious reason; it represents much more than a response to surrounding events (if it even relates to them), and may persist despite whatever external actions are taken until the proper medical and pharmacological treatment is given. (At that point, treatment can be extremely successful, and eliminate great suffering). We have other things to say about biological depression and mood swings, and potential effects on awareness and creativity. (See Chapter Five.) But the current point is a very different one.

Yes, for Karen, her negative mood state was potentially a positive thing! She saw the warning signal, was awakened from her stupor, and was able to react. A warning system became activated which overrode her basic "healthy" personality traits. Something wasn't right. Something needed to be changed. How did this register first in her immune system? In her hormone levels showing dips in meaningful bonding with others? (fn) How much we might like to know this. But whatever the answer, Karen's survival and coping strategies had once again come to the forefront. And she developed a more active and rewarding life plan.

Three Vastly Different Experiences of the Same Thing

We may be as different as can be, one from another, in how we see something. Because three people go to the same play, doesn't mean that these three people have equally seen it. Perhaps one was daydreaming, another was seeing only the costumes, and the third was attending with great concentration to the action.

Or let us return again to Karen's retirement neighborhood -- and now imagine yourself there, in a car, out on a windy coastal highway below her house, on a low steep ridge where the land curves along a rocky shoreline. You are chauffeuring a friend who has flown in from the Midwest, from a land bound area, and who is in town on business, along with a young child. What a difference there is in what each of you may see.

The child, first, is reacting dramatically to the novelty. She has never seen the ocean and she's high in her seat, looking out the back window. She needs to see the ocean, to make its acquaintance. The rocks, the spray, the sparkle of sun, the wind in her face, the crash of the waves, the seagulls, the precipitous drop from the cliff, the ocean steamer in the distance—motionless, but trailing in its wake a line of white.

It's great, she thinks; it's amazing. The child just can't believe it, can't stop marveling at it. In its beauty and complexity is perhaps an intrinsic message: Attend! This vista is life-giving, to be revered. These are the oceans we grew from -- they speak to us still. Don't just catalogue this one, O Growing Mind, but place it among the deepest repository of memories that will continue to resonate with every other thought.

And so—gently—it is put into its place.

In this moving encounter, aesthetics beats deeply in the impulse to look, to savor, and to remember. And perhaps, ultimately, to survive.

But now here is the Midwestern adult friend, sitting more straight and businesslike in the front seat. "This," he says sincerely, "is a stunning view." He keeps looking back, stops for a snapshot, lets the child run around a bit on a beach, makes a number of other comments (meanwhile thinking how nice it is back in his peaceful farm country, with rugged hills and the silence of the mountains). This is not someone who is seeing the ocean for the first time, nor for that matter this part of the country. Yet there is much that is novel. He is still tuned in for an ocean "refresher course." His attention is nonetheless divided; he keeps turning away from the view to an ongoing conversation about a multicity business project—the real reason he has made this trip to the coast.

And now here is the driver, the host, it is finally us—a timeworn adult who has passed this vista many times before. We feel hassled and rushed—will we make it to the Marriott in time for the friend's luncheon meeting with two business associates? We already know all about the ocean—the spray, the rocks, the sun. We've got this under control. But what about that approaching car? How fast should we go? How fast should we take this turn? Our needs are much more immediate—focused in part on just living through this moment. As with a hunter in the jungle, it is not the beauty of the palm fronds that catches our attention this time. It is the lion about to pounce.

We are, all three, attending to different things, and for very different reasons. Yet, even for the child, these may include some ultimate purposes of survival.

Yet how far indeed we adults may have travelled from the wonder of the child. And how significant indeed if this fresh and aesthetic seeing—translated to adult form, along with the habits of awareness it can generate—have become, more than any business luncheon at the Marriott, what we really need to survive.

Blindness to Environmental Dangers

For now let us move beyond trees, beaches, and seagulls to a broader stage -- to our readings of our world and its imperiled status. I was taken aback when I read Robert Ornstein and Paul Ehrlich's book, *New World, New Mind: Moving Toward Conscious Evolution*, because I was doing many of the same things they described (and still am, although I'm trying). As they put it, "a paranoid visitor from outer space might assume that television was deliberately trying to keep Earthlings from discovering what is really transpiring on their planet."

Where the earth is concerned, we once again tend to react to sudden and major changes, meanwhile overlooking steadily mounting dangers. Of which there are a great many. And of which a great many are potentially lethal.

We, instead, are reading about the marital problems of a well-known royal couple, the details of the murder of a celebrity's wife, and the surprise marriage of a pair of young people, one the daughter of "The King of Rock 'n Roll." Think about it. This is what is being stuffed into our neurons—both by ourselves and by others. This is indeed what sells.

Meanwhile, think of some of the steady insidious forces which it is so easy (and so convenient) to forget. They creep right up on us, moving so continuously that we think they're not moving at all. So steadily do they come from our fast-frame-changing perspective, that we may not even notice. Never mind that we may not really want to know. Or feel "there's nothing we can do anyway."(See Ch. 10, "Seeing Beyond") Spreading pollution, global warming, resource depletion, for example, and the vast multiplier effect of an expanding population.

The slower it is—or the slower it seems—the more dangerous it can be. We habituate to it, we numb out. The 1993 bombing of the World Trade Center? Six people killed. A ready front-page item. The poisons we will be breathing over dinner tonight? "Just a price of modern life, you know." "We are learning how to deal with these." "We have always had these problems." (Since when?) "Look, our lifespan is actually increasing—you've got to look at the big picture." (We do indeed.)

If it happens quickly, we tend to catch it. But if the scale is years, then watch out, because it might just catch us.

Our misperceptions may be abetted by the monstrous scale of some of these problems. We're very good at thinking in tens and twenties. We do have our fingers and toes. And even in thousands and tens of thousands. But try thinking about millions of new people and how they'll be fed. Or millions of acres destroyed. A thousand or a million? A million does seem a lot bigger, doesn't it?

Or consider a problem that seems far away geographically. Seems far away. Again, we were evolved to think in terms of our immediate environs much more readily than about events transpiring in a faraway part of the planet.

Yet consider the ongoing destruction of the world's rain forests. Not a distant problem at all, not one to be put out of mind—but an immediate threat to everyone of us. Among a great many other things, the rain forests trap radiant energy from the sun, produce oxygen and absorb massive amounts of carbon dioxide—the opposite of what we do, as oxygen breathers and carbon dioxide producers—and help stabilize the world's climate and the release of greenhouse gases. The rain forests have had an effect, from all across the world, on the air that you're breathing right now. And these forests are disappearing.

How do we frame this problem manageably in a way that we can understand? With small numbers and dramatic consequences. In this case, it is all too easy. How much of the planet's forests were lost between 1970 and 1990, over a mere twenty year period? More than one quarter. How fast is the rain forest now being destroyed—often by burning? At the rate of 10 city blocks per minute. *Ten city blocks per minute.* Just imagine that destruction in your own home town.

And, meanwhile, we sit around reading about the marital separation of "Princess Di" on the cover of *Newsweek*.

Adapted to *What?*

We're quick to spot the dramatic and sensational, the noisy, fast, and explosive danger. We even hone this ability to perfection, if young enough, and so inclined, in video arcades and home *Nintendo* games. How absurd. Massive dangers meanwhile are looming up and threatening to engulf us. Our perceptual and conceptual apparatuses were formed back in prehistoric times, and for entirely different purposes; they just aren't working for us now. Our environments have vastly changed—yet our genes have remained the same. In many important ways, we are adapted to the wrong environment.

One can see this phenomenon in a different way in the events selected for *Time* magazine's feature "The Most Amazing 60 Years in History" (1923-1982), as reported by Ornstein and Ehrlich in *New World, New Mind*. Here, one should recall, were the candidate events of thoughtful journalists who gave lengthy reflection to our history. Their selections included the New York stock market crash, The Marshall Plan, the Cuban Missile Crisis, and the end of Watergate and resignation of Richard Nixon. No argument here.

Yet during the same period, unprecedented events occurred that were not reported at all. These included a doubling of the world's population, environmental deterioration at a level never before seen, and an increase in the U.S. federal budget deficit by a factor of ten.

Two more ongoing events did at least make the pages of *Time*, so "eventful" were these: the most destructive war in human history, and the appearance of nuclear weapons.

Toward Conscious Evolution

Ornstein and Ehrlich called for a new kind of educated evolution, an evolution of information (or memes)—truly a conscious evolution. It would involve the schools, the media, and many other institutions in society. The goal would be/ finally/ to teach us to see. To learn to circumvent our perceptual and conceptual limitations and distinguish what is still "natural" in our evolution from what has become dangerous. Dangerous yet partially invisible. Because we can still learn to see it/ and can hope to alter it in time.

Processes we need to learn might certainly involve skills in original thinking discussed under "integrative complexity" (see Chapter Five). The freeing our minds and imaginations will be aided further by "Breaking Down Barriers/"the title of the next chapter. Finally our overall awareness of our situation and our world may be better served in the long run by a heightened caring and aesthetic awareness than by a sole confrontation with the "facts" accompanied by fear and panic (and reactions of helplessness or denial). We pursue this further in Chapter Ten and also introduce some of the concepts below.

An Aesthetic Sense Can Help

This notion may seem removed or impractical/ perhaps. Yet / significantly/ a higher aesthetic sensitivity could provide one major hope as we flounder about blindly in a dangerous world. There are three linked considerations: awareness, understanding, and caring. Beauty (or elegance, "rightness"or "fit") provides a sometimes subtle but also pervasive source of awareness that can penetrate our automaton-like stupor.

This effect may be most crucial, in fact, where fear may be crushing, and serves mainly to drive us away.

An aesthetic moment may not be equal to a flash of fear in its intensity, or adrenaline-shock. Yet instead, it has every potential to be nurtured and enjoyed, rather than fled from or neutralized. This willing form of awareness can also make the abstract more real, more concrete and particularized, and can feed our understanding. We look and we notice. As Emerson said, "Therefore does beauty... remain for the apprehension and pursuit of the intellect." How much more intensely we may connect to the plight of a rain forest, and the fire which is threatening it, after seeing glossy photos of the sun streaming through the forest canopy, into a world of symbiotic orchids and colorful tropical birds.

And finally we have caring. Being attracted to something of ten implies that one cares at least in some particular. A greater understanding can feed into that feeling of involvement, investment, and concern. As Paracelsus said: "(The person) who understands also loves, notices, sees.... The more knowledge is inherent in a thing, the greater the love.... anyone who imagines that all fruits ripen at the same time as the strawberries knows nothing about grapes."

One looks more closely because one cares. One looks back again because one cares. As one understands, invests oneself, becomes intimate with some knowledge, process, or being, to which one is attracted in some way, one typically wants to know what will happen to it. The outcome matters. One becomes connected. This, indeed, pertains to survival.

As with our connections with other people (see Chapter Ten), which can lead to better health and even longevity, we have every reason to propose that greater connection to the world in general can enhance personal health and well-being, our sense of efficacy, and yet a further discrimination and appreciation of many aspects of our world -- and, indeed, of ourselves. We'll most certainly return to this.

Misperception: What We See, But See Wrong

But there's more we are missing. "You ain't seen anything yet." What we do finally perceive is not necessarily what we get. We have ways of packaging the data we receive—and then throwing away the data, and just keeping the package.

Automatic Accommodation

Consider Piaget's accommodation, at an extreme—as an automatic phenomenon that can turn off our minds. Here is over-accommodation, where one automatically adjusts one's inner reality to, in essence, what the outside world is saying. "Yes," you say, "I will buy the Brooklyn Bridge." Lots of luck. One slaps in a piece of outside information without any processing or critical judgment. This is a tiny touch of brainwashing, and we all get taken in by this one from time to time.

By listening to an "expert," for instance. The expert says you have a bad cold. No X-rays or medicine will be necessary—go home, get some rest. So you're sure you have a bad cold. That night you run a high fever and it turns out you had pneumonia.

Or the expert says that you're no good at algebra because you didn't do well on the test. Now you think you're no good at algebra. In fact, you had been doing fine on all your homework and were enjoying the problems. It was just a lousy test.

Or the expert says that a particular canvas is a great work of art. You didn't much like it, but now you think maybe you "should."

Or—to make things worse—that these are the scientific advances of the decade which count, the "winners, "in a competitive sense. The others, when one takes the extreme view, therefore don't count, and may fade from our awareness. It's the dichotomy of the winners and the losers. If you don't win, then you lose.

Or we have a "professional" saying you really should be enjoying your retirement; "almost anybody would love a life like this." Similar to Karen, in the example above, you end up feeling guilty. You may conclude that it is you who is lacking.

Or we have the experts telling us we really have to fight this war.

Mindless Assimilation

Now let's take, in a little more detail, Piaget's assimilation—the fitting of new outside data to what one already expects, what one is already programmed to receive—and the important example of abstractions and categories. As Ellen Langer says in her book, *Mindfulness*: Mindlessness sets in when we rely too rigidly on categories and distinctions created in the past (masculine/feminine, old/young, success/failure).... We build our own and our shared realities and then we become victims of them—blind to the fact that they are constructs, ideas.

Ask someone, "What do you see across the street?"

They reply something like, "A house, a car out on the curb, a tree near the sidewalk, sunshine, a person through the front window."

They may be particularly proud of adding the person through the window. But, we have good survival equipment to notice just such a person; we don't want to miss people who are skulking around, barely visible, showing us just a flash of motion.

Now turn this observer around and distract her or him with something else for a few minutes, so the visual impression fades on the retina. At this point, you might ask some other questions, keeping these open-ended. No peeking now.

"What," for instance, "did the car in front of the house look like? The house? Where was the tree exactly—how did it fit into the sidewalk? Or did it? And so on. You might get a few labels back. Some other categories. The car's brand name. The color of the house or the car. But you might also find—on some particulars—that the observer really doesn't have a clue.

Was the house white or beige, was there a chimney, a porch, large windows, wood or stucco, a stairway up, one two or three stories, they really have no idea. They registered "house"—click, check off one house—and maybe something about it's being big or little, or light or dark, or something else of personal relevance. Then they switched off the viewer, and went on to the next "thing." And if they didn't actually mention the tree out in front of the house the first time, don't be surprised now if they don't even know it's there.

Thus, we may assimilate new data to the categories we already have, and stop there, rather than making the effort to take in some new, and unique, information. Prejudice is an excellent example. They're all "gjksiws" and that's that. Prejudice is not just about blurring true differences between unique individuals who, among other things, happen to be "gjksiw's," but also about creating false differences by making entirely too much of a category, and what one thinks it implies. (See Chapter Six.)

The "Erasing" Power of Categories

The power of categories actively to erase other information was brought home to me after moving back to California from the East Coast of the United States. This is another instance of a vanishing tree.

Nearby in my neighborhood, was an amazing flowering tree, a gargantuan tree, much taller than any rooftop in the vicinity -towering over the houses—a tree such as I'd never seen before, with large robust deep green leaves and, most amazing of all, these immense white flowers opening out all over it. You had to crane your neck to see the whole of it.

I just couldn't believe it.

Here was a flowering tree transported from the land of the giants. It should have been a tenth that size. It should have been a small bush. It seemed absolutely magic. One was dwarfed by this product of nature, which looked as if it carne from a place far, far away, if such a place even existed. I was reminded of the huge ground ferns you see in a rain forest—lush and expansive—nothing like their smaller cousins up north. Each day I would look at this tremendous tree with wonder; I would sometimes linger in my car and stare at it. I still couldn't believe it.

Until one day someone said, "Oh! That's just a magnolia."

You could hear the air rush out of my popped balloon. Just a magnolia. I'd even lived in a place with a magnolia tree. How foolish of me. The flowers there did look quite similar to these. Sure, this tree was an awful lot larger, it certainly was a large magnolia, but now everything was falling into place. It really wasn't all that amazing.

It was just a magnolia.

Nonetheless, I still stop my car to look. I try to recapture the magic feeling. I'm fighting against habituation, as well as the simplifying effect of a powerful term, an accurate summarizing name. With effort, I can still recapture a bit of the amazement I felt. Yet I also hear, immediately, ringing in my head, "it's a magnolia." And the magic is gone.

Social Conventions

These are just some of the blinders we wear when we see largely in categories. And who issues these blinders? Why, society, in large part, our culture, all the better to understand our world and communicate with each other.

But also all the better to exclude certain things from our awareness and thoughtful consideration. A great many things. As Eric Fromm put it: "This system works, as it were, like a socially conditioned filter: Experience cannot enter awareness unless it can penetrate this filter..."

Generally speaking, it may be said that an experience rarely comes into awareness for which the language has no word.

Nor is this only a question of vocabulary, but of grammar, of syntax, the whole flavor of a language. For instance, we tend to use a lot of nouns, so well packaged do we think we have things (or want them to be). Yet if we're not thinking in "verbs, "how much we may miss of all the motion, process, and dynamism, around us!

"A car, a house, a tree." That was the description in the example above. One didn't hear about the breeze blowing the tree in front of the house, the clouds gathering above, the birds scurrying for shelter, the orange cat that skulked across the yard to where the birds were now retreating, the wisps of smoke from the chimney, wafted away almost immediately before they even became visible. Never mind the four cars and the truck that whizzed past on the street during the whole exercise. When one is looking through a still and not a video camera, the pictures are quite different.

Other Languages

And we haven't even mentioned languages other than verbal ones! There can be tremendous losses when one ignores or fails to integrate these rich modes of experience. What about the vast world of visual images? We were actually quite good with these as children. In the rain forest situation above, a visual image was mentioned as a way of bringing in aesthetic awareness.

If a picture is "worth a thousand words," the value also goes far beyond issues of quantity. Whole emotional dimensions of experience may be lost. Think of the poignancy of a photograph of a man openly weeping. Doesn't this twist something that might not otherwise be touched in the same way? (Now we have returned to our artistic school subjects unfortunately called "electives," which are left primarily for "artists" to master. One might argue that we are voluntarily putting out our eyes.)

Think of the vocabulary of colors we may know best when we dress ourselves -- but not necessarily when we express ourselves. Or the vocabulary of line and shape and pattern. An angry line. A joyful line. A patch of color "so dense and solid it would be hard to penetrate it with a chainsaw." The flight of a bird that is lighter than air. These are all expressive possibilities, and ones that a child might be more comfortable with than many an adult.

Yet listen to logician, philosopher and educator Susanne Langer, who spoke to the essential language of the arts. These non-discursive symbols give us a direct and intuitive knowledge of life patterns through feelings and emotions which ordinary discursive language cannot convey.

As Langer said: "... the intuition of artistic import is a high human function which so far both psychology and epistemology have completely bypassed. Yet its roots lie at the same depth as those of discursive reason, and are, indeed, largely the same."

Langer was not speaking to the arts as some optional frill, or some prettification of life. Rather, to the expression of a complex pattern of meaning, an summation of currents of emotional feeling, which runs under the surface of every single thing we do. They col or our every experience, our every judgment, memory, and future plan, every step of our lives. Do we really want to leave these messages uncoded?

Langer again: "Feeling is a dynamic pattern of tremendous complexity.... all sorts of processes may culminate in feeling with or without direct regard to each other.... Our best identification of such phenomena is through images that hold and present them for our contemplation; and their images *are works of art*" (emphasis mine).

Or consider the sounds of music, broadly defined -- the rhythms of our lives, the swinging of doors, the sounds of traffic, the crowds in the store, the dripping of a light spring rain. Sound was one of our first and most basic contacts with the world, back in utero, before we were even born.

Did you know that a near-term fetus can hear quite well, and has been living for months in a world of pulsing rhythms, of mother's heartbeat and breath, surrounded by the whooshing of blood coursing through the uterine blood vessels? Check the book *The World of the Newborn.* Or did you know that sounds from "outside" are transmitted quite well through the amniotic fluid? That newborns can already recognize their mother's voice, right after they are born?

We were, none of us, in a stupor back then. We were already, very carefully, listening. And for good reason. As Carl Seashore said: "... from the beginning music, as the expression of emotional life not reducible to logical language, has been a medium for communicating ideals or urges as contrasted with ideas."

You, as an observing employer, employee, teacher, parent, friend, spouse, partner, and so on, have likely discovered how very much more one can learn from not just what is said, but how it is said. Indeed, this is a part of good clinical training. Subtle intonations can sometimes tell much more than the words do. This is the music of our speech, and these are the messages of this music. But do we usually study this music?

Here then is another general process are that can be undervalued, undertaught, or fully overlooked, the process of sound and its many meanings. Sound can tap into so many dimensions of our experience, stringing itself out beguilingly over time. We are certainly used to screening this information out. What about bringing it in? Think about the sounds surrounding you right now. Even, perhaps, some music that you deliberately put on.

Of course, verbal language can help reconnect us with some of these other rich dimensions of experience—never mind help connect them with each other. Eric Fromm noted how in some languages, the verb form "it rains," is conjugated very differently than it is in English. Here's what we may think: It rains or it doesn't. A fact is a fact is a fact.

But somebody else may care very much whether you say it rains because:

     * You have been out in the rain and gotten wet (felt it)

     * You have seen it raining from inside your shelter (saw it)

     * Somebody has told you that it is raining (heard it)

The source of the information can be extremely important to the experience of it, and there are different verb forms reflecting this. It is a fair assumption that these people may get a lot more out a rainstorm than we do.

Part-People, Glamour, and Emptiness

We end this section with a discussion of some limited ways in which we may perceive other people. This is related to issues of categorization and simplification, but it is also a very important special case in itself.

Here we are now at a department store during a busy Christmas rush. People are everywhere, noise, Christmas carols, shoving, we somehow make our way to the counter. Now we ask the saleswoman to get a bottle of a certain perfume. Then we rush off to the next thing on our agenda. Ten minutes later, how well do we even remember that saleswoman? Did we even see her at the time as a person, or merely some creature who could help fulfill a particular need for us at a particular time. This is a very important point.

OK, you say, we didn't have time for that. We were in too much of a hurry. But what about when we intentionally seek the part-person, or in mental health terms, the so-called "part-object," for reasons of our own gratification. When we reject what is true for an appealing caricature.

Here is one common and almost drug-like response to the alienation, loneliness, and anonymity of modern life: identification with the cast of famous and glamorous characters found in the movies, television, tabloids, and popular magazines. This is almost the obverse of the "self-in-relation" (see Chapter Nine), of our full selves in mutual connection with authentic others. It is a fascination with the one-dimensional. Here is instant excitement, sex, love (of some obscure sort), adventure, power, glamour, and prestige, all in the time that it takes to turn on the television set.

Be a princess, an adventurer, a superhero, a millionaire. It's like a drug high, a powerful drug of abuse. For one thing, this doesn't take much work, if any. And it satisfies quickly, as with the most addictive substances. Bringing what? Excitement, belonging, self-esteem and hope through identification be it a quick fix for achievement, power, fame, or romance. Or just a self-ablating escape. As with any good drug of abuse, it erases, just a bit, the anonymity and helplessness of self.

Yet underneath all of this—and we know this instinctively when we are mourning at a funeral, or are fully present at a birth underneath all of this, these images are empty empty empty.

This is a world of part-objects. Of things and beings that exist only for what they can do for you. Here's a person who only serves you dinner at a restaurant. Does one wonder what their home life is actually like, or what books they like to read? Likewise the figure in the newspaper, the hero in the movies, and sometimes a spouse or a child.

Why this fascination with celebrity, with people who are cardboard pastiches, with no reality whatsoever? In fact, it's fascination with the bare impressionistic outlines of their caricatures, caricatures which one might don like a costume, with their trails of fame, power, prestige, or glamour. It is not the reality of the person at all but rather the lack of reality, highlighted and intensified, with all the trappings of reality erased.

It's the spin doctor's dream, and the psychotherapist's nightmare. We don't want to know that these people go to the bathroom—or perhaps, to know them at all. That they have bad days, rotten tempers, problems with their kids, and that their house is a mess. That they're really not as nice as their screen images. And that they really don't look that good, after all, without their makeup.

And again, one may realize, someone has been doing the creating for us. Some marketing magnates have created an artificial image out of their imaginations and our wishful thinking, and we've bought it. At the supermarket checkout stand, on the evening news, at the pulp fiction rack in the drugstore. It is time for us instead to bring this creativity actively into our own, real and genuine lives, which are rich and three-dimensional, and dense with promise and feeling.

An Aesthetic of Caring

Awareness, understanding, and caring—the aesthetic above—we apply these this time to the full human being. To be aware consciously of the identity of another person, to understand that person in his or her complexity, and with his or her own needs and wishes. To grow to care for that three-dimensional living being, in an interaction of sharing and reciprocity. At best, this can be a connected awareness, and an aesthetic of caring.

Included here is another conceptual and perceptual shift, and a key to our conscious evolution. To see the world through different eyes: to see ourselves in relation. Three-dimensionally in relation. As we shall see (in Chapter Ten), it is both physically and psychologically healthy to do so. It is adaptive. It is sometimes lifegiving. Our own human nature is saying to us, is begging of us, to Please Do This.

Caring and being cared for. Belonging, holding, embracing, nurturing, responding. No longer isolated a t om-creatures running after little part-objects to satisfy our needs. Now we are afloat in a world full of interconnected creatures, creatures fee ling, breathing, hurting, like ourselves, and demanding of our attention, our watchful careful listening, and our caring and truest love.

CHAPTER 9

BREAKING DOWN BARRIERS

Something we were withholding made us weak.
Until we found it was ourselves.

--ROBERT FROST

Proposition: We all—you and I and everyone else—have major splits between parts of ourselves, and within parts of our experience. Unlike the automatisms so far discussed, these distortions may be rooted in a fixed mental picture of ourselves and our world—one we want to preserve even if it's not true. Some patterns of distortion carry the flair of the individual's personality, and others seem part of the human equipment we all carry (at least in this time and culture). When these distortions receive strong cultural, or consensual sanction, especially when "everyone is doing it, "it may be a great challenge not to do it. Here are yet other ways we may learn not to see. We may often gain creatively, and gain in general, by healing these splits.

Talk about seeing the world anew—seeing it in different ways. Here is something I wrote several years ago, after seeing a children's film I had certainly seen before. But this time I was seeing it with my very young daughter, and was amazed by how upsetting it was. I was truly seeing it for the first time. I apologize for any discomfort. But my motive is to look at how we see the world—or don't—so we can do it better.

In fact, some people agreed at the time with my assessment of this movie. But others couldn't see what I was making such a fuss about. This children's film is still one of the most popular ones around. Only recently at a local drugstore, I saw dozens of them for sale, displayed prominently on a shelf above the checkout stand.

Cruelty to a baby. Why would we watch this? Why would we have our children watch this?

Yet many of us have, at some time, seen this movie.

First we see baby come into the world, and the delight of the new mother. We witness joy and tenderness, hugs and caresses. The tiny helpless infant looks up through at-first blurred eyes to find strength and devotion, and endless love, in the locked gaze of mother, with the promise of safety and strength, and satisfaction of all needs. The wide blue baby eyes in a sweet round head that's at least as large as the little body. The innocent gaze, the oh-so-willing smile, the need to be loved and to be cared for.

Can we help it? We're programmed to respond to these little people. Our hormones flow; we bond, we commit to the care of the baby.

But then this story gets awful.

A problem appears. The baby is deformed—part of the face is distorted in size. This doesn't at all deter mother, who is devoted and all the more protective. We see mother become understandably rude when some cruel female acquaintances turn on her and mock the child, with only a pretense at sensitivity. Speaking of baby, they spell, rather than say, words like F-R-E-A-K.

Next, we see some young boys discover the baby. They mock and poke at the infant, making fun of how he looks, and, when mother protests, they even try to drag baby away from her and into their view. Mother becomes furious, and she frantically tries to protect baby, even overthrowing and thrashing one of the youths. As her helpless baby watches, wide-eyed and uncomprehending, people come running, with ropes and loud voices, and mother is apprehended, tied down, declared insane, and carried away.

The one essential constant in the world of the helpless newborn is betrayed. The all-powerful parent is neutralized and eliminated.

Now this helpless baby is left with the very female acquaintances of mother's who earlier mocked this baby. Worse yet, they ultimately blame baby, or baby's abnormalities, for mother's behavior, and baby is shunned and excluded from the group. All alone, confused, and frightened, baby creeps away.

Child abuse. What else can one call it? And the story continues, getting worse, not better (and better in only its last few moments). The name of this frightening film? *Dumbo*—a much beloved cartoon classic from Walt Disney Productions, the story about the little elephant with the oversize ears; it has now been a favorite of many children, and many families, for decades.

I began watching this drama for the first time in many years, to my great dismay, with my toddler daughter who greeted each new appearance of the infant elephant with a delighted "Baby!," only to see this baby degraded, mocked, humiliated, shunned, scorned, and in essence abandoned by the one single figure who represented stability in a frightening world. She just couldn't understand it.

My daughter absolutely insisted on seeing this film to the end, her attention total, her little face filled with terrible concern, and almost nearing hysterics when I several times stopped the movie, or attempted fast-forward.

Meanwhile, I foolishly kept waiting for the "good parts," to balance what had gone before. This is a child, incidentally, who loves the film *The Jungle Book*, based on the Rudyard Kipling classic, with all its "law of the jungle" realism. She growls like the tiger and hisses like the snake. This she can start to master and understand.

But the cruelty and abuse in the present movie was totally beyond her comprehension—and her mother's. What is the excuse for all this? Are we really seeing the price of individuality, of nonconformity, of resilience? The message here, at least for 90% of this film, was not in the least about the triumph of being different. It was about the cruelty of human beings (no, Dumbo was not really about elephants), about the lack of social acceptance of deviance, and the inability of parents and caring people ultimately to protect even the weakest and most innocent of us. It was horrible.

Yet we show this film quite uncritically to our children. Why? There's something very important here. Something about how we really feel about our lives, our safety, our esteem, our tolerance of others, and -- something deep and hidden which we must somehow feel a need to deal with, but can only stand to confront, and can only tolerate, in this indirect and disguised way.

There will be more about *Dumbo* later. But how are we able to breeze through a movie like this? Or watch mythical film characters abusing each other or shooting innocent victims through the head? Partly by desensitization -- by tuning out after a steady diet of violence. Also by selectively perceiving. Through focusing on what we want and dispensing somehow with the rest. These skills -- or rather, defenses -- are not in themselves bad. Their use can be very adaptive. Indeed that's how they got there.

But their misuse can also cause us to distance from a reality that is truly our lives. And to create splits within ourselves, within our own minds. Our awareness and creativity can be stifled at times when we really need to act, and this can be very bad indeed.

Putting Up the Walls

Splits within ourselves? This may not sound familiar. But this too may be part of our everyday experience. Below we consider some examples. One may even imagine fences between different parts of one's mind, because the separated-off material is still there. (In its totality, this process is to be distinguished from the shattering experiences of individual trauma survivors; there are qualitatively different features and adaptive functions.)

In the present case, first, we have specific thoughts or fee lings we don't like, and so we make them go away. Included is a form of disjunction between our thoughts and feelings; we may, for instance, stay intellectual about some area, and downplay its feeling side. This can all be very socially acceptable, and we may fall into it, at times, the same way we fall into bed. In addition, there are general *types* or categories of feelings or thoughts we may prefer to keep hold of, while we banish others. Indeed, there are whole fields of endeavor we may tend to keep separate from each other, because they draw strongly from different sides of these splits.

We will argue it is often healthier not to maintain these splits. But we must also deal with why we would have the splits in the first place if they are really not all that good for us. Finally, we look at some special—and creative—ways to finesse our minds' first tendency, and take a closer look at the world.

Go Away: Unwanted Thoughts and Feelings

Our psychological defenses can be quite useful. The point is often to distance us—at least for a time—from something disturbing within our individual selves. To forget it exists, or at least not be bothered too much by it. Yet our defenses have their time and place, and also their price.

Let us say you have a particularly demanding in-law who is coming to visit and you feel inadequate to the situation. Deep inside, you are already feeling nervous, stressed, and irritated that you have to deal with this person. Yet you are also torn that you should feel so unwelcoming, so inhospitable. Your guest is someone you would like to have feel welcome. You would wish for this person to have a good time.

Nor do you like seeing yourself as someone so burdened and spiteful, so lacking in patience and generosity (you think self-critically), that you would not welcome them. This may not fit with your image of yourself at all.

The above are very common sorts of feelings, and common "mixed feelings." In this sense, they are quite normal. We human beings are complicated indeed.

Certain conflicts within our own minds can be alleviated by a few psychological tricks which the mind pulls out of its hat. These tricks, or psychological defenses, are extremely common, and at times quite adaptive. Here, for instance, is one approach. With the unwelcome in-law, the goal is to put aside one's negative thoughts and feelings, at least until the visitor has gone home. One can perhaps suppress these thoughts and feelings as they arise. Or even avoid them completely.

Another approach deals more directly with content than feelings; it twists this information around to make it more acceptable to one's view of the world and oneself. One starts rationalizing, or pseudo-reasoning that this unwelcome visit is really a great opportunity." It is actually very good for me," one thinks, "to learn to deal with this difficult person. And it is good for them too," one adds, "to be where every need isn't immediately met." And so on. Perhaps. Yet here too is a certain amount of hogwash, because you would really prefer that the two of you got along without so much trouble. Or that the visitor didn't come at all. But you don't want to think about that.

The strategy of not thinking about something can be abetted by pushing aside or isolating the emotions that would normally go along with these thoughts. One doesn't deliberately or consciously decide to banish these feelings; the defense is working silently in the background, and the feelings simply fade or disappear.

Intellectually, you are well aware that this visiting in-law will be difficult. But—with your defenses switched on—you no longer have to deal with all the annoyance you might otherwise feel toward the person, or the nervousness within yourself. You have perhaps sensed just a bit of this feeling already—you know its potential and power—way down there in the subterranean depths of your mind. Yet you somehow, most luckily, you don't have to confront the full brunt of this.

Finally, at what might seem a more extreme level of defense, consider denial, or the refusal to believe that something is happening at all. This may seem truly extreme, or "out of touch with reality," but we all do this at times as well.

Let's say you have just lost somebody who was very dear to you. Denial is a common first response to the death of a loved one. The loss can be so intense and terrible that it is asking way too much of a person to take it in all at once." I can't believe it," one commonly hears people say. And indeed they can't quite believe it, although if push comes to shove, they are aware that something is going on. And they will believe it soon enough. In the meantime, the defense of denial helps to soften the blow.

Some Costs of This Selective Experiencing

Denial, avoidance, suppression, rationalization and isolation—these are only a fraction of the psychological defenses that people have named and studied. These defenses are not things, as their noun names might suggest, but common processes, or particular ways of processing information. Certain patterns have been observed with some frequency in people, and have been clustered into these and other human-made categories. People tend to differ in the particular defenses they use, even as they may differ in general.

Our focus here is not so much on the specific patterns of defense as the general phenomenon of selective perception—of distortion of and dissociation from parts of our reality. At times, our psychological defenses serve us well. They provide one further mechanism for triage of the information that reaches "consciousness"—such that the conscious mind is faced only with that information that is really needed. At best, our defenses permit little mini-distortions of our experience that help us smooth things over at critical points, focus on what we must do, and defer full awareness of an overwhelming situation until it can finally be managed.

But there are times when these defenses may go too far. There is energy involved in maintaining these mental barriers. Plus the world goes on turning outside of these defensive walls, whether one sees it or not. However, our bodies often know. For instance, suppressors of certain emotions - - for instance people who present an "everything is fine" attitude, no matter how bad things get -- may find themselves more vulnerable to certain sorts of physical disease.

On the other end, people who deliberately break down certain barriers and access those forbidden thoughts (in a stepwise and controlled manner, not through unsolicited and explosive confrontation) may not only end up feeling better psychologically, but physically as well. They may have a stronger resistance to disease. We look at an example of this below. Our bodies are sending us some very important messages.

Creative Expression, Psychological Openness, and Health

Creative processes may be extremely effective ways to heal oneself, to learn more about who you are, how you got that way, and where you want to go. Take writing, painting, or singing (and rapping), for example. Or moving and dancing. These expressions can open the psychic doors, and also provide a means of control for working with whatever comes in.

In the safety of your room or office, you can take out those difficult feelings and painful conflicts, and have a good look at them. You can explore all they may mean to you, and where they have come from. If you keep a private journal of your writing, or portfolio of your drawings, for instance, you can also have a record of the road you have travelled. In retrospect, this can be tremendously empowering. It is amazing how some of those intensely painful feelings and conflicts come to fade. And each success you have makes the next exploration potentially easier.

Listen to Virginia Woolf, from her diary: "Why is life so tragic; so like a little strip of pavement over an abyss. I look down; I feel giddy.... But why do I feel this: Now that I say it I don't feel it... Melancholy diminishes as I write."

You can also try out those feelings, if you like, on writing about another person. A fantasy person. This person may attempt a few things that you've always wanted to do. There's no limit after all on what they can do or say. It isn't real. Truly, anything goes. This time, you've got the control. Many a novel or play had its beginnings in an artist's life circumstance which they wished had been different.

Creative writing and Immune Response

Be there any doubts about the healthy effects of creative confrontation, consider research by Pennebaker, Kiecolt-Glaser, and Glaser, in which college students were asked to write creatively about some of their most traumatic experiences, ones they had discussed very little (if ever) with anyone. Each writing session was only twenty minutes long. There was also a control group which wrote about something more neutral, such as what their shoes looked like.

At the end of only four days, not only did the first group end up feeling better psychologically, but made fewer health center visits over the subsequent weeks. In addition, they showed evidence of stronger immune system function.

Only four days, and a few minutes of writing a day! This is amazing. It sounds actually like a cardiac regimen. Get at least three days of exercise a week, the doctor tells the patient, twenty minutes a day. As with this cardiac program, the exercise of creative confrontation, and its healthy effects could truly be lifesaving.

Why might this occur? One woman who had been sexually abused as a child wrote first about her embarrassment and guilt. But with time, this transformed into anger at her victimization, and finally gave her a broader perspective. "Before," she said, "I'd lie to myself. Now I don't feel like I even have to think about it because I got it off my chest."

This woman's working through happened extremely fast; it might well have taken years, and never been fully complete. Yet, in any case, her success freed valuable mental energy for other things. This woman also built mastery, confidence, and coping skills that could help immunize her, physically as well as psychologically, against future assaults.

The Other Side: A Potential Edge-of-Chaos, and Falling off the Tight Rope

It's only fair to look as well at the bumps in this road. As well protected as the creator may be, psychologically, the entrance of new information from one's own mind can happen unpredictably. This information is, after all, upsetting. Just how upsetting is it?—that is certainly the question. On the one hand its entrance may start uncontrolled cascades of new insights and personal realizations this may threaten to put one's true self on the line. On the other hand, the process may end up being simple, benign, and limited. Yet one doesn't know what exactly to expect when one opens the floodgates.

What is likely, however, is the more regularly one "stays in t ouch with oneself," the fewer the very big surprises. And the more resources one will have for handling these. Metaphorically, this process may also be where the "edge-of-chaos" meets "ego-strength." It is the other side of "creative insight" it is indeed a creative insight, but it's the insight one doesn't want!

Here is the unwelcome personal realization that may go on and on and on. You can get one with the other.

But it also helps to know that a certain amount of this instability, self-doubt, and personal surprise is normal! It is expectable. It is also part of how we, all of us, are troubled and imperfect. And how we are tremendously variable, and "abnormal," as part of our normality, all of this without being "pathological."(See Chapter Five.) If this sort of exploratory creative process were more normalized in our society exercise before breakfast if we routinely did it as a healthful we might all of us, not only be more psychologically open, but be more comfortable with what this openness is able to "tell us."

Ego-strength, and Playing the Game One's Own Way

Creativity does ask that one be "open to inner experience," (see for instance, Carl Rogers, *On Becoming a Person,* or Frank Barron, *Creative Person and Creative Process*), and can use a process of "regression in the service of the ego" (most notably, see Ernest Kris), as a font of creative inspiration. One opens the mental gates to a range of thoughts and thought-forms, some quite primitive—hence the term "regression"—as we discussed in Chapter Four. This opens the gates once again to those thoughts which may be threatening. Recall the similarities in conceptual style between creative writers and blatantly manic patients, in Chapter Five. All showed overinclusive and colorful modes of thought. But the writers were more ready and waiting for these. In a general sense, the thoughts were expected, if not exactly solicited. Still, this is where some people may confuse "abnormality" with "pathology." One may recall the creative writers also came out stronger in abstract and cohesive thinking; they could pull it all together, and do so for adaptive real-world reasons. We see this process may in some ways, not only be far removed from pathology, but at times may represent its opposite. In conjunction with ego-strength here the ability and courage to look deeply within oneself and deal with whatever comes up -- one's harboring of unusual thoughts could be tremendously healthy indeed.

Yet, in all fairness, one may at times also be walking a kind of tightrope. It is healthy to get to the end of the tightrope, but unpleasant at times when one falls off. One may still recover, yet it can hurt. Indeed, any of us can fall off the tightrope, and be awash in the anxious overload of too much insight, too quickly. It is almost guaranteed. Here is one way in which illness and health may seem intertwined. Yet if one sees such conflict, in small doses, as "part of life," and of growth, it becomes less of an issue. Less of an illness. And less of a catastrophe.

So here now is our more open, cheerful creative person. Let us say, a courageous artist or writer. She or he orders up some of those odd thoughts, in a general direction, but type unspecified, ready or not. This creator is set to circumvent those defenses, along with automatisms, habits, conceptual blocks, and blindnesses we all have. Hopefully, this willing artist or seer will stop and show us a thing or two as well, along the way. The creator can perhaps help speak for the future, along with a present we are currently not seeing.

Go Away Bad Mood, stay Awhile Good Mood

Here's another whole area of defense—but of a more generic type. We all, in this culture, do it. And we help each other do it as well.

Indeed, there are people who like to wallow in a bad mood. And people who thrive on turmoil and conflict. But most people, most of the time, like to feel good. To be happy, relaxed, confident, and at peace. This is a strong enough need for this that a bad mood tends to be sent packing whenever practical. This is helped by a human tendency to keep thinking along the same mood-l inked lines of thought. This is called mood-congruent recall. Our invoking this tendency, when an unpleasant thought erupts, "chasing the blues away" can, indeed, become a way of life.

Here are some examples of this editing process, of what has been called negative mood repair. Surely we've all done this. "Oh, that was nothing." "I'm not going to think about that." "It's going to get better, just wait and see." No one says this can't be adaptive. Once again, it's a question of degree.

At the same time, we may go out of our way to hang onto the good moods. We link them to more and more of the same feelings. We embroider our webwork of associations with the good stuff, just as long as we can keep squeezing it in. This is positive mood maintenance. Some examples: "What a beautiful day!... The sky is sunny... Things are looking better and better.... It's just like last summer... I remember that happy time we had at the beach..."And whatever, again, is wrong with this? Nothing, if we sooner or later get up off of that beach.

It is a question, overall, of how clearly we are seeing. While we are having a good time, we may be missing important events we need to think about, and turning our back on chances to act creatively in the world. True, we might rather be sipping that cool drink under our beach umbrella. Yet, accepting the challenge can lead later to an even more profound satisfaction and joy, as well as a greater personal sense of creative power and efficacy.

One part of what a creative journal writer may be doing is intentionally jumping those mood congruent divides in the mind. Letting in a little negative air, but then turning it around, shaping it and sending it back again with a new appearance. This creator is learning that facing a negative situation can feel good, and sometimes, even feel terrific.

Furthermore, this creator is leaving in his or her mental wake, new associations -- new mental roads, freeways even, in the brain -between those positive and negative compounds of thought and fee ling. This will make travel between these relatively isolated collections of mood-linked thoughts easier in the future. One can imagine the creator's attention moving through this domain of possibility—now joyous, now despairing, now angry—whatever best suits the purposes of the moment. This creator, be this a writer, artist, singer, or even scientist or mathematician, will be painting with a fuller emotional palette.

The Glowing Past Empowers the Future

Indeed, to step out on the mental tightrope to begin with, and not to look down all the time, requires a good reason for continuing. Here again comes ego-strength, along with confidence, and empowerment—and a sense of purpose. Here are the trails of glory of adversity overcome, with wonderful feelings of triumph at the end. There may certainly be parallels with courageous physical actions.

Recall Ralph Waldo Emerson on the intrinsic beauty of great acts. "The high and divine beauty... is that which is found in combination with the human will. Beauty is the mark God sets upon virtue.". He illustrates how the setting and the details of the moment come to glow in the memory of human courage and greatness.

Lasting Benefits

One needn't always take the hardest road; one must pick one's moments, and one's personal battles. But should one succeed, there may be a future payoff as well as an immediate one. Some advantages in summary:

    1. Feeling more empowered, and more in control, on a personal issue, at least in symbolic, creative form.

    2. Finding related health effects, such as improved immune cell function.

    3. Building a stronger creative process, a richer associative network and imaginative potential, for the next time around.

    4. Building a greater motivation to be creative -- to take the creative route, and risks -- the next time around.

    5. Feeling more empowered, more healthy, more imaginative, with stronger immune function... and on and on, as the process builds on itself.

And also, as we shall discuss further in Chapter Ten:

    6. Increasingly coming to unite personal discovery with universal themes and conflicts, and weaving one's struggles into a broader web of meaning that can further validate one's humanity, and can help not only oneself but others too.

    7. Finding one's continued imaginative activity happens more and more out of the joy of creating, and the impetus of growth and discovery, without needing to flee from pain or be conflict-driven.

What We Are Fleeing From

But now let's practice what we're preaching, and break with this mood for a moment. Consider, for instance, the advances of science that may occur without much input from our feelings or our value systems. We often think of science as "objective," "factual, "and therefore perhaps straightforward. Can science take care of itself? Well, it hasn't so far. Here may be a very dangerous instance of a defensive split, in our minds and out in the world.

Lewis Thomas stated a common misconception about science: "Even today... the impression of science that the public gains.... is first of all a matter of simply getting all the numbers together.... If only they had enough robots and enough computers, the scientists could go off to the beach and wait for their papers to be written for them."

Thomas suggests the scientists are partly at fault. First for teaching biology, as if, say, it were a foreign language. Starting with fundamental laws, and teaching superstructures of facts as if these were it, the whole thing, simple, clear, finished, and tidied up. Or at least with only a little more tidying up to do. Then, he suggests, we teach this science as if it is better. Somehow superior to other disciplines. Here are the real answers, and not just some speculations.

Science and Certainty

Not just the work of some "fuzzy minded social scientists," as I heard people say, and said myself as well, back as a physics major in the "space race" era, when large educational resources were devoted to "beating the Russians." What a laugh that seems now.

We, the golden physics majors, with serious courses aplenty to fit into our bulging schedules, were allowed to cut way back on our "breadth requirements." Five or six courses at most, as I recall. Fewer courses than people in non-scientific fields. Some advisors were actually apologetic. You need to do this, it's rules after all, but at least "they've" recognized that you don't need to do so much of it. "And you also can get a lot of math if you take a special section of Economics."(I did this, in fact -- and the math really broadened the power of the economic theory. But one hidden message was "you don't have to stray that far from your field if you watch out, and you duck down this academic alley.")

And heaven forbid that we "science types" should have sacrificed any portion of advanced electromagnetism or an experimental physics laboratory for a novel or a poem or a song. These efforts were, after all, purely subjective, and possibly, they weren't even true. Now, I can't guarantee that every last science major was as bad as I was -- I certainly hope not. But I did at least keep doing some art, on the side, and eventually even added to this picture some traits of a "fuzzy minded social scientist."

Yet I must also confess that, back then, I was really rather afraid of those "humanities types," and this fed into a split in my own mind. I was an uncertain adolescent who found myself, or at least my place, in the elegant precision of those very numbers and formulas, problem sets, and computer programs. Here was a world I could understand and master.

And now I'm wondering, as I write this, how many other fledgling scientists, or senior scientists for that matter, are feeling this same love of the certainty.

Science and its Mysteries

Lewis Thomas suggests that, in teaching science, we "concentrate the attention of all students on the things that are not known." And that we do so from the earliest age. Science is a mystery. We really don't know anything about it. We really and truly don't. And that is what we need to deal with, scientist and artist alike.

"Twentieth-century science, has provided us with a glimpse of something we never really knew before, the revelation of human ignorance.".... We have a wilderness of mystery to make our way through in the centuries ahead, and we will need science for this but not science alone. Science will, in its own time, produce the data and some of the meaning in the data, but never the full meaning.... we shall need minds at work from all sorts of brains outside the fields of science, most of all the brains of poets, of course, but also those of artists, musicians, philosophers, historians, writers in general.

Thomas stresses the importance of teaching science to people we really need to have think about it. These are not the scientists, but "pretty much everybody else." His hope is that out of these many, a few people, "a much smaller minority than the scientific community and probably a lot harder to find," will be able to somehow tell us what really is going on. To "imagine new levels of meaning that are likely to be lost on the rest of us."

Let it be understood that the earth's life is a system of inter-living, interdependent creatures, and that we do not understand at all how it works. The earth's environment, from the range of atmospheric gases to the chemical constituents of the sea, has been held in an almost unbelievably improbable state of regulated balance since life began... and we do not know that that one works, even less what it means. Teach that.

What, one might ask, are we doing with our science, and technology, what are our goals, our values. We may be smart enough to map the human genome, but are we smart enough to alter it? What problems should we be solving in the next twenty years? How have we come to so misuse technology? How does this relate to the values of our society? How indeed can we save our earth? Can science do this alone—or do we need something entirely different.

Thomas again: "There's a lot to be answered. An appreciation of what is happening in science today, and of how great a distance lies ahead for exploring, ought to be one of the rewards of a liberal-arts education.... a feel for the queernesses of nature, the inexplicable things. And the poets, on whose shoulders the future rests, might, late nights, thinking things over, begin to see some meanings that elude the rest of us."

Are We the Mistreated Child?

We return finally to Dumbo, the unhappy little elephant, and mistreated baby in the Disney movie, but also a symbol of many of the harsh realities we avoid. A symbol as well of the abuse that is being done to us.

This baby animal is indeed being abused. Even our watching the movie is a form of abuse, an assault on us that we are accepting and tolerating invoking as best we can our various defenses to soften the blow. Even to the extent that I, for one, used to think this movie was OK. One very critical difference from the experience of the individual trauma survivor is that we may never even know we are doing this—that something has happened to us. We are consensually and unknowingly playing our little mind games, passing them on to our children, learning them by osmosis, agreeing with each other without ever saying anything. This, we infer, is the way to see the world. Us and everyone else.

Isn't this also a way we survive the anger and the violence in our own streets, and in our homes, and sometimes even perpetrate these outbursts ourselves out of desperate impulse, where the feelings have been building up without any outlet. If we see them, it may sometimes feel as if there is nowhere else to turn, nothing else in life, and no one who could ever understand.

We are confronted day after day with so many unspeakable horrors, on TV, in the newspaper, and in our own defense, we may sometimes treat these as seriously as the comic strip on the same page. What is fantasy and what is reality? They don't seem truly real; they don't really touch us. We're so numbed out, so deadened to the horrors in the world, because if we weren't, then perhaps we couldn't stand it.

It may all seem too overwhelming—the avalanching conditions of overpopulation, pollution, environmental degradation. And at our very doorstep, the hunger, the poverty, the drug use, the violence. We may occasionally give to a cause (or we may not), but our actual human appreciation of the problem, of what it's like, say, for a homeless mother and child on a day to day basis, may be extremely limited. For you and me and for all of us.

Here, our defenses, our evolutionary limitations, and our mood modulating strategies stand us in good stead. They further a collective and consensual dissociation (and indeed a psychosis) from some of the most painful realities. These are not interesting psychological phenomena we should just take note of and accept. Or perhaps memorize for a college class.

Rather, they are indicators of the amount of trauma which we, as individuals and a society, have come to endure and tolerate.

A Great Deal of Hope

Could it sound much grimmer? In fact, there's still a great deal of hope for us all—there is so much farther our human potential can take us. So much farther. But this will require our conscious evolution. And this will involve effort, creativity, openness and risk, and, before all else, the courage of awareness.

CHAPTER 10

SEEING BEYOND

There is no one but us. There is no one to send, nor a clean hand, nor a pure heart on the face of the earth, nor in the earth, but only us, a generation comforting ourselves with the notion that we have come at an awkward time, that our innocent fathers are all dead—as if innocence had ever been—and our children busy and troubled, and we ourselves unfit, not yet ready, having each of us chosen wrongly, made a false start, failed, yielded to impulse and the tangled comfort of pleasures, and grown exhausted, unable to seek the thread, weak, and involved. But there is no one but us. There never has been.

--ANNIE DILLARD

Most people want to care, and they want to help. If it were a matter of walking across the street to a neighbor's house, they would be on their way. But where "big" issues are concerned, they may feel much too hassled with other things, sure they couldn't make much difference anyway, and often unaware—thanks to our ever effective defenses and automatisms—of just how bad things have gotten.

Yet in reality, if every person had just a tiny attitude change, and a slightly altered vision of the world around us, then things would change, and dramatically. The votes would be cast. Quickly, like a change of slides in a projector, we could see ourselves in a new place. The smallest attitude change, if widespread enough, could be amplified in astonishing complexity, through the ceaseless and interlocking webs of human creative activities, be these conversations with friends, decisions at work, messages to one's children, or "official" works of art or of science.

Such changes seem to be building even now. I'd like to suggest four reasons why creative people—potentially, all of us—may be especially able to move into this flow, to "see beyond" and envision new ways of being in this world.

As prelude, I wish to give an example of several recent shifts in my own perception I might not have had several years ago. Indeed, I have studied creative ways of being for quite a few years. Yet I have only recently begun to sense their profound potential. Many people have contributed to this, directly or indirectly, only some of whom are mentioned in this book.

The confluence of these many efforts will hopefully keep feeding into a growing movement toward a more open, exploring, aware, exciting, creative, collaborative, process-oriented and growth-oriented view of human potential. If so, then the time couldn't be riper.

Trip to Lake Tahoe

This was not particularly on my mind during a trip last year to visit friends at Lake Tahoe, a deep clear lake on the California-Nevada border, high in the Sierra Nevada Mountains. The trip was a break, a vacation, and a chance to relax. We ended up slightly to the Nevada side, at South Shore Lake Tahoe, site of gambling casinos and spectacular winter ski runs, as well as beaches, mountains, and hiking trails.

I was also returning to a special place of my childhood. There were joyous childhood memories of the deep blue lake, sidling into the chilly water, with especially strong memories of early morning waterskiing, the rush of the motor and water churning up behind the boat, the still sky, and lake ringed by tall mountains profiled against the sky.

That was it. Mountains, lake, cold water, warm sun, high mountains, thousands of trees. I had it packaged. It had been there many times, and now I was back. Would it be any different? Of course not.

So here I am, many years later now, and well into a relaxing day, at a small secluded beach down a long hiking trail from the road. I am easing out into the water, jumping on my toes to avoid that cold splash above the midriff. Out and out, amidst waves and mountains and a brisk wind. A motorboat is anchored, tossing and tipping. A beautiful hot sun, bright sand, children digging holes and making sand castles, faint squeals and shouts across the water from the shore. How I wish this vacation were longer.

And here again are the waves, now off to my left, bursting high against a cavern in the rocks, wave after wave, rushing steadily inward, striking and roaring to crescendo, with joyous explosions of white foam. I'm looking up at the sky. Looking back at the shore. And at trees upon trees upon trees.

Then something snaps, the scene shifts. It is incredible because I didn't see it at all before. And now it is so obvious. The brownish trees, the dying trees. Needles a reddish tan, tree after tree. The others white, skeleton-like, all bristles and even branches now gone, standing skeletons and heralds of a death to come.

And there are so many of these trees, so many stricken, maybe one out of three at this lovely little beach. I'd missed them all from the shore. As if I were unable to see at all. Now with a shift in perspective, looking back from the water, I can finally see them. This is the first shift.

It is the drought, I thought. Dehydration. For this is what I had been told. First the dryness, and then the beetles come and eat the trees. And this explains it? Now it is all right? It wasn't this way when I was a child. It wasn't even vaguely like this. And now this lovely forest, this lake country of high mountains and trees that were so breathtaking parental, godlike, awe inspiring -- which I could only admire -- are endangered.

And endangered by what? By whom?

Now I look at the water. Before it was blue. The water is supposed to be blue. And out from the shore it is eternally blue, in shades of blue-purple, of royal, and of Caribbean aqua toward the shallows. It is clear and it is gorgeous.

Yet suddenly, where I stand and look back, the water becomes something else. Here is the sandy rot of death, the orangey col or like a fire, spread out on top of the water, reflected above the blue, almost like an oil slick. It is everywhere, the reflection of these trees. I hadn't even noticed it before. Blue water—I knew all about it. But now it is turning brown, and the scene is dying. This is another startling shift.

Now back to shore, back to town, first up a long hiking trail, up a mountain. Once you open your eyes, it gets worse and worse. A valley is almost wall to wall with orangey-yellow dryness. Why there? Why is it happening? Shouldn't the valleys be filling with water? And I look up at the faraway hills. It's like New England in the autumn. Sort of. The colors aren't as brilliant. Not by half. But they're as scattered and omnipresent. It is the autumn of something much more menacing.

Then there is another shift, perhaps the most profound, bringing tears to my eyes. For I've thought about nature, I've recycled my trash, I've read books, I've discussed. I could surely do better, but I haven't been all that bad.

Now suddenly, I see these straggly trees, these loving creatures of my youth, standing there back then, ever so proud as I grew with pre-teen awkwardness, worried about my weight, toppled on my water skis, and then finally sailed forth proudly, dipping on one ski, jumping the wake in a glory of spray. Proud were those trees in my memory of the time.

And now here they droop, they wilt, they try so hard against the assaults of their surrounds. This includes the increasing bludgeons of society, even the fumes of those same motor boats I enjoyed so much. And those tall proud mountains that stand to infinity compared with our moments on earth, are themselves covered with those same gasping trees (the ones that give us air), as we putt putt our cars in a traffic jam down past the casinos, with the air conditioners blasting away at what ozone layer remains.

Now we are back from the beach, and off to the lakeside day camp of the son of our hosts. Here the trees are almost OK. It is a park, it is a playground, a picnic area, a library, and a nearby RV campground. They've cut down the trees that didn't make it, or lopped off a few lower branches here and there. I sigh a sigh of relief. It almost looks OK. It is OK. It's back to the lake I remember.

But no, it isn't. Here is one tree starting to turn which they haven't caught yet. And another, and another, really quite a few, looking further up a hill. There is a creeping, pressing blight, and it cannot be disguised.

Yes, the trees will still be here when I'm gone. At least some of t hem. But they are also my children, my precious charges. And what am I doing, I thought, what am I really doing, to help them. This was a shift, not to ownership, but something closer to friendship, and to friendship betrayed.

And to parenting betrayed. Of our ever so wise, and long lived, but terribly vulnerable children.

Now some people will say that there are seasons of drought, and there are seasons of rain. And that what I saw was not out of the cycle. These are the constantly changing patterns of weather over the years, and the drought was but one part of the picture; it was natural enough.

Not a result, let us say, of industrialization, atmospheric pollution, and global warming. Indeed, the following winter was a very wet one.

I cannot solve this. But I do know there are countless other ways in which we are harming our environment, including acts that cause acid rain to fall on these very same trees. When we talk about acres of rain forest in a country far away, it may not hurt as poignantly as watching the gentle giants, the very trees of one's youth, gasp and wither. Suddenly one knows that one desperately cares.

Not Hopeless

Sometimes it feels hopeless. But it is not hopeless. If every person committed himself or herself to even a slight change, as was suggested above, it could shift things that tiny amount that could s tart the whole landscape evolving in a different direction.

This could occur even without a sudden surge in awareness. But now, for good measure, let us add in a sudden chain reaction, a catastrophic change for the better. With luck, it could even be an edge-of-chaos effect. This might occur if a "critical mass" were reached of people who found new meaning and purpose in life, new efficacy, personal connection, and health through bonding with the world and with others. Through opening to these struggles we all share, and committing to something greater. This can feel very good to do. And it is definitely healthy.

Here are four qualities of a creative caring that can surely help. Some have been alluded to earlier. These four qualities can all come at a cost, but also carry tremendous benefits. They might be looked at as ways of investing in one's self. Interestingly, they are not "guaranteed" to come automatically to someone who is personally creative. But personal creativity can make them more likely. These are:

I. A feeling we're in this together

II. A widening awareness

III. A loving potential

IV. Creative courage

Each quality is discussed below, along with ways in which creativity may help bring it to fruition. We also look at how creativity may sometimes sail on carelessly -- or even destructively without these qualities. But we shall suggest, in most cases, and in the long run, that creativity tends to work in the service of health. Health for us individually and together.

Creative Caring—Four Qualities

1—A Feeling We're In This Together

If you feel this connection, you will, first of all, not feel alone. Indeed, you won't be alone. You will belong to a powerful and growing group of people, and without so much as leaving your chair, or leaving the room. Your ongoing efforts will tend to be connected, sometimes in subtle and imperceptible ways, to this life force. Our attitudes are able to guide us both consciously and unconsciously.

We need this connectedness. None of our societal or global problems can be solved by one person alone. When piled on our individual shoulders, they will surely crush us. If one's defenses are working on overtime, one may not even be able to keep them in mind in to begin with.

Yet, similar to voting for a president, if one can visualize one's individual opinion or effort as adding on to the contributions of many other people, one can inherit the power of the whole. One can identify with this whole, and feel—in fact, be—less isolated, vulnerable, and helpless.

Everyone has some degree of connection with a group larger then oneself, be this a family, an organization or club, a class, a working group, or a neighborhood or town. This situation is comparable, perhaps, to the environment of evolution. People functioned in small hunter-gatherer bands, knew everyone else, and existed in a comfortable web of reciprocity. People had their individual identities and roles, but also a group identity and obligation. And what one person did for another very readily returned in kind to that first person. People were "all in this together."

And so are we.

Yet our sense of "community" can be weakened by many things. One in particular is a strong focus on competition. For a group to work well together involves drawing on the strengths of all, and not handicapping each other by setting up artificial contests in which people are in opposition, and where some will be vanquished, in a zero-sum game. "Divide and conquer" is still an effective principle. Again, as in Chapter Three, this does not mean that people's unique strengths cannot be celebrated, or that excellence cannot be sought. In fact, this is essential to the best uses of our diverse potential. The question is how this is to be done.

Identifying with a larger group. The next crucial step is to take a leap from a small group to a larger group. And a larger group after that. And even a larger group. And finally to all of humankind. Yet how easily such groups–even more than individuals can become pitted against each other. We have also been programmed for this. Those people are different? Then they must be the enemy.

Dr. Seuss's book on the "Zooks" and the "Yooks" (who buttered their bread differently) shows this clearly. In *The Butter Battle Book*, these Zooks and Yooks end up in an arms race, building ever more elaborate and nonsensical weapons. When the only real question is buttering your bread, the absurdity jumps out at you.

In a comparable way, we need to identify not only with all humans, but with all living organisms, with the web of life that exists on the earth. And also with the earth itself, of which we are an inextricable part. And how little we know about this amazing system. As Lewis Thomas stressed, "teach that." Don't teach about the certainties of science, but the uncertainties. And about our own role in the mystery.

And also about the urgency. As Norman Myers put it in *The Gaia Atlas of Future Worlds*: "We are changing the face of the planet with all the impact of a geologic upheaval. In the past... they have usually extended over periods of thousands if not millions of years. Now they are all happening at once, and within the space of just a few decades the flicker of a geological eye.... yet whatever the changes humanity has wrought to date, they are a pale portent of what is to come within the lifespans of most readers of this book—unless we start to recognize our responsibilities as managers of the planetary ecosystem."

We need to think in larger and larger terms, and visualize ourselves on a larger and larger stage. This also means challenging our cherished attitudes, beliefs, and habits. We're so strongly conditioned. We all need to do this -- to keep challenging ourselves and to keep on doing it.

Do we think habitually of preserving the earth? Or do we at times see the earth as a storehouse of unmined resources for our use. Do we fancy the land, the oceans, the air, as extending to infinity—as unlimited repositories for all the wastes, the refuse, the chemicals and gases we want to dump—as we happily manufacture, consume, zoom around, and "shop' til we drop"? Or are we all living in a small closed box with each other and wishing that person over there would put out his cigar? Do we see other living organisms as cohabiters in a cooperative system, or existing as things or somebody's property?

Indeed everyone may do some of this new thinking already. But the way many of us were brought up, the totality is a tall order indeed.

Bad news and good news. There is some "bad news, and some good news." The consequences of a broader awareness may seem alarming indeed. Who needs all of this? It feels like too much. To make matters worse, when one identifies more strongly with other people, and their problems, it makes yet other problems one never thought about before become super-conscious. They too can become one's own problems.

So here again are our disappearing forests. Our reverse lungs. Our climate stabilizers. Our metabolizers and recyclers of carbon dioxide and of water. Our buffers of the greenhouse effect. And much more.

Now consider the farmer who, in desperation, is burning down the rain forest. Without planting new crops on the cleared land, he and his family cannot live. His desperation may become our own. What can he do? What can we, as individuals and citizens, do? Can we help provide any other way to make a living? Would it help to donate money? To whom? Do we buy certain products and avoid others? Do we change who we vote for? Do we support family planning options? Do we encourage tourism bringing greater awareness to tourists and riches to the inhabitants? And so on.

Of course, we as individuals cannot do everything on every issue. It is too much, it is unrealistic, and we would just burn ourselves out. But each of us can choose more limited places to help that are personally meaningful.

The country of Sweden, looking toward a more "sustainable future," has endorsed a four-point program called The Natural Step, which has been distributed to every school and every household. Its guidelines and specific suggestions have been applied to everything from individual family decisions, to city water, to ski resort management. In brief, the points involve preserving mineral resources, conserving green land, limiting persistent unnatural compounds (such as PCB's), and creating a just and efficient metabolism of resources. This model might be one sort of place to start.

The "bad news" mentioned above was the pain of awareness of our far-reaching problems. But the "good news" is that these were always our problems. The difference is that we are now more aware of them, and can work to turn things around.

An education in *creativity* can help. A creative style is really essential. We need to keep seeing the big picture. We need to be thinking holistically—to keep bringing in truckloads of "integrative complexity," to process our complex world and our creative options. We need to keep learning what we are apt not to see. And learning how to think in slow changes, in large numbers, in vast distances, and in multiple causes. How to nip an automatism in the bud—or more realistically, how to decide which ones to keep and which ones to dump.

There are so many places, actually, where we could be learning all of this -- in the schools, in the family, in the community, on TV, in the media generally. In *New World, New Mind,* Ornstein and Ehrlich give some excellent examples. Think about it. Conscious Evolution 101. Creativity 101. We should be learning these skills as readily as we learn English. And at the same time as we learn English.

Creativity and connection. A creative style carries many potential advantages for "connection," for broader and more profound ways of relating with each other. Such connections can deepen caring and our identification with all people. Indeed, creative persons may at times experience transcendent feelings, said Frank Barron in *Creative Person and Creative Process,* even of "awe and of oneness with the universe..." In the humanistic view of self-actualization as expressed by Abraham Maslow—a goal of full personal development—an object can be experienced with complete and selfless absorption. There may be mystic and oceanic aspects. Indeed, using whatever terms one prefers, the creative mind is able to reach across many barriers, and communicate in universal languages and forms.

A creative style also specifically raises the chance of empathy, that is, of "sharing in and comprehending the momentary psychological state of another person," Psychologist Judith Jordan and associates develop this further in *Women's Growth in Connection.* Yet it is not just for women. Empathy is a complex capacity. Further, it is not something which only highly creative people possess. We all have some capacity for empathy—in fact, it is a quality of primates in general, and not just of human beings. And surely it is a strength in survival. Whether or not one's empathetic capacity is strong, creative people often have some related qualities. These include emotional sensitivity, intuition, psychological mindedness, and ego-strength. These can be building blocks for empathy, or further increase the power it has. At best, these qualities can help one to identify and to give, and as Rosenhan put it, to "experience the role of a needy other... and to experience joy because the receiver will be happy." We can surely advance best as a group if we can do this—to as share our worries, and rejoice with each other's good fortune.

The other side: Creativity is no guarantee. Neither creativity nor empathy are guarantees of a caring or universal connection. There must be a separate valuing of this. Here are two examples of where they needn't go together.

It is well known how some creative people may "stand apart," with a fierce autonomy, independence, preoccupation, nonconformity, and sometimes antisocial posture and stern resistance to group norms. Certain creative people are even frankly antisocial and "could care less." For some people, creative activity is as much an escape as anything else.

Can this fit with the above vision of community? It very much depends. What are the reasons for the creator's aloofness? How nurturing is the culture? In a culture that ostracizes the person who is "different," these "creative characteristics" could be big trouble. The creator becomes problematic for the culture, and the culture for the creator. The friction could well push some creators further away—and perhaps rightly so.

Yet, in the bigger picture, and from where they sit, they may still deeply care.

One can also imagine a open happy culture with a celebration of differences that could draw in many standoffish creative persons, who really want to connect, and not compromise their individuality in the least.

Empathy is something else again. It can be wonderful, but it doesn't automatically mean caring. In the worst case, it may hold the opposite potential. Imagine the professional terrorist. Here is someone whose empathetic skills are probably excellent. Where to put the bomb to scare the most people? To cause the most uproar? To make them feel the least safe in their own cities? How well the terrorists can probably imagine the fear. The fear they are also seeking to create. Similarly, creativity doesn't have a value label attached to it. The user can be destructive as well as constructive. A terrorist may be creative indeed. Or think of a despotic leader. A wager of brutal wars. Or closer to home, consider the sabotager of someone supposed to be a friend. The deceiver -- the very clever deceiver—in a "trusting" relationship. The incredibly effective liar, sabotager of books, embezzler of funds. The examples run on and on. Clearly, something more than creativity, and more than empathy, is needed for a caring capacity and for a larger view of our connection and interdependence in this world.

2--A Widening Awareness

We've discussed this in part—how to keep a linked intellectual emotional awareness of human problems. You can't solve a problem until you can see it. And also until you can feel it. Our full awareness depends on a creative gathering of evidence, and suspension of closure on our "integrative complexity," as above—and on our connecting at many levels, and in many "languages" of thought and feeling, with the world. Toward this end, we can learn to get around our automatisms, defenses, and perceptual deficits.

But this is especially hard when a problem seems to go on and on. How much, after all, can one take? And why bother anyway, one may find oneself thinking, if there is nothing you can do?

One way to combat this, and to keep yourself feeling and thinking, is to connect with other people. And to keep doing something something concrete, specific, and probably at the local level—where you will be able to keep seeing the results. Recycling your trash at the curbside each week can be a tremendously empowering experience, if you become aware of what this means. If you think holistically of where all the materials are coming from each week, and where they are going. And where they might have been going instead if you, and others, weren't recycling them.

With this attitude, one's perceptual field can continue to open up.

There are also international ways to expand one's connections and awareness. As the "information highway" starts running through more living rooms, more people will connect up by computer, all over the world. The country they live in can become less important than their particular interests. Consider an interest group on our conscious evolution—cross-cultural idea-sharing on what we humans are really like! Across oceans and continents, ideas can whiz, circle the globe, multiply and bring people together. The world will shrink accordingly.

Here's another local approach, and one that starts young. Even small children can be involved. Take the problem of homelessness which, when viewed all at once, is complex and overwhelming, and is intertwined with so many other issues. Yet classes from one California preschool, *The Duck's Nest,* mentioned earlier, are helping. Their focus is at a personal level, working with children who live at a nearby shelter for families. The preschoolers really come to feel, as well as see, the problem.

The preschoolers go to the shelter for shared activities such as singing, and the shelter children in turn visit the preschool. This is a personal connection. In addition, the preschoolers' parents donate money toward holiday dinners and other supports. Yet it is not really clear who is helping whom the most. The shelter children have some new connections and opportunities. Meanwhile, the little preschoolers learn firsthand that these homeless families are not all that different from their own. They learn that they themselves are lucky. "There but for the Grace of God..."

These preschool children feel connected, and they also learn they can do something. They can carry this empowerment, warmth, and connection forward with them, and will be much less apt that some other child to say, "There's nothing I can do."

The other side: Awareness without caring. But there's still a less pleasant side of this particular street. There are people who are well aware of social and global problems. They scan them carefully, maybe chart them and graph them, and do creative surveys and projections. But only to make the wisest decisions concerning, let us say, corporate profits abroad, or to plan an effective political campaign.

Such activities can certainly also help a society. But some of their perpetrators identify a great deal less with the unfortunate than with their own groups and agendas. One can feel empowered, and creatively aware, but it doesn't necessarily mean that one will care.

3—A Loving Potential

This is about an ethic of caring. It is one of the oddest things that some people think that ethics, principles, morals, and the like are inevitably: (a) rigid; (b) punitive; (c) not very interesting; (d) authoritarian; (e) uncreative. Indeed, if you have a list of "do's and don'ts," ones you didn't make up, and which you cannot change, it may indeed seem this way.

But let's toss these terms aside for a moment and move to the idea of loving someone. Consider a romance that is developing. One is learning about the other, and vice versa. Sensing, intuiting, feeling, wondering, learning, wishing, yearning, and dancing a dance of two. Caring and giving freely out of this caring. Wanting the best for this person, and for the relationship. And sensing the aesthetic in all of this: the understanding, the beauty, the passion, the interaction that becomes more than the sum of its parts. And the creativity.

Hopefully, this image is neither rigid nor boring. It is rich with implicit values that are flexible and adaptive. As Ashley Montagu put it: "Love implies the possession of a feeling of deep involvement in another, and to love means to communicate that feeling of involvement.... Love is most needed by the human organism from the moment of birth. Love is reciprocal in its effect and is as beneficial to the giver as it is to the recipient. Love is creative. Love enlarges the capacities of those who are loved..."

Love enables the person to treat life as an art.

Love as an attitude of mind and as a form of behavior is adaptively the best and most efficient of all adjustive processes.... For the person and the species love is the form of behavior having the highest survival value.

The Relational Self. Love may be "natural." But it doesn't mean that it's easy. What does it take to care? A willingness to risk and to give. To be authentically oneself, and to feel comfortable in doing this, without any falseness or pretense. Indeed, to feel generally wonderful about this process. To be willing to risk occasional rejection, misunderstanding, and conflict, with a fundamental faith in oneself, this process, and the other.

Doesn't it sound as if some qualities of creative living might be helpful?

When relationship is concerned, it will certainly also "take two." There needs to be an ultimate trust in the beloved other, even though there may sometimes be a conflict here or a misunderstanding there. Over time, it will all straighten out. The ultimate commitment of both parties—in the ideal, at least—will not be to "my view" or "your view" but to a mutuality, to a mutual understanding at the level of thoughts and feelings, an empathetic sharing and giving, and to working out the differences that get in the way. Theorists of the crucial "self-in-relation" model of human development, including Judith Jordan and associates, have worked such qualities out in detail.

Does this picture sound unusual? "As rare as hens' teeth? "These are, after all, ideals. They are something to work for. Relationships which work are work, and relationships are hard. Yet when there is genuine love operating, one can at least move in this positive direction. One may even come to see conflicts as a good and welcome thing! Is this amazing? This does not refer to every single conflict, nor to every single moment. But, when there is an underlying commitment to someone, the coming together of different points of view can create a new dialectic, a chance for a new and deeper understanding. And it can (hopefully) enlarge a climate for working together to achieve it. When this does happen, it can feel very good indeed.

Ethic of caring: Moving out from two people. What if one can somehow extend this sort of caring from a firm basis one establishes with another to encompass more and more people?

We have been living largely within a morality of principles. Consider, for instance, Lawrence Kohlberg's model of moral development. The highest stage involves principles of conscience. These are logical, universal, consistent, just and fair. There is an overriding respect for the rights of others.

What is wrong with this? Let us, rather, reframe this question, and add another dimension. Carol Gilligan challenged a principled morality as more typical of men, with a focus on separation and the individual. No one, in this view, should be intruding on another's rights, or threatening their dignity. Gilligan, author of *In a Different Voice,* saw women as more concerned with the relationship, and with the responsibilities rather than rights of connection. As Gilligan said of one research subject, "While Kohlberg's subject worries about people interfering with each other's rights, this woman worries about 'the possibility of omission, of your not helping others when you could help them.'"

But no one has demanded that we play "either-or" with these guidelines for living. Alfie Kohn, in his important book, *The Brighter Side of Human Nature*, proposes joining justice with caring. He thus unites principles and empathy; one can truly have the best of both. This also helps to reintegrate the intellectual and emotional dimensions of morality, and the personal with the universal. One might wonder if our original environment of evolution, based on a small-group reciprocity, didn't use such a system.

The joining of justice and caring also reunites some stereotypically male and female qualities. One may recall that the most highly creative people often abandon these artificial sex-role stereotypes. These creators can revel, when they wish, in an androgyny which draws broadly from all manner of human behavior. Similarly, there need not be a "male" morality and a "female" morality. A "human" morality will be quite good enough.

Some very odd things could happen with a morality of caring without the component of justice. For instance, consider a beloved person who gets repeated heart transplants while anonymous others do not get a chance. On what basis does one decide with whom to empathize? Some fairness, please.

On the other end, extremely odd things can happen with a morality of justice without a more personal and emotion- linked caring component. In the Kantian view, which has been influential since the Enlightenment, not only are one's principles primary, but they may seem even more honorable if they go against one's feelings. Kant said: "(If one acts) only from duty and without any inclination-then for the first time his action has genuine moral worth."

This is the point about how being good is supposed to hurt. What a life! This approach doesn't draw much on the mutual satisfactions of love, or caring, or even of a cheerful reciprocity. Worse yet, it casts one's feelings in the role of the bad guy. An important book, by neurologist Antonio Damasio, *Descartes's Error*, confronts this problem, along with contributions of other thinkers to this worldview, most certainly including Descartes.

Here is Damasio: "Thus, absence of emotion appears to be at least as pernicious for rationality as excessive emotion.... emotion probably assists reasoning, especially when it comes to personal and social matters, and eventually points us to the sector of the decision-making space that is most advantageous for us.... new neurological evidence suggests that no emotion at all is an even greater problem. Emotion may well be the support system without which the edifice of reason cannot function properly and may even collapse."

Let us now return to love. How significant that great world religions across cultures and continents have talked about loving one's fellow human being as oneself, and about universal love. If our connections are grounded in this ethic, surely they will have the power to endure.

The other side: Creativity without caring. We turn again for a moment to creativity gone sour, but also to how it may ultimately transform itself.

Consider the embezzler who cavalierly appropriates millions that belong to others. The dealer who hooks innocent young people on addictive substances—helping to condemn them, and perhaps their unborn babies—to lives of disappointment and despair. The house burglar who is a regular at breaking and entering, in order to feed his own drug habit.

To some, this activity may seem less a sought-after choice, or moral decision, than the only way to eat, or to stay alive. To others, it may also be a route to thrills, self-esteem, belongingness, a feeling of power in a world flying out of control, and a chance to feel clever and accomplished. Indeed, one can find a lot of creativity displayed. How tragic that this same potential could not have gone into something much more constructive. And that the creator could not have enjoyed more fundamental personal satisfactions. Yet for whatever reason, this was the only doorway that seemed open. It perhaps offered an escape from a terrifying fate that only this person could know.

Let's also add into this mix, some famous politicians turned criminals. And some heads of state—and don't these come readily to mind—who massacred huge numbers of their own populations. Weren't these leaders people whose very role was to care for their citizenry? Who were even designated to be "acting for us."

How creative is "Destructive Creativity"? If creativity is supposed to be so "healthy," then it becomes important to ask this question: "How creative is 'destructive' creativity?" In a just world, wouldn't a "destructive" person somehow be finessed out of having full creative powers?

One might like to believe this, but it is far from clear. Carl Rogers, the humanistic psychologist, felt that the underlying creative process was essentially the same for destructive creativity. The difference was in the degree of non-defensiveness, or openness to experience, found in the more constructive creator.

One could perhaps argue that this defended creator would run up against more mental roadblocks, compared to the open, freewheeling creator, a person who was less afraid of her or his own mind. The destructive person would find, perhaps, fewer raw materials for creating. Perhaps.

But one can also imagine, without too much trouble, a defended, yet very creative, criminal working freely within a well-compartmentalized domain of knowledge. This person knows very well how to rob a bank. One hundred different kinds of banks. What a fun puzzle this is! In fact, when unpleasant thoughts intrude, it is the very thought of a clever break-in that makes this person feel better. How motivated this person may be to seek a triumph in crime.

Opting for self-deception over caring. We, of course, are not really split into "the good guys and the bad guys." It is only fair to think of ways in which this phenomenon may play out in the rest of us—in which our psychological defenses get in the way, and to someone else's detriment.

Let us imagine, first of all, that our defenses prevent our understanding some issue. To understand it, we would have to learn way too much about ourselves. And now, secondly, that we end up being unkind to somebody, so that we can put this issue out of our minds, and avoid even the risk of seeing behind our defenses. Our behavior may not seem very nice—indeed it's been called worse (see M. Scott Peck, for instance). But I imagine we all can think of a time when we've done at least a little of this. And there can be very creative ways this plays out. Here's an apt example for this section.

Tom denies we have much of a problem with atmospheric pollution. OK, that's Tom's opinion. But next Tom takes pot shots at some people he's just met who are working on air quality. He doesn't listen at all to what they have to say. In fact, Tom really gets going and becomes a riot. He's so very funny. He makes people look like clowns in the way they would have to drive around, dress themselves, or act, in order to "save the air." And "did the air even say 'thank you'?" You get the picture.

In Tom's world, this response is a bigger choice than it might seem. Underneath, it's a choice between making fun of someone, and potentially challenging a whole embedded belief system of his own. At risk are a great many parts of his lifestyle and, in fact, even of the occupation he chose. Tom risks being bowled over by one of those unwanted creative insights about who he really is. And so he opts instead to let someone else bear the brunt of his discomfort.

There are certainly more extreme examples of this type of scapegoating phenomenon, where instead of a little casual ribbing, the behavior toward others involves outright discrimination or abuse. But let us turn instead to how creativity can be healing—how it can help to break down these internal barriers of mind, and help people be more open, feeling, caring, and giving.

Creative coping, health, and caring. Here is a big ray of hope. People who create not every last person who creates -- but a great many people, find it keeps opening them up a little bit more. Their mental roadblocks get more and more elastic. They find a little bump in the road, a gasp, an unwelcome thought, but only at certain times. The overall payoff is worth it. They can move a little further along, ease out into the corners of their minds.

Here indeed comes the healthy potential of creativity. One can also add an extra dose of integrative complexity each time one rides over a rough mental place. The latter quality can make the next creative encounter even easier. We looked at this phenomenon in the last chapter, where people who wrote creatively about difficult life experiences not only felt better, but showed a strengthened immune system. This is important indeed. Our minds don't want to stay t angled and trapped. Indeed, the arts may be a particularly good vehicle for this psychological growth. Let's take an example.

D-Creativity to B-Creativity. Here now is Lesley, who is writing a poem about a childhood friend. Lesley was playing with her friend in a vacant lot. Suddenly Lesley's mother calls her. In the poem, that is. Lesley wasn't planning for her mother to call her. But back there, recorded in Lesley's mind, along with those childhood games and vacation days and afternoons with friends, is her mother calling her. And now Lesley's hears her mother's voice, fearful, she feels herself shrinking, sees the surprise on her friend's face. She remember s how angry her mother got, how frightened Lesley was, and how little her mother wanted the kids out of her sight.

Mom was awfully overprotective, Lesley muses. And suddenly, Lesley feels just a little bit freer in her own modern world of adults.

Now we follow Lesley to another healthy junction. She begins to move from "D-creativity" to B-creativity." That is, she starts moving from *deficiency-creativity* to *being-creativity*, as defined by Celeste Rhodes, by analogy with humanistic psychologist Abraham Maslow's D-love and B-love. Rhodes's work appeared first in *The Creativity Research Journal* and is being reprinted by Mark Runco and the present author in our forthcoming edited book, *Eminent Creativity, Everyday Creativity, and Health.*

Maslow's first kind of love is more needy, clinging, and tied to one's own needs. The second comes from the more fully actualized person, and is giving, selfless, fluid, and non-demanding. Yet, as deficiency needs are met, the first type of love may come to shade into the second.

As with love, Rhodes has suggested that creative activity could start from a deficiency need, one which it is attempting to remedy. And why ever not? What an excellent idea! One might be writing a poem about one's mother, for one's own purposes. And then one eventually moves onward from there in a natural upward spiral of personal growth, and then of giving.

So here we have Lesley, who starts getting interested in where some of her childhood fears came from. Soon she also explores the fears of others, young adults like herself, who had an overprotective mother. She investigates, talks with others, does more writing, and shares this, feeling more and more empowered, as her fears appear increasingly empty. This is great, thinks Lesley. But just think of all the other people walking around with this baggage. I don't want them to be so dragged down with these fears. I want to help them.

And so Lesley does. This includes writing a story for a small literary magazine. It is still about Lesley and her mother, in disguised form. But more generally it is about children who run and hide, and those who jump and shout. It's about the messages of childhood, and the child in the adult. Lesley is finding universal currents and connections in her message. She is transcending her own particular situation, and sharing with others in a spirit of caring, and a very giving love.

4—Creative Courage

Rollo May said, in *The Courage to Create,* "If we let ourselves experience the evil, we will be forced to do something about it." Hopefully—but it is not necessarily so. The added ingredients include a belief in one's own effectiveness, and a strong dose of creative courage. In one study, Berman showed about half of the high school seniors surveyed over more than a ten year period agreed fully or largely with the statement, "I feel I can do very little to change the way the world is today."

The interesting group, though, is the other half. Why do those students feel empowered while the first group does not? There are many possibilities. For one, there is the gradual empowerment discussed above—where little kids are already learning they can help, and that this feels good, even when they are 3 or 4 or 5 years old.

Of course, there is also an adult involved somewhere in this effort. Some adult teacher believes in herself or himself, enough to take a stand, and to model this for the child. The modeling influence is tremendously important. Do you want a verbal problem-solving child or a Mighty Morphin' Power Ranger? Watch out, because the Power Rangers can really kick.

Adversity, creativity, and resilience. Some people who lacked the modeling or early exposure still seem to have forged their own creative confidence and courage. They overcame adversity and become resilient survivors. This is extremely interesting and important. It is remarkable how many eminent creative people have led troubled lives including traumatic childhoods, poverty, traumatic loss, physical disability, or mental illness. Surely this is not an accident.

These are people who have, essentially, been thrown into the pool and learned to swim. They somehow overcame their problems, or at least carried on despite them. Sometimes, in the arts, creative expression was used directly to deal with these problems. For some people, creativity may indeed have been part of the secret. Often, there was something else as well one supportive adult outside or inside the family, for instance. Or some special opportunities.

However it is generated, success can lead to the feeling that you can overcome adversity the next time. Or that you can be "different" than others and still succeed. Or that having negative feelings shouldn't necessarily lead to running away -- either mentally or physically. That one can actually make things better, can turn these negative feelings into positive ends. Blaney has shown that one can even make this part of one's personal style, and one's basic conviction.

Yet doing this will take self-confidence, plus. Hitting a wall of adversity is not a good prescription for survival in general. Or for creativity. It is thus that Goertzel and Goertzel, authors of *Cradles of Eminence,* who studied 400 eminent 20th century figures—85% of whom came from troubled beginnings—cautioned parents not to take their results as an indication that they should mistreat children as a means of stimulating creativity. What an incredible thought this is, in any case.

But for each person who sails forth resiliently from a hard early life, a great many more will fall at the wayside, or at least have parts of their human potential stunted. Brute force will tend to take its toll. There are better ways than this.

Creative "immunity." The best way to build creative courage—the ability and willingness to act, to approach instead of avoid difficulty, and to creatively transform it—is slowly. This can work for people of any age, adult or child, but can be particularly effective for impressionable young children. It may be likened to acquired immunity, like a vaccination for mumps or measles. Or perhaps to a slowly administered series of desensitizing shots for allergies. It may cause a little discomfort at the time, but can greatly soften a blow later on. Now here is a child perhaps who already has a creative edge. Maybe this is a girl or boy who is encouraged to be independent, to ask questions. Maybe this youth plays freely, and is given many resources for doing so. Maybe this child has a high need for novelty, and indulges this, along with a touch of reasonable risk-taking, with a like-minded parent.

Or maybe this is the resilient creator in miniature, a young person who already has some problems, but finds creative outlets. Perhaps there is a family uprooting, a sibling death, a parent's divorce. The troubled youth comes to write, draw, or play with puppets. Often it works and this troubled young person feels better. Sometimes, the youth even feels wonderful.

The message for the future: Don't run. Stay and do something. It's a little rough at times, but things can end up much better in the long run. And at times, it can even feel great.

One possible result of this approach is the style of integrative complexity. The young person -- or the willing adult -- learns to value delay, risk, and hope, and to place less stake in her or his immediate comfort and closure than in a better future.

"The Child is the World." What's above is all easy to say. But it is not always easy to do. Let me end with a personal anecdote, where the issue was the difficulty of "taking that unpopular stand." The episode may sound relatively minor to some people. But it felt anything but minor to me at the time, and that is part of the point.

Sometimes it is the seemingly small stand that may count most. When one's principles don't seem fully challenged, when you may think they don't even fully apply. When others may call it trivial. When they won't agree or even help you. When you could argue the moment away, for a little acceptance, simplicity, and a false peace. How easy it is to give in.

This one time, you think, won't make all that much difference. This is only a little retreat. If things were really serious, well, then, I would take a stand.

But it doesn't really work that way. We all know deep inside when something is important to us. Plus the insidiousness of habituation will get us in the end. One can get into the habit of making these little retreats, choosing, in essence, the anonymity and death of inaction to the aliveness, and trouble, of creative response. And it is often in an instant that one must decide.

The following incident occurred at a party with some boisterous and determined friends and associates. My young daughter was with me at the time.

A large moth was flying around trapped, dark brown and flapping over our heads, near the fan of the vaulted ceiling of the home where the party was being held. The owner wanted it out, and so a not her guest obliged by getting a hand vacuum.

"Just suck it up," said the owner.

And bye bye moth -- trapped alive in the bowels of that machine. Should I just let this one go? You can't save every moth, I thought. We're always stepping on bugs. Shouldn't I just let them do it?

But I didn't. "Why not save the moth," I finally said." It's simple to do, and "there's no need to harm it."

As I feared, I became a target for humor. "Do you want to save everything? Do you want to save the smallpox virus? And so on.

I used a little humor in return. "Mosquitos are the natural enemies," I replied, and added, "even if they don't strike first." (How much of a cop out was that, I wondered)

And then I added that my mother had always done this, had always saved the creatures. Invoking my mother had helped. I then invoked Albert Schweitzer, whom I recently learned had also done this, and that helped a little more. To a "respect for life" explanation, which I voiced a couple of times, I got only dismissal.

But my daughter, my dear daughter. I'd almost forgotten! Her eyes were wide. "We should save it, right? We should take it outside and let it go free!" She waved her arms and bounced about." That's right, isn't it, Mom?" She gave an excited little leap, her head turned back toward me, eyes wide, hands gesturing as if to cradle the bug.

"Yes," I said, "it is right."

My God, the precious lesson, the moment, almost forgotten, overlooked. And a confrontation with the self that I boldly present to my daughter at other, more convenient, times. Had this self almost taken a leave? A leave of my senses?

The child is the world. The bug is the world.

And so the moth obliged. It truly did. It swooped down and flickered a bit near the light by the host's easy chair, right near me, while the terrible humans converged, flashing a vacuum, and grabbing and chasing.

But I was closest. Among reaching hands, I simply scooped up the creature. "It knows who the good guys are," I joked. I cupped the moth between my hands.

"Hooray," said my daughter, and ran for the door. She knew what was next—now—we would let it go. I asked that the outdoor light be turned on, so we could see it fly away.

The host made a joke about letting in a lot more moths. No problem. I laughed right along. The moment -- and the life -- had been saved

AFTERWORD

In summary, here are ten propositions to consider:

1) We create, we adapt. We are all part of an evolving process of life forms and information. Indeed, our biology, most certainly our genes, are yet other forms of information. As with biodiversity, the diversity we generate through our life choices, actions, and the information we produce is our ultimate advantage for survival. We as human beings can think up something f or every occasion. Herein lies our essential creativity.

2) We survive. Creativity is a key to our survival, as creatures, a species, and as parents of thoughts and feelings, of the world of information. This is our creative birthright—and our personal and shared culture. We are not, just a few of us, doing this. All of us together, whether we know it or not, or like it or not, are contributing to a creative and evolving process of information. Indeed, a survival edge can't be the sole result of a few people, however influential these people may be. Survival is ultimately a grass roots matter, operating out from the level of the everyday person. We human beings will survive only if we are in survival mode.

3) We can enjoy being unique. This evolution is fueled by our individual uniquenesses, including our colorful outbursts of "abnormality" and "deviance." We may frequently be opposed by the powerful forces of conformity. Yet the climate of a time may determine how much of this "abnormality" will be labeled "creative" versus "pathological," and how rapidly things can change. As with biodiversity, it is our collective diversity that will help assure the process will continue.

4) We create worlds. Indeed, creativity gives rise to the broad worlds we inhabit, far beyond the confines of our room and our neighborhood, and our concrete physical reality. Creativity links our past, present, and future, and also worlds existing only in fantasy. Creativity is not a weekend hobby. It is the essence of our lives as human beings.

5) We can be happily off balance. The creation of new information involves a conversation—a metabolism of new information with the old, a dialectic. This involves both Jean Piaget's assimilation to the old ways of looking at things, and accommodation to the new. But there will not always be a Piagetian ideal of balance or equilibrium. The creator may

voluntarily spark thought processes, including more primitive and childlike ones, that may throw things way out of kilter. And happily so, for at a metaphorical, and perhaps literal, "edge-of-chaos," a whole new order of thought and understanding may be determined, at times in a crashing moment of insight.

6) We can feel it. How do we know what to notice, what to do? We sense those critical junctures in the life flow, through our innate aesthetic sensors, another and more subtle survival tool. When we put fear aside, and tune up our aesthetic responses, a vision may enter carrying meaning and satisfaction. Beauty, or elegance, may be the key—a sense of rightness, urging us to get involved, to care, to make a difference. It may help drive a process of creative growth and development—a joining and issuing of new information into the world—even as sexual attraction can drive a genetic mating.

7) We can sense our rewards. These rewards are personal satisfaction, happiness, and a sense of wellbeing both physically and psychologically. Nature likes us to do this, and may even at times prolong our lives if we are actively involved in this endeavor. We chase those ideas, we love those ideas. We marry them together, and we marry them within us. We will keep doing it until we die.

8) Yet sometimes we miss it. We are blinded to much around us through an evolutionary mismatch of our capacities and modern times. And then blinded again through our conceptual shortcuts and simplifications. And again through our massive psychological defenses—especially when something gets tremendously bad, and needs our attention. Then again through our built in schemas that make the facing of dangers a little harder to do—favoring the illusions of happiness over less comfortable realities. Or splitting off needed parts of our experience one from another: our range of positive and negative feelings, our feelings from our thoughts, or our interrelated human endeavors such as the sciences and the arts.

9) We can stay blissfully ignorant together. In the story of the blind men and the elephant, the blind men put together a composite picture of this massive creature, each from his own perspective. A leg, a tusk, a side of the animal, and so on. To us, these widely differing perspectives seem amusing, because we, the readers, can "see" the "big picture." Yet, in our present dilemma of understanding ourselves and our world, most people's misperceptions are biased in similar ways. To make matters worse, we may support each other in these limited

views. Who has a clue as to what the "big picture" really looks like? This situation can be dangerous.

10) Or we can evolve consciously. There is no time to evolve genetically. But memetic evolution can be near instantaneous. We need new levels of awareness of how we see, think, and feel, of global problems, and of new forms of cooperation and awareness of global interdependence. The same defenses that can distort our individual lives distort our vision of our community and our world. This might be called a massive consensual delusion. Talk about *pathology*—that's what's being called the *normality*. Things need to be stood on their head. We need not stand around automatically saying yes or no to what we hear. We can be cheerful creative challengers of the status quo, exercising our integrative complexity the same way as we might exercise our muscles. Saying stop!, there's a better way to go. And banding together to take bigger and bigger bites of the problem.

For better or for worse, we are also teaching what we are learning to our young. The "Three R's" are fine, but perhaps it is time as well for "Three C's": *creativity, caring,* and *connection.* These may help us discover the "what, why, and how" of the 21st century.

BIBLIOGRAPHY

From Richards, R. (1997). Conclusions: When illness yields creativity (final integrating chapter). In M. Runco & R. Richards (Eds.), *Eminent Creativity, Everyday Creativity and Health* (pp. 485-540). Greenwich, CT: Ablex Publishing Corporation.

Ackerman, D. (1994). *A natural history of love*. New York: Random House.

Adler, W. Jr. (1991). *The whole earth quiz book*. New York: Quill.

Akiskal, H. & Akiskal, K (1988). Reassessing the prevalence of bipolar disorders: Clinical significance and artistic creativity. *Psychiatry and Psychobiology*, 3, 29-36.

Akiskal, H. & Akiskal, K. (1992). Cyclothymic, hyperthymic, and depressive temperaments as subaffective variants of mood disorders. In A. Tasman & M.B. Riba (Eds.), *Review of psychiatry*, Vol. 11, (pp. 43-62). Washington, DC: American Psychiatric Press.

Akiskal, H. S. & Mallya. G. (1987). Criteria for the "soft" bipolar spectrum: Treatment implications. *Psychopharmacology Bulletin*, 23, 67-73.

Albert, R. S. (1971). Cognitive development and parental loss among the gifted, the exceptionally gifted and the creative. *Psychological Reports*, 29, 19-26.

Albert, R. S. (1983). Family positions and the attainment of eminence. In R S. Albert (Ed.), *Genius and eminence*, (pp. 141-153). New York: Pergamon Press.

Albert, R. S. &, Runco, M. A. (1986). The achievement of eminence. In R.J. Sternberg & Davidson (Eds.), *Conceptions of giftedness*. New York: Cambridge University Press.

Andreason, N. (1978). Creativity and psychiatric illness. *Psychiatric Annals*. 8, 113-119.

Andreasen, N. (1987). Creativity and mental illness: Prevalence rates in writers and their first-degree relatives. *American Journal of Psychiatry*. 144, 1288-1292.

Andreasen, N. & Canter, A (1974). The creative writer: Psychiatric symptoms and family history. *Comprehensive Psychiatry*, 15, 123-131.

Andreasen, N. & Glick I. D. (1988). Bipolar affective disorder and creativity: Implications and clinical management *Comprehensive Psychiatry*, 15, 113-131.

Andreasen, N. & Powers, P. (1974). Overinclusive thinking in mania and schizophrenia. *British journal of Psychiatry*, 125, 452-456.

Bailin, S. (1990). Societal creativity: Problems with pathology. *Creativity Research Journal* 3, 100-I03.

Barron, F. (1963a). The disposition toward originality. In C. W. Taylor & F. Barron (Eds.), *Scientific creativity: Its recognition and development*, (pp. 139-152). New York: Wiley.

Barron, F. (1963b). The needs for order and disorder as motives in creative activity. In C. W. Taylor & F. Barron (Eds.), *Scientific creativity: Its recognition and development*, (pp. 153-160). New York: Wiley.

Barron, F. (1969). *Creative person and creative process*. New York: Holt, Rinehart & Winston.

Barron, F. & Bradley. P. (1990). The dash of social philosophies and personalities in the nuclear arms control debate: A healthful dialectic? *Creative Research Journal*, 3, 237-246.

Bu, P. & Chen, K (1991, January). Self-organized criticality. Scientific American, 46-53.

Barron, F. & Bradley, P. (1990). The clash of social philosophies and personalities in the nuclear arms control debate: A healthful dialectic? *Creativity Research Journal* 3, 237-246.

Becker, G. (1978). *The mad genius controversy: A study in the sociology of deviance*. Beverly Hills, CA: Sage.

Berman, S. (1991). The real ropes course: The development of social consciousness. *ESR (Educators for Social Responsibility) Journal* 1, 1-18.

Blaney, P. H. (1986). Affect and memory: A review. *Psychological Bulletin*, 99, 229-246.

Bogen, J. & Bogen, G. (1988). Psychiatric Clinics of North America. (Vol 2, No.3). Philadelphia: WB Saunders.

Bower, G. H. (1981). Mood and memory. *American Psychologist*, 36, 129-148.

Brent, D. A., Kupfer, D. J., Bromet, E. J., & Dew, M. A. (1988). The assessment and treatment of patients at risk for suicide. In A. J. Frances, & R E. Hales (Eds.), *Review of psychiatry*, Vol 7, (pp. 353-385). Washington, D.C.: American Psychiatric Press.

Brown, L. R., Brough, H., Durning, A.., Flavin, C., French, H., Jacobson, J., Lenssen, N., Lowe, .M, Postel, S., Renner, M, Ryan, J., Starke, L., & Young, J. (1992). *State of the world, 1992: A Worldwatch Institute report on progress toward a sustainable society*. New York: Norton.

Brown, L. R, Durning, A., Flavin, C., French, H., Jacobson, J., Lenssen, N., Lowe, M., Postel S., Renner, M., Ryan, J., Starke, L., & Young, J. (1991). *State of the world: A Worldwatch Institute report on progress toward a sustainable society*. New York: Norton.

Carroll, J. (1993, July 20). The barriers obliterated by the Holocaust. *Boston Globe*, 15.

Cropley, A. J. (1990). Creativity and mental health in everyday life. *Creativity Research Journal*, 3, 167-178.

Csikszentmihalyi, M. (1988). Society, culture, and person: A systems view of creativity. In R. J. Sternberg (Ed.), *The nature of creativity*, (pp. 325-339). Cambridge, England: Cambridge University Press.

Dawkins, R. (1976). *The selfish gene*. New York: Oxford University Press.

Dertouzos, M. L. (1991). Communications, computers and networks. *Scientific American*, 265, 62-69.

Donald, M. (1991). *Origins of the modern mind: Three stages in the evolution of culture and cognition*. Cambridge, MA: Harvard University Press.

Dudek, S. Z. & Verrault, R (1989). The creative thinking and ego functioning of children. *Creativity Research Journal*, 2, 64-86.

Eckblad, M., & Chapman, L.J. (1986). Development and validation of a scale for hypomanic personality. *Journal of Abnormal Psychology*, 3, 214-222.

Ehrlich, P. R., & Ehrlich A. H. (1991). *The population explosion*. New York: Touchstone.

Eisenberg, D., Kessler, R C., Foster, C., Norlock, F. E., Calkins, D. R, & Delbanco, T. L. (1993). Unconventional medicine in the United States. *New England Journal of Medicine*, 328, 246-252.

Eisenman, R (1990). Creativity, preference for complexity, and physical and mental illness. *Creativity Research Journal*, 3, 231-236.

Eysenck, H. (1993). Creativity and personality: Suggestions for a theory. *Psychological Inquiry*, 4, 147-178.

Eysenck, H. (1994). *Creativity Research Journal*, 7, 209-216.

Feldman, D. H. (1990). Four frames for the study of creativity. *Creativity Research Journal*, 3, 104-111.

Flach, F. (1990). Disorders of the pathways involved in the creative process. *Creativity Research Journal*, 3, 158-165.

Fobes, J. L. (1989). The cognitive psychobiology of performance regulation. *Journal of Sports Medicine and Physical Fitness*, 29, 202-208.

Forrest, S. (1991). Emergent computation: Self-organizing, collective, and cooperative phenomena in natural and artificial computing networks. In S. Forrest (Ed.), *Emergent computation*. Cambridge, MA: MIT Press.

Forrest, S. & Miller, J. H. (1991). Emergent behavior in classifier systems. In S. Forrest (Ed.), *Emergent computation*, (pp. 213-227). Cambridge, MA: MIT Press.

Freud, S. (1908/1958). The relation of the poet to day-dreaming. In S. Freud, *On creativity and the unconscious* (collected writings) (pp. 44-54). New York: Random House.

Freud, S. (1920). *A general introduction to psychoanalysis*. New York: Boni and Liveright.

Freyd, J.J. (August, 1991). Memory repression, dissociative states, and other cognitive control processes involved in adult sequelae of childhood trauma. Paper given at the Second Annual Conference of the Program on Conscious and Unconscious Mental Processes, University of California, San Francisco.

Frijda, N. H. (1988). The laws of emotion. *American Psychologist*, 43, 349-358.

Gardner, H. (1993). *Creating minds*. New York: Basic Books.

Gardner, K.G. & Moran, J. D., III (1990). *Creativity Research Journal*, 3, 281-286.

Garmezy, N. & Rutter, M. (1983). *Stress, coping, and development in children*. New York: McGraw-Hill.

Gedo, J. E. (1990). More on the healing power of art: The case of John Ensor. *Creativity Research Journal*, 3, 33-57.

Glance, N. S. & Huberman, B. A. (1994, March). The dynamics of social dilemmas. *Scientific American*.

Glantz, K & Pearce,]. K (1989). *Exiles from Eden: Psychotherapy from an evolutionary perspective*. New York: Norton.

Gleick, J. (1988). *Chaos: Making a new science*. New York: Penguin.

Goertzel, V. & Goertzel, M. G. (1962). *Cradles of eminence*. Boston: Little, Brown.

Goldstein, K. & Scheerer, M. (1941). Abstract and concrete behavior: An experimental study with special tests. *Psychological Monographs*, 53, Whole No. 239.

Goodwin, F. K. & Jamison, K R. (1990). *Manic-depressive illness*. New York: Oxford University Press.

Goswami, A. (1993). An idealist theory of ethics. *Creativity Research Journal*, 6, 185-196.

Gould, S. J. (1989). *Wonderful life*. New York: Norton.

Gruber, H. (1985). Giftedness and moral responsibility: Creative thinking and human survival. In F. D. Horowitz & M. O'Brien (Eds.), *The gifted and talented*: Developmental perspectives (pp. 301-330), Washington, D.C.: American Psychological Assoc.

Gruber, H. (1988). Creative altruism, cooperation, and world peace. In T. J. Hurley (Ed.), *The greater self: New frontiers in exceptional abilities research*. Sausalito: CA; Institute of Noetic Sciences.

Gruber, H. (1989). Creativity and human survival. In D. Wallace, & H. Gruber (Eds.), *Creative people at work* (pp. 278-287). New York: Oxford University Press.

Gruber, H. (1993). Creativity in the moral domain: Ought implies can implies create. *Creativity, Research Journal*, 6, 3-15.

Guyton, A. C. (1976). *Textbook of medical physiology*, Philadelphia: W. B. Saunders.

Harrington, D. (1990). The ecology of human creativity: A psychological perspective. In M. A. Runco and R. S. Albert, (Eds). *Theories of creativity*. Newbury Park, CA: Sage Publications.

Haste, H. (1993). Moral creativity and education for citizenship. *Creativity Research Journal*, 6, 153-164.

Hausman, C. R. (1990). The origin of creative achievement: Spontaneity, responsibility, and individuals. *Creativity Research Journal*, 3, 112-117.

Hirsch, D. (1993). WRKO's Victoria Jones. *Talkers*, 43, 1, 3, 11.

Hoffman, R. E. (1987). Computer simulations of neural information processing and the schizophrenia-mania dichotomy. *Archives of General Psychiatry*, 44, 178-188.

Holland, J. H., Kolyoak, K J., Nisbett, R. E. & Thagard, P. R. (1986). Induction: *Processes of inference, learning, and discovery*. Cambridge, MA: MIT Press.

Holzman, P. S., Shenton, M. E., & Solovay, M. R (1986). Quality of thought disorder in differential diagnosis. *Schizophrenia Bulletin*, 12, 360-372.

Hoppe, K. (1988). *Psychiatric Clinics of North America*. (Vol. 2 No.3) Philadelphia: WB Saunders.

Hoppe, K. & Kyle, N. (1990). Dual brain, creativity, and health. *Creativity Research Journal*, 3, 150-157.

Horowitz, M. J. (1988). Unconsciously determined defensive strategies. In M. Horowitz (Ed.), *Psychodynamics and cognition*. Chicago: University of Chicago Press.

Isen, A. M. (1984). Toward understanding the role of affect in cognition. In R. S. Wyer, Jr., & T.K. Srull (Eds.), *Handbook of social cognition*, Vol. 3, (pp. 179-235). Hillsdale, NJ: Erlbaum.

Isen, A. M. (1985). Asymmetry of happiness and sadness in effects on memory in normal college students: Comment on Hasher, Rose, Zacks, Sanft, and Doren. *Journal of Experimental Psychology: General* 114, 388-391.

Isen, A. M., Daubman, K. A., & Nowicki, G. P. (1987). Positive affect facilitates creative problem solving. *Journal of Personality and Social Psychology*, 52, 1122-1131.

Isen, A. M., Nygren, T. E., & Ashby, F. G. (1988). Influence of positive affect on the subjective utility of gains and losses: It is just not worth the risk. *Journal of Personality and Social Psychology*, 55,710-717.

Jamison, K. R., Gerner, R, Hammen, C., & Padesky, C. (1980). Clouds and silver linings: Positive experiences associated with primary affective disorders. *American Journal of Psychiatry*, 137, 198-202.

Jamison, K. R. (1989). Mood disorders and patterns of creative in British writers. *Psychiatry*, 52, 125-134.

Jamison, K. R. (1990), Manic-depressive illness, creativity, and leadership. In F. K. Goodwin, & K. R. Jamison, *Manic-depressive illness*. (pp. 332-367). New York: Oxford University Press.

Jamison, K. (1993). *Touched with fire*. New York: Free Press.

Jordan, J. (1990). *Courage in connection: Conflict, compassion, creativity*. Wellesley, MA: Stone Center for Developmental Services and Studies, Wellesley College.

Jordan, J. (1992). *Relational resilience*. Wellesley, MA: Stone Center for Developmental Services and Studies, Wellesley College.

Jordan, J. V., Kaplan, A. G., Miller, J. B., Stiver, I. P., & Surrey, J. L. (1991). *Women's growth in connection*. New York: Guilford.

Kagan, J. (1989, April). Temperamental contributions to social behavior. *American Psychologist*, 668-674.

Kantrowitz, B. & Ramo, J. (1993, 31 May). An interactive life. *Newsweek*, 42-44.

Kohn, A. (1986). *No contest: The case against competition*. Boston: Houghton Mifflin.

Kohn, A. (1990). *The brighter side of human nature*. New York: Basic Books.

Kreisberg, S. (1992). *Transforming power: Domination, empowerment, and education*. Albany, NY: State University of New York Press.

Krystal, H. (1981). The hedonic element in affectivity. *Annual of Psychoanalysis*, 9, 93-113.

Kuhn, T. S. (1970). *The structure of scientific revolutions*, 2nd Ed. Chicago: University of Chicago Press.

Kyle, N. (1988). *Psychiatric Clinics of North America*.

Langer, E. (1989). *Mindfulness*. Reading, MA: Addison-Wesley.

Lawlor, G. J., Jr., & Fischer, T. J. (Eds.). (1988). *Manual of allergy and immunology*, 2nd Ed. Boston: Little, Brown, and Co.

Lifton, R. J., & Markusen, E. (1990). The *genocidal mentality: Nazi holocaust and nuclear threat*. New York: Basic Books.

Lifton, R. J., & Falk, R. (1982). *Indefensible weapons*. New York: Basic Books.

Locke, S. E., & Colligan, D. (1986). *The healer within*. New York: Dutton.

Ludwig, A. M. (1990). Alcohol input and creative output. *British Journal of Addiction*, 85, 953-963.

Ludwig, A. M. (1992a). Creative achievement and psychopathology: Comparison among professions. *American Journal of Psychotherapy*, 46, 330-353.

Ludwig, A. M. (1992b). Culture and creativity. *American Journal of Psychotherapy*, 46, 454-469.

Lumsden, C. J., & Findlay, C. S. (1988). Evolution of the creative mind. *Creativity Research Journal*, 1, 75-91.

Martindale, C. (1990). Innovation, illegitimacy, and individualism. *Creativity Research Journal*, 3, 118-124.

Matthysse, S. (1991). Mood disorders and the dynamic stability of the system of memories. In, J. Madden IV (Ed.), *Neurobiology of learning, emotion, and affect*. New York: Raven Press.

McLaren, R. (1993). The dark side of creativity. *Creativity Research Journal*, 6, 137-144.

Minkoff, E. C. (1983). *Evolutionary biology*. Reading, MA: Addison-Wesley.

Ornstein, R. & Ehrlich. P. (1989). *New world, new mind: Moving toward conscious evolution*. New York: Touchstone.

Ornstein, R. & Swencionis. C. (Eds.). (1990). *The healing brain, A scientific reader*, New York: The Guilford Press.

Osborn, A. F. (1963). *Applied imagination*. New York: Scribner's.

Oswald, P. (1991). *Vaslav Nijinsky: A leap into madness*. New York: Lyle Stuart.

Pennebaker, J.W., Kiecolt·Glaser, J. K. & Glaser, R. (1988). Confronting traumatic experience and immunocompetence. *Journal of Consulting and clinical Psychology*, 56, 638-639.

Peterson, C. & Bossio. L. M., (1991). Health and optimism: *New research on the relationship between positive thinking and physical well-being*. New York: New York Free Press.

Peterson, K. C. Prout, M. F., & Schwarz, R. A. (1991). *Post-traumatic stress disorder*. New York: Plenum Press.

Redondi, P. (1987). *Galileo: Heretic*. Princeton. NJ: Princeton University Press.

Rhodes, C. (1990). Growth from deficiency creativity to being creativity. *Creativity Research Journal*, 3. 287-289.

Richards, R. (198l). Relationships between creativity and psychopathology: An evaluation and interpretation of the evidence. *Genetic Psychology Monographs*, 103. 261-324.

Richards, R. (1990). Everyday creativity, eminent creativity, and health. *Creativity & Research Journal*. 3, 300-326.

Richards, R. (1991, August). Everyday creativity and the arts, paper presented at the Annual Meeting of the American Psychological Association, San Francisco. CA. Version in *Psychologie Heute*. (1992. December), 58-64. (German). Version in A. Montuori & R. Purser (Eds.). (in press). Social creativity: *Prospects and possibilities* (vol 3). Creskill, NJ: Hampton Press.

Richards, R. (1993a). Seeing beyond: Issues of creative, awareness and social responsibility. *Creativity Research Journal* 6. 165-183.

Richards, R. (1993b). Everyday creativity, eminent creativity, and psychopathology. Commentary on "Creativity and psychopathology" by Hans J. Eysenck. *Psychological Inquiry*, 4, 212-217.

Richards, R. (1994a). Acceptable and Unacceptable Research. *Creativity Research Journal* 7, 87-90.

Richards, R. (1994b). Creativity and bipolar mood swings: Why the association? In M. Shaw & M.A. Richards, R. (1996a). Does the lone genius ride again? Chaos, creativity, and community. *Journal of Humanistic Psychology* 36(2), 44-60.

Richards, R. (l996b) Beyond Piaget: Accepting divergent, chaotic, and creative thought. In M. Runco (Ed.). *New· Directions for Child Development*. 72, 67-86. San Francisco: Jossey-Bass.

Richards, R. & Kinney, D. (1990). Mood Swings and creativity. *Creativity Research Journal* 3, 203-218.

Richards, R., Kinney, D., Benet, M. & Merzel, A.P.C. (1988). Assessing everyday creativity: Characteristics of the Lifetime Creativity· Scales and validation with three large samples. *Journal of Personality and Social Psychology*, 54, 476-485.

Richards, R., Kinney, D., Daniels, H. & Linkins, K. (992). Everyday creativity and bipolar and unipolar affective disorder: Preliminary study of personal and family history. European Psychiatry, 7, 49-52.

Richards, R., Kinney, D., Lunde, I., Benet, M., & Merzel, A. P. C. (1988). Creativity in manic-depressives, cyclothymes, their normal relatives, and control subjects. *Journal of Abnormal Psychology* 97, 281-288.

Rifkin, J. (1990). The global environmental crisis. In J. Rifkin (Ed.), *The green lifestyle handbook*. New York: Holt.

Roe, A. (1963). Personal problems and science. In, C. W. Taylor, & F. Barron (Eds.), *Scientific creativity: Its recognition and development*, (pp. 132-138). New York: Wiley and Sons.

Rolf, J., Master, A. S., Cicchetti, D., Nuechterlein, K. H., & Weintraum, S. (Eds.) (1990). *Risk and protective factors in the development of psychopathology*. New York: Cambridge University Press. Rothenberg, A. (1990). Creativity, mental health, and alcoholism. *Creativity Research Journal*, 3, 179-201.

Rubenson, D. L. (1990). The accidental economist. *Creativity Research Journal*, 3, 125-129.

Rubenson, D. L., & Runco, M. A. (1992). The psychoeconomic approach to creativity. *New Ideas in Psychology*, 10, 131-147.

Runco (Eds.). *Creativity and affect* (pp. 44-72). Norwood, NJ: Ablex.

Runco, M.A. (l993). Creative morality: Intentional and unconventional. *Creativity Research Journal* 6, 17-28.

Runco, M. A. (1994). Creativity and its discontents. In M. Shaw, & M. A. Runco (Eds.), *Creativity and affect* (pp. 102-123). Norwood, NJ: Ablex.

Runco, M A., Ebersole, P., & Mraz, W. (1990). Self-actualization and creativity. *Journal of Social Behavior and Personality* 6, l61-167.

Sandblom, P. (1989). *Creativity and disease: How illness affects literature*. Philadelphia: G. B. Lippincott.

Schou, M. (1979). Artistic productivity and lithium prophylzxis in manic-depressive illness. *British Journal of Psychiatry* 135, 97-103.

Schuldberg, D. (1990). Schizotypal and hypomanic traits, creativity, and psychological health. *Creativity Research Journal* 3, 218-230.

Schuldberg, D. (1994). Giddiness and horror. In M. Shaw, & M. Runco (Eds.), *Creativity and affect*. (pp. 87-101). Norwood, NJ: Ablex Publishing Co.

Simonton, D. K. (1984). *Genius, creativity and leadership: Historiometric inquiries*. Cambridge, MA: Harvard University Press.

Simonton, D. K. (1988). *Scientific genius: A psychology of science*. New York: Cambridge University Press.

Simonton, D. K. (1990a). Political pathology and societal creativity. *Creativity Research Journal* 3, 85-99.

Simonton, D. K. (1990b). Monsieur appends reflections. *Creativity Research Journal*, 3, 146-149.

Skarda, C. & Freeman, W. J. (1987). How brains make chaos in order to make sense of the world. *Behavioral and Brain Sciences*, 10, 161-173.

Smith, D. W. (Ed.). (1977). *Introduction to clinical pediatrics*, 2nd Ed. Philadelphia: W. B. Saunders.

Smith, G. J. W., & Van der Meer, G. (1990). *Creativity Research Journal*, 3, 249-264.

Solovay, M. D., Shenton, M. E., Gasperetti, C., Doleman, M., Kentenbaum, E., Carpenter, J. T., & Holzman, P. (1986). Scoring manual for the Thought Disorder Index (revised version). *Schizophrenia Bulletin*, 12, 483-496.

Spender, D. (1982). *Women of ideas*. London: Pandora.

Stariha, W. E., & Walberg, H. J. (1990). Psychological mediators of the inverse pathology-creativity effect. *Creativity Research Journal*, 3, 130-133.

Stein, M. I. (1990). Anabolic and catabolic factors in the creative process. *Creativity Research Journal*, 3, 134-145.

Styron, W. (1990). Darkness visible: *A memoir of madness*. New York: Random House.

Tooby, J. & DeVore, I. (1987). The reconstruction of hominid behavioral evolution through strategic modeling. In W. G. Kinzey (Ed.) (1987). *The evolution of human behavior: Primate models*. (pp. 183-237). Albany, NY: State University of New York Press.

Wallach, M. A. & Kogan, N. (1965). *Modes of thinking in young children*. New York: Holt, Rinehart, & Winston.

Wender, P. H., Kety, S. S., Rosenthal, D., Schulsinger, F., Ortmann, J. & Lunde, I. (1986). Psychiatric disorders in the biological and adaptive families of adopted individuals with affective disorders. *Archives of General Psychiatry*, 43, 923-929.

Waldrop, M. M. (1992). Complexity: *The emerging science at the edge of order and chaos*. New York: Simon and Schuster.

Wilson, E. O. (May 20, 1993). Is humanity suicidal? *New York Times Magazine*, 24-29.

Wilson, E. O. (1992). *The diversity of life*. New York: W. W. Norton.

Wilson, D. (1992). Evolutionary epidemiology. *Acta Biotheoretica* 40.

X, Malcolm, & Haley, A. (1964). *The autobiography of Malcolm X*. New York: Ballantine.

Yoffe, E. (December 13, 1992). Silence of the frogs, *New York Times Magazine*, 36-38, 64-66, 76.

ABOUT THE AUTHOR

(1995)

Ruth Richards, M.D., Ph.D., psychiatrist and psychologist with the University of California, San Francisco, and Harvard Medical School, has a broad multidisciplinary background, including work in behavioral, biological and physical science, medicine, psychiatry, and educational psychology. She is also a visual artist and credentialed teacher of art, and has, in addition, studied creative writing with the poet, writer, and Pulitzer Prize nominee (and student of Robert Lowell), Kathleen Spivack.

Dr. Richards has studied, taught, and written extensively about human creativity for over twenty years. She sees creativity as a vital force in our evolution, and her holistic approach integrates the many perspectives above. Relevant to Everyday Creativity, Dr. Richards has been exploring aspects of the "relational" model of women's development, developed at the Stone Center at Wellesley College by Judith Jordan, Jan Surrey, Irene Stiver and colleagues (with whom Dr. Richards has worked), and Carol Gilligan, Jean Baker Miller, and others. Dr. Richards has worked clinically with the relational model in the Boston area and California (with both men and women) and, last summer, taught a graduate course, "Self-in-Relation," at the University of California, Berkeley.

Dr. Richards has spoken at professional meetings, public gatherings, and on television. Her work has been covered in over two dozen periodicals, including *The New York Times, Miami Herald, Los Angeles Times, and Asahi Weekly* (Japan).

With co-editor Mark Runco, Editor of the *Creativity Research Journal*, Dr. Richards has an edited book in press with Ablex Publishing Corp., entitled Eminent Creativity, Everyday Creativity, and Health. Recently, she has consulted for a potential Museum of Creativity. Dr. Richards also serves on the editorial board of *The Creativity Research Journal*, and is very much in touch with the latest ideas and findings in the study of creativity.

KEY CONCEPTS

EVERYDAY CREATIVITY: Coping and Thriving in the 21st Century
(April 1995, alternative structure)

How can we be more creative, and why do we care so much about it in the first place? What exactly is creativity? Is there really any point in thinking about innovation if we're not talented in art, or music, or some other "creative field"? If it's actually so good for us to be creative -as many people think -- then why are we hearing so much about creativity and pain, depression, mood disorders, abnormality? Might creativity even hurt or unbalance us? Hadn't we better find this out?

How can we fit such concerns with reports that creativity can enhance our physical and psychological health? Didn't Freud find that creativity comes from pain and unconscious conflict? How does this mesh with the evidence that each of us already shows abundant "everyday creativity"- - even if this tends to be underdeveloped, unrecognized or unrewarded.

What of reports that we can all become greatly more creative, and quite comfortably so, as part of our evolutionary birthright. Or that we can use this creativity to awaken ourselves to a reality we now shut out, learn to connect more fully with those we love, care more actively about our world, and even "evolve consciously" toward more creative modes of living for the 21st century. There is a great deal to untangle here.

Everyday Creativity looks at the latest research and thinking on creativity, including the author's studies from Harvard and McLean Hospital on the nature of creativity in everyday life, and its sometimes surprising relations both to mood disorders and positive mental health. The book addresses critical modern issues, forging a unique synthesis of material from humanistic psychology, evolutionary biology, and the new "self-in-relation" model of development from the Stone Center at Wellesley College.
There are two ongoing themes:

(1) Originality: Through our uniqueness and diversity, we all take part in an ongoing flow of originality -- in an "evolution of information."

(2) Awareness: We all have many areas of blindness and mental distortion; creative living and thinking hold both a means and reward for awakening.

In this summary, a number of new ideas are noted only briefly. Some are discussed in the next section. Also, note that Parts 1 & 2 might be combined ("what we miss").

I. The Creativity of Everyday Life: Consciousness-raising about what everyday creativity is, how we overlook it, and how we can rediscover it, using principles from The Lifetime Creativity Scales. We see that originality is everywhere in our daily lives -- from the office to the backyard -- and that its functions include survival itself. We draw parallels between biological and cultural evolution, and the idea that our varied creative "memes" (NB re psychodiversity) help fuel an "evolution of information." We each take part in more ways than we realize.

      Chapter 1 - Psychodiversity
      Chapter 2 - Seeing Everyday Creativity

II. So Much We Miss: Consciousness-raising continues, in this case about the many deadening qualities that plague us: our habitual, evolutionary, conceptual, defensive, and consensual blindnesses and distortions. We can do much to raise our awareness, as part of our "conscious evolution." We are not all that we can be.

      Chapter 3 -- Death by Automatism
      Chapter 4 -- Distortion and Defense

III. The Subtle Attraction: A way out -- a new perspective on awareness and our motivation to create. We may escape our mindless stupor through painful warning signals such as fear, anxiety, and anger -- these quickly awaken us. But nature can call us in a gentler way, even seduce us, into wide-eyed awareness and creation of new forms. The pull is beauty, or elegance, fitness, "rightness." This view, grounded in longstanding wisdom, bounds cheerfully over Freud, and gives life to modern humanistic views of human potential and our need for self-actualization.

Chapter 5 -- Creative Libido

Chapter 6 - Personal Growth and Creativity

IV. Diversity, Health, and Change:
We leap further into the unknown, toward a figurative "edge-of-chaos." We can be wild, and creatively so. This may be an evolutionary imperative -- to be, at times, unusually aware, unusually original. Piaget's cognitive "equilibrium" may not be the only/ultimate goal. Our fullest creative potential can draw from what some call "immaturity," "abnormality," "moodiness," and even "illness." There is openness to all manner of experience - but there is also creative control. This can improve our health and wellbeing. It may hold a key to creative insight. And to knowing ourselves and accepting others.

Chapter 7 - Freeing the Child in Us

Chapter 8 - Our Healthy "Abnormality"

Chapter 9 - Mood Swings, Depression, and Creativity

Chapter 10 - Pain and Creative Coping

V. Caring Ever More Deeply:
Now we extend the "self-in-relation" model, and see that creativity, at its best, can connect us more deeply and consciously with the world, and with the special people in our lives. It can help us to work with, rather than against, each other, and to educate our young to be all they can be. It can aid our "conscious evolution," empowering us in an ever more endangered world. Everyday creativity can broaden the meaning of caring, and give us new reasons for living.

Chapter 11 - Valuing Differences

Chapter 12 - Valuing Each Other

Chapter 13 - Nurturing Creativity

Chapter 14 - Seeing Beyond

An Evolution of Information

Our exploration takes us through the rich generation of diversity in our world. For convenience, we might speak of "psychodiversity," by analogy with the biodiversity of living organisms. This current term refers to the outcomes of our rich and fantastic array of mental processes, in their varied modes and preferred styles of operation, of intercommunication, and states of consciousness, including the vast landscapes of knowledge, ideas, emotional expression, questions, and constructions of wish and fantasy that we have created over the years as individuals and as a culture. This diversity of content and process forms the basis for an ongoing evolution, going beyond genetic coding of organisms to the entire world of information. Originality, as the key to creativity, is a catalyst for these endless new products of our minds and imaginations.

Other comments expand on the five focal areas in the Table of Contents:

I. The Creativity of Everyday Life

An "evolution of information" is a grass roots matter and so, too, will be the creativity which feeds it. We are each a part of this everyday process. Whether managing an office, writing an article, teaching a child, developing a new medication, repairing a home, or campaigning for political office, we are constantly changing, adapting, improvising -- creating. As part of a complex and inter connected web of human interaction, we are also having an influence far beyond our immediate neighborhoods, perhaps much farther than we think.

Yet how many people think that creativity is only about painting a picture, singing a song, of doing a science experiment. And how many think creativity only "counts" if it is done professionally, or perhaps wins an award. No one says such things about breathing or sleeping or eating. Yet our creativity, which helps us adapt to changing terrains and life threatening conditions, may be just as important to our survival. How amazing that this essential innovative quality may often go unrecognized, underdeveloped, and unrewarded.

Everyday creativity is not at all an "extra" or a luxury, but a major life theme and force. It allows us to adapt and survive physically, and also to grow psychologically. It is both a happy reward of our humanness and an innate responsibility. Creativity enables our biological evolution, and also our psychological and cultural evolution. We do a certain amount of creating without even thinking, but how much better if we can stop and do this consciously.

II. So Much We Miss

How much more of our lives we also miss! Look around you right now. Did you see that cup on the table, that plant, that window, or hear the soft murmur of music in the background? How completely unaware we can be of a person standing right beside us, a tree above our heads, the words of a colleague, or the meaning of our own lives. We are shackled by an incredible range of blindnesses and automatisms—evolutionary, habitual, categorical, defensive, and consensual, including delusions we in society collude in sharing with each other.

There are times for such limiting habits and defenses—without them our day would be too complex to process. Yet we don't want each day to look exactly like the last one. We sometimes are awakened, but the signals are often unpleasant: fear, anxiety, anger. When our survival is threatened, we quickly take notice.

But there are happier ways out of our stupor. We find an important one in our creative thoughts and lifestyles. Here comes the happy thrill of the new twist, the new vision, the excitement and challenge, and ultimately the joy of living. Now we can hear the music in the rain, see the wonder on a child's face, and speak movingly to a loved one. We can notice afresh, and we notice that we've noticed. Now too, we can quietly sense a problem and take a careful action that can save us.

III. The Subtle Attraction

But how do we start, do we begin to wake up? We propose a subtle attraction, in an argument which draws from modern humanistic and "relational" psychologies (and is also based, interestingly, in the wisdom of Plato, Ficino, Santayana, and others). We suggest that the world of information -- of our minds and hearts -has its own unique drive similar to the drive of sexual attraction. This manifests in the subtle pull of beauty, viewed in the broadest sense, including intuitions of elegance, fitness, or "rightness." It stops us. It wakes us up. It arouses us.

The result, this time, is the creation of new forms or information, and not biological organisms. This is no longer a Freudian universe of homeostasis, or a wound-down stability. Things can get wild. The sexual drive is not the only reproductive urge of interest (or pleasure), and creativity is not merely an eruption under duress that resolves a neurotic conflict or problem.

Our creative horizon involves more than physical survival. It is also one of curiosity, growth, and ongoing striving, a quest which is healthy and fulfilling. This process links creativity, however it may start out, to growth and self-actualization. And, viewed as part of the big picture, this is a force generating ever more elaborate complexity in nature, and emergent structures in our minds.

IV. Diversity, Health, and Change

Creative living can free many parts of ourselves and weave them back integrally into the richness of who we are: the child in us who appeared too immature, the thoughts we had that seemed too "weird," the mood swings that felt too "wild," and even some forms of pain and illness, when these led to growth and learning, rather than flight. How much more we can grow with this attitude. We need to expand greatly the boundaries of what we consider "normal."

One problem may still be fixation with a homeostatic model of thinking, rather than, say, an emergent structure model, reaching ever outward to greater heights of elaboration and synthesis. We are often cheerfully off balance in our roaming minds. Our greatest progress may even come at such times. This can also help us understand a creative style called "integrative complexity," an exploratory means of mentally balancing - - without falling - - amidst a world of possibilities. As we accept these many parts of ourselves, we will also cherish more readily the richness in the world around us. We can all surely be many diverse things at once - - child and adult, wild and well-grounded, hurting and healing -- at our richest and most buoyantly creative. In this diversity lies our hope for the future.

Our bodies also tell us that creative openness is good, good for our psychological freedom, our health and wellbeing, our immune systems, perhaps even our longevity. Here, evolution is sending us a very important message. This stuff is good for us. Even when the root of creativity lies in mental illness -- as in a bipolar or unipolar depressed mood disorder -- or in incredible stress and adversity, its healing qualities may still shine through. Such "pathology" may also tell us more about how to increase our own "normal" and healthy creative process.

V. Caring Ever More Deeply

Finally, this growth does not happen impersonally. It happens because we care. This "subtle attraction" attracts indeed, pulls us closer, and urges us to notice and to change. To interact with something, to touch it and, in doing so, to touch ourselves. To connect, and to transform. We needn't just love our fellow creatures; we can love all of creation. We can work together, support each other, and improve the world. If this process truly "works," then we will be moving on to create more beauty. If we have evolution in action, then it attracts, pulls, and moves others to care in turn, to transform, create, and carry forward the process of growth.

We are not talking rarities. We are all doing this—we are constantly "conceiving" new information. Sadly, this process is not always growth- producing, and "good" for us or our world. We must deal with this "other side" too. How much more powerful then if we can consciously hear the call to creativity, know what is calling us, and how to respond. If, more generally—and not only in the world of our personal relationships—we can learn to make the right choices, and for the right reasons.